D0559760

The WORLD in a CITY

BALLANTINE BOOKS

NEW YORK

The WORLD in a CITY

—

TRAVELING THE GLOBE THROUGH THE
NEIGHBORHOODS OF THE NEW NEW YORK

—

Joseph Berger

DEER PARK PUBLIC LIBRARY
44 LAKE AVENUE
DEER PARK, NY 11729

Copyright © 2007 by Joe Berger

All rights reserved.

Published in the United States by Ballantine Books,
an imprint of The Random House Publishing Group,
a division of Random House, Inc., New York.

BALLANTINE and colophon are registered
trademarks of Random House, Inc.

LIBRARY OF CONGRESS CATALOGING-IN-PUBLICATION DATA

Berger, Joseph.
The world in a city : traveling the globe through the
neighborhoods of the new New York / Joseph Berger.
p. cm.

ISBN-13: 978-0-345-48738-4 (hardcover : alk. paper)

1. New York (N.Y.)—Description and travel. 2. Ethnic
neighborhoods—New York (State)—New York.
3. Immigrants—New York (State)—New York—Social life
and customs. 4. Berger, Joseph—Travel—New York
(State)—New York. 5. New York (N.Y.)—Social life and
customs. 6. City and town life—New York (State)—
New York. 7. Pluralism (Social sciences)—New York
(State)—New York. 8. Cosmopolitanism—New York
(State)—New York. 9. New York (N.Y.)—Ethnic
relations. I. Title.
F128.55.B46 2007
917.47'10444089—dc22   2007017314

Printed in the United States of America
on acid-free paper

www.ballantinebooks.com

2 4 6 8 9 7 5 3 1

FIRST EDITION

Book design by Barbara M. Bachman

To Brenda and Annie,
my traveling companions for life

The Global City

. . .

WHEN I WAS EIGHT YEARS OLD AND HAD BEEN AN IMMIGRANT IN New York City just three years, still something of a stranger to its wondrous streets, I came across a cut-rate guidebook to Manhattan. Leafing through it left me with an itch to explore the sights of midtown and downtown, one of those impulses that eight-year-olds find impossible to resist. I felt as possessed as Magellan must have been when he set out to circumnavigate the globe. Soon I enlisted my six-year-old brother, Josh, and my nine-year-old friend Maury from across the street to take the journey with me. On a sunny fall day we actually walked all the way from my home at 102nd Street down to Chinatown and back up to the United Nations, a trek of probably ten miles or so. It was our most adventurous adventure up to that early point in our lives and not so unimaginable for children our age in the snug New York of the early 1950s, the world depicted so evocatively a few years before in E. B. White's *Here Is New York*.

As we hiked along, we took in the Museum of Natural History with its glassed-in grizzly bears, wax Indians, and colossal dangling whale. We gazed at the plump, smug Oldsmobiles and Pontiacs in the row of car dealerships along Broadway, the Camels smoker in Times Square blowing perfectly round smoke rings, the elevated and escalated bazaars of Macy's and Gimbels, and the unrivaled tallest building in the universe, the Empire State. We sailed on to the dazzling model train panoramas of the A. C. Gilbert toy-train building, the stalls of bric-a-brac and tchotchkes along Canal Street, the swarming warrens of Chinatown, and, after we turned around and walked north through the uncharted territory of the East Side, the brand-new sparkling glass slab of the UN. There was such a feast of streetscapes—gritty to honky-tonk to majestic—and a variety of *Homo sapiens*—Irish bus drivers, Italian bricklayers, Jewish garment workers, Puerto Rican doormen, WASP bankers, black elevator operators (migrants no doubt from the dying cotton fields of the South), and secretaries and actors escaping the Midwest—that it seemed we took our time savoring every block. We were so engrossed that by the time we came home my mother had asked the police to search for us.

That explorer's wanderlust has never left me, and I've been lucky enough to use it to my advantage in my career as a reporter in New York City, most especially in recent years as a kind of roving correspondent for *The New York Times* in the city's neighborhoods. What has changed—stunningly and magnificently—is the city itself. The New York of the late 1940s and 1950s, the decorous, congenial metropolis of E. B. White where a mother would allow an eight-year-old to wander miles away, is an artifact for the museums. So is a New York where most of the faces we saw were slightly different shades of European beige dappled by only a few spots of ebony and bronze. Even the New York of the 1970s and 1980s, where grown-ups would stay clear of large parts of the city for fear of attack or humiliation, and where suspicion and fear among races isolated from one another was the background music of the day, that too is gone.

The city today is polyglot and polychrome, more cosmopolitan than the Casablanca and Shanghai of the movies, without the hovering air of noirish menace. The whole world can be found in this city. I can do interviews in such exotic places as Ecuador and Uzbekistan and Bangladesh simply by getting on the subway for the cost of a MetroCard. When I took that walk around Manhattan, there were half a dozen sizable ethnic groups, with the rest of the world barely represented except in tourist oddities such as Chinatown and Astoria. But the descendants of those 1950s groups are by now largely settled in genteel suburbs and have been replaced by people born abroad in dozens of countries. Sixty percent of the city's residents are either immigrants or children of immigrants. There are now at least twenty-five new nationalities with significant representations—Dominicans, Chinese, Jamaicans, Guyanese,

Mexicans, Ecuadorians, Haitians, Trinidadians, Colombians, Russians, Uzbeks, Koreans, Indians, Poles, Filipinos, Bangladeshis, Pakistanis, Salvadorans, Nigerians, and Ghanaians, to name the largest. Most of the new immigrants entered the United States as a result of the Hart-Celler Act of 1965, which ended forty-year-old preferences for immigrants from countries such as Britain, France, and Germany that had historically shaped the American population and established quotas of 20,000 for each country in the Eastern Hemisphere.

A 2005 analysis by the New York City Department of City Planning shows that New York stands atop the globe in its ethnic variety. Los Angeles has more people born abroad—40.9 percent compared with 35.9 for New York—but most are from Mexico. A handful of world cities rival New York in its proportion of the foreign-born—Toronto's is 49.4 percent; Sydney, 33.4 percent; London, 27.4 percent—but their ethnic stew is not as varied.

As a result of New York City's newcomers, almost every neighborhood has been transformed from what it looked like at mid-twentieth century. In the 1950s, the city was a checkerboard of provinces clearly carved out by a half dozen ethnic groups, so that the Grand Concourse, Forest Hills, and Midwood were Jewish, the Bronx north of Fordham Road Irish, Bensonhurst Italian in the north and Jewish in the south, and the like. Today Flushing is Chinese and Korean, Jackson Heights is Indian, Ecuadorian, and Colombian, Washington Heights and the West Bronx are Dominican, Richmond Hill is Guyanese, East Flatbush is Caribbean, and Rego Park is Russian and Uzbek. Astoria is still Greek, but far less so and increasingly Arabic, Brazilian, and Bangladeshi. Bensonhurst is still Italian but now a third Chinese. There are also far more melting-pot neighborhoods, such as Ditmas Park, Brooklyn, where no ethnic or racial group is dominant and where a substantial amount of intermingling takes place. Such places exemplify the utopian vision the city had of itself a century ago but that was then actually something of a myth.

Many neighborhoods are also very different places than they were as a result of the seismic shifts in the American economy, from greasy nuts-and-bolts factories to cleaner service- and computer-based workplaces. Factory buildings in Queens and the Bronx are now more likely to produce films than white bread, graphic designs for pots and pans rather than pots and pans themselves. The Garment Center now designs and markets dresses rather than actually sews them. The Lower East Side is now less a stop for immigrants from Bohemia than for bohemians. And such innovations as satellite television and videoconferencing are narrowing the anguishing distance the immigrants of Jackson Heights and Flushing feel from their homelands and the families they left behind, changing the very experience of what it means to be an immigrant.

New York, colossal as it is, has become more than ever a collection of villages, scores of virtually self-reliant hamlets, each exquisitely textured by a particular ethnicity, history, politics, even housing stock. In the pages that follow, I'll take you to some of those villages, for me the city's most beguiling neighborhoods, and chat with some of their most emblematic and charming inhabitants. We'll meet Claudio Caponigro, the last Italian barber of East Harlem, and I'll tell you about the old, flavorful world of politicians and padrones of which he is a relic and of the changes taking place in the Latino world around him. We will visit the cobbler of Bayard Street in Chinatown, who has set up a shoemaking shop right on a rent-free sidewalk of New York. Wielding his timeworn tools in the frost of winter and the steambath of summer, he is re-creating a kind of commerce common in his homeland but that here is a novel twist on the wily immigrant freelancer who scrapes out a living catch-as-catch-can. In a more significant example of immigration's impact on the city's economy, I'll show you how Filipinos in humdrum corners of the city such as the Bronx's Norwood have come to dominate the nursing industry. I'll take you along to another once nameless corner of the Bronx, Bedford Park, to meet Intesar Museitef, a Palestinian woman who for many years traveled four hours a day by subway and bus for a part-time job that paid $7 an hour. She'll give you an idea of the hard lives of some of the newcomers that people neighborhoods like hers.

I'll take you to Little Neck, Queens, where the waves of ethnicities slapping up against each other produce tension over something as banal as the signs on shops; to the Grand Concourse, where new waves of African Americans, Ghanaians actually, are saving up their hard-won earnings to buy houses, not in the Bronx, but back home in Ghana; to Brighton Beach and Midwood, where Russian women keep the past alive by draping themselves in fur for the winter and dragging their children to ballroom-dancing lessons; to Rego Park, Queens, where another breed of Soviet Jews, from Uzbekistan and other southern lands, are grappling with a homeland throwback that is not so welcome here—wife beating; and to Richmond Hill, Queens, where Guyanese of indisputable Indian descent are spurned by Indians from India.

I'll show you neighborhoods filled with piquant streets and cheeky characters that are being transformed as I write, neighborhoods such as Bensonhurst, which is no longer as Italian as it was when Tony Manero swaggered about, strutting his third-generation version of Italian American life in *Saturday Night Fever*. These older migrations are, in predictable fashion, trading factories and diners for college classrooms and corner offices, forsaking their brick row houses and concrete backyards for suburban greenery. Yet I'll also show you two neighborhoods that have barely changed at all, seaside colonies known as Gerritsen Beach and Broad Channel, where the populations of white ethnic firefighters, garbage collectors, and subway conductors are as timeless as the seagulls wheeling across somber marine skies.

Along the way, to give readers some perspective, I will confide at points what I remember of those neighborhoods from my childhood as an immigrant newly plunked down in a dazzling, daunting city and my years as a young striver trying to earn his footing in its rugged urban terrain. As you'll see, Claudio, the Italian barber of East Harlem, stirs me because he reminds me of Boris, the last Jewish barber in the pocket of the Grand Concourse where we lived during my teenage years. The chill between Guyanese immigrants of Indian ethnicity and those who come directly from India recalls for me how the children of the Eastern European immigrants of the late nineteenth century seemed to keep apart from the Holocaust survivors who came over in the late 1940s and early 1950s. In New York, the exuberance of immigrant ascent and the heartbreak of exclusion seem to flow in tandem. I also want to let you know something about the history, landscape, and politics of these neighborhoods, their sights and smells and flavors, some of the spots where I might have enjoyed an unaccustomed meal or a serendipitous purchase.

Those who live in the city but rarely venture out of their snug corner of New York would enjoy safaris to these vivid, sometimes astonishing neighborhoods that they may pass under by subway in blissful disregard. But so would strangers to the big city who deprive themselves of a fuller sense of its personality by confining themselves to meeting other tourists at old standbys such as the Empire State Building and the Statue of Liberty. Everyone should know about this rapidly transmogrifying New York because it's coming soon to a theater near you.

Though New York is far out ahead of other metropolises in its colorful palette, Chicago, Philadelphia, Los Angeles, and practically every other American city—small as well as large—and many other world cities have been deeply tinged by waves of immigration. The U.S. Census Bureau released data in 2005 that showed that immigrant populations are growing rapidly in American heartland states such as Indiana, South Dakota, and Colorado. In Deep South Georgia, the foreign-born made up 9 percent of the state's residents. Overall, the 35.7 million immigrants made up 12.4 percent of the nation's population in 2005, a jump of 1.2 percentage points in just five years.

While usually one or two ethnic influxes are responsible for change— Los Angeles' diversity is mostly Mexican and Chinese—once uniform cities such as Toronto and London are now certifiably polyglot, and other homogenous cities such as Paris and Rome are becoming polyglot. The riots by Arab and North African youths discontented with their treatment by the French, and the bombings of the London subway by Muslim fanatics were stark declarations of these changes. New York is the future they all will share. With a tolerance bred in the bone and a long experience in grappling with immigrants, it has become the world's "global laboratory," as Oz Almog, a sociologist in Israel who studies that country's ethnic groups, put it. It is the place where the mixing of contrasting tribes is being tested like nowhere else.

A vivid example of the universality of the country's ethnic metamorphosis occurred to me in the summer of 2005 when I took a long weekend trip to Block Island, purportedly a bastion of flinty Yankee ways though heavily touristed in summer, with my wife and daughter and some friends. One afternoon we stopped to have lunch at an Italian bakery called Aldo's. Outside there was a two-man Peruvian band. Each player was wearing a rainbow-colored poncho and playing Inca folk standards, but the songs were interspersed with cosmopolitan kitsch including "Shalom Chaverim," a traditional Israeli melody. Here were Peruvians playing Israeli music at an Italian restaurant in a stronghold of Yankee traditionalism. What more need be said about the new America?

And it's not just ethnicity, but changing tastes and intellectual perspectives that are altering the landscape—of New York and the rest of the world. Take the Lower East Side—that fabled immigrant neighborhood that gave birth to so many of the great comedians, songwriters, labor leaders, and intellectuals of the past century. The people who fled the Lower East Side as a festering warren of disease and poverty are witnessing their grandchildren and great-grandchildren moving back to the old neighborhood. Those gritty, jagged streets have become a magnet for another generation of strivers, this one speaking English without an accent. Young people who grew up seeing sunsets over mountains prefer to see them over water tanks, tar-covered rooftops, and cross-hatched steel bridges. The proof is in the soaring rents that those forefathers and foremothers could never have imagined paying. Go figure.

Change is bewitching and bewildering, but we must snatch what we see before it flickers into something far different or fades into memory. This book is an effort to seize the New York moment.

Contents

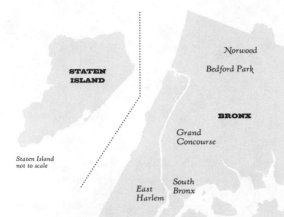

STATEN
ISLAND

Staten Island
not to scale

Norwood

Bedford Park

BRONX

Grand
Concourse

East
Harlem

South
Bronx

MANHATTAN

Astoria

Jackson
Heights

Flushing

Douglaston

Little
Neck

Garment
District

Lower
East
Side

Rego
Park

QUEENS

China-
town

Richmond
Hill

Gowanus

Red
Hook

BROOKLYN

Ditmas
Park

Midwood

Bensonhurst

Gerritsen Beach

Broad
Channel

Brighton
Beach

The **WORLD** in a **CITY**

Chapter 1

So You Thought You Knew Astoria

. . .

FOR HALF A CENTURY, ASTORIA IN QUEENS HAS BEEN A NEIGH-borhood of cafés where dark-haired Greek men sip strong coffee and smoke strong cigarettes while talking in Greek late into the night. It is a place of quiet sidewalks lined with tenderly fussed-over brick and shingle row houses, where a solitary widow in black can be glimpsed scurrying homeward as if she were on the island of Rhodes.

The cafés are still teeming, the houses tidy. But the Greek hold on the neighborhood has slowly been weakening. Successful Greeks have been leaving for leafier locales. As a result, there are moments when Astoria has a theme-park feel to it, a cardboard façade of a Greek Main Street with cafés named Athens, Omonia, and Zodiac and Greece's blue and white colors splashed everywhere, but a diminishing number of actual Greeks living within.

That's because other groups have been rising up to take their place. On a Friday on Steinway Street, one of Astoria's commercial spines, several hundred men from North African and Middle Eastern countries were jammed into Al-Iman Mosque, a marble-faced storefront that is one of several Muslim halls of worship that have sprung up in Astoria. Some wore ordinary street clothes, some white robes and knit white skullcaps. There were so many worshipers that thirteen had to pray on the sidewalk, kneeling shoeless on prayer mats and touching their foreheads and palms to the ground. When the prayers were over, El Allel Dahli, a Moroccan immigrant, emerged with his teenage son, Omar, telling of the plate of couscous and lamb he had brought as a gift to the poor to honor the birth that morning of his daughter, Jenine. "I am very happy today," he told me.

He could also have been happy that, as his visit confirmed, the immediate neighborhood was turning into New York City's casbah. Not only was there his flourishing mosque, but down Steinway Street, as far as his eyes could see, there were Middle Eastern restaurants, groceries, travel agencies, a driving school, a barber shop, a pharmacy, a dried fruit and nuts store, a bookstore—twenty-five shops in all. In the cafés, clusters of Egyptian, Moroccan, or Tunisian men were puffing on hookahs—tall, gaudily embellished water pipes stoked with charcoal to burn sheeshah, the fragrant tobacco that comes in flavors such as molasses and apple. Sometimes these men—taxi drivers, merchants, or just plain idlers—play backgammon or dominoes or watch Arabic television shows beamed in by satellite, but mostly they schmooze about the things Mediterranean men talk about when they're together—soccer, politics, women—while waiters fill up their pipes with chunks of charcoal at $4 a smoke. In classic New York fashion, Steinway Street is a slice of Arabic Algiers on Astoria's former Main Street, renamed after a German immigrant who a century before assembled the world's greatest pianos a few blocks away.

And it is not just Middle Easterners and North Africans who are changing the neighborhood's personality. Those settling in Astoria in the past decade or two include Bangladeshis, Serbians, Bosnians, Ecuadorians, and, yes, even increasingly young Manhattan professionals drawn by the neighborhood's modest rents, cosmopolitan flavors, and short commute to midtown Manhattan. More vibrant than them all seem to be the Brazilians, who have brought samba nightclubs and bikini-waxing salons to streets that once held moussaka joints. When Brazil won the World Cup in 2002, Astoria's streets were turned into an all-night party, and when the team lost in 2006, the streets were leaden with mourning.

New York can be viewed as an archipelago, like Indonesia a collection of distinctive islands, in its case its villagelike neighborhoods. Each island has its own way of doing things, its own flavor, fragrance, and indelible characters. But, as a result of the roiling tides of migration and the unquenchable human restlessness and hunger for something better and grander, most of these neighborhoods are in constant, ineluctable flux. Some transform with astonishing swiftness as if hit by a flood; a few suffer erosion that is scarcely detectable until one day its inhabitants realize that what was there is gone.

Astoria was an appropriate jumping-off point for my three-year-long ramble around the city because it is a classic New York neighborhood, a place that has long had a sharply defined character and a distinct place in the city's landscape, but one that has been turned into a Babel of cultures by the waves of immigration set off by the 1965 law. When New Yorkers dropped the name Astoria, it was understood they were talking about an enclave where Greek was spoken and Greek folkways were observed. So it was striking to me as I walked the streets how much of that accent had faded. Astoria's Greek population has been cut by a third in the past two decades, by some unofficial estimates, to 30,000 from 45,000, with official, if undercounted, census figures even gloomier, putting the number of people who claimed Greek ancestry at just 18,217, or 8.6 percent of the neighborhood's residents.

The decline of the Greeks can be seen as an old New York story, no different from the shrinking of the Jewish population on the Lower East Side or the number of Italians along Arthur Avenue in the Bronx. As immigrants of one nationality make it, they forsake the jostling streets, and newer immigrants, hoping to make their fortunes, move in. "It's an upward mobility kind of thing," said Robert Stephanopoulos, dean of Holy Trinity Greek Orthodox Cathedral on East Seventy-fourth Street and father of George (Bill Clinton's press secretary and now an ABC broadcaster). But the fact that it is an oft-told story is scant consolation for longtime Greek residents who have tried to rekindle the old country in this new one. They find a bittersweet quality to the changeover. On the one hand, it affirms their community's upswing; on the other, their village in New York is withering.

"In New York everything turns around," Peter Figetakis, forty-eight, a Greek-born film director who has lived in Astoria since the 1970s, told me. "Now the Hindus and Arabs, it's their time."

For the newer residents, the mood is expansive. On a two-block stretch of Steinway between Twenty-eighth Avenue and Astoria Boulevard, there is a veritable souk, with shops selling halal meat, Syrian pastries, airplane tickets to Morocco, driving lessons in Arabic, Korans and other Muslim books, and robes in styles such as the caftan, the abaya, the hooded djellaba, and the chador, which covers the body from head to toe, including much of the face. Indeed, a common street sight is a woman in ankle-length robe and head scarf—hijab—surrounded by small children. Laziza of New York Pastry, a Jordanian bakery, may have baklava superior to that made by the neighborhood's Greeks. With two dozen such Arabic shops, the Steinway strip outpaces the city's most famous Middle Eastern thoroughfare, Brooklyn's Atlantic Avenue, which was started by Lebanese and Syrian Christians, not Muslims. In cafés and restaurants once owned by Greeks and Italians, television shows from Cairo and news from Qatar-based Al Jazeera are beamed in on flat-screen televisions. Some cafés are open round-the-clock so taxi drivers can stop in and have their sheeshah and an espresso.

Noureddine Daouaou, a taxi driver from Casablanca who has lived in the United States for more than twenty years, said he prefers Astoria to other places in New York where Arabs cluster because the neighborhood has a cosmopolitan mix of peoples. "You don't feel homesick," he said. "You find peace somehow. You find people try to get along. We can understand each other in one language."

The number of Arab speakers in the neighborhood the city designates as Queens Community Board 1 (the city is broken into fifty-nine community boards that offer advice on land-use and budget issues) rose from 2,265 in 1990 to 4,097 in 2000, an 80 percent increase, and will be far larger in the next census. For the Middle Easterners, the attraction to Astoria seems to be the congenial Mediterranean accent: foods that overlap with such Greek delicacies as kebab, okra, lentils, and honey-coated pastries, and cultural harmonies such as men idling with one another in cafés. "They feel more comfortable with Greeks," George Mohamed Oumous, a forty-five-year-old Moroccan computer programmer, said of his fellow Arabs. "We've been near each other for centuries. You listen to Greek music, you think you could be listening to Egyptian music."

Ali El Sayed, who is Steinway's Sidney Greenstreet, the man aware of this mini-Casablanca's secrets, was a pioneer. A broad-shouldered Alexandrian with a shaved head like a genie, Sayed moved to Steinway

Street in the late 1980s to open the Kabab Café, a narrow six-table cranny filled with Egyptian bric-a-brac, stained glass, and a hookah or two. It sells a tasty hummus and falafel plate. "How's the food, folks?" he'll sometimes ask, displaying his American slang. "I'm just an insecure guy, so I need to ask." He found Astoria congenial because it was easy to shop for foods, such as hummus and okra, that he uses in his cooking. Within a few years the neighborhood had enough Arabs and other Muslims to support its first mosque, which was opened in a onetime pool hall on Twenty-eighth Avenue.

Sayed told me that Egyptians in Astoria are proud to be Americans, proud to blend into American society. Indeed, Egyptians and other Arabs and Muslims are assimilating in the United States with as much enthusiasm as earlier immigrant groups. In London, Paris, and Hamburg, there is far more ambivalence. Even two and three generations after they began settling in those cities, the Muslim underclass tends to remain outside the mainstream, whether by choice or because of the hostility they encounter from their long-rooted European neighbors. In the aftermath of the September 11 attacks, those communities have been fertile soil for homegrown terrorists. But in American cities such as New York, Muslims have been "pretty much immune to the jihadist virus," according to an assessment by Daniel Benjamin, a former National Security Council official quoted in *The Atlantic* on the fifth anniversary of September 11. Across the United States, Arab immigrants have a median income higher than the overall American one and a larger proportion of graduate degrees, something that is not true in France, Germany, and Britain. Moreover, Arabs and other Muslims are pouring into the United States in larger numbers than ever, despite the dip in the first years after 9/11, searching for jobs and personal freedom just as immigrants have always done. In 2005, for example, there were almost 5,000 Egyptians admitted as legal permanent residents, more than in the years before 9/11.

But assimilation can be a Trojan horse, a gift full of dangers, and those perils are appreciated in Arab Astoria. Many of the neighborhood's Egyptians and other younger Middle Easterners are marrying non–Middle Easterners. Sayed is married to an Argentinian, and his seven-year-old son, Esmaeel, speaks English and Spanish, not Arabic.

"There are lots of fears that their culture is getting destroyed," Sayed said.

Though in many patches of Astoria, Arabs are supplanting Greeks, the transition, by most accounts, has been without overt bitterness or conflict. George Delis, district manager of Community Board 1, said, "I get complaints from Greeks that the streets are dirtier, the properties not as well kept. I say to them, 'When you came to this country, the Italians and Irish were saying there goes the neighborhood.' And that's how I feel. This is a community of immigrants." Indeed, Oumous, the Moroccan computer programmer, said there was some suspiciousness after September 11 and landlords were likely to inquire more scrupulously into newcomers' backgrounds, but generally there has been no antagonism.

I HEARD AN ENTIRELY different beat just ten blocks south—the samba sound of the Brazilians. The Brazilians stand out in the smorgasbord of New York Latinos, who generally come here poor, half educated, and willing to spirit across borders. Brazilians in New York more often tend to come from bourgeois backgrounds; they are well schooled, and many held professional, managerial, or highly skilled jobs before they left their homeland. The 2000 census revealed that 30.8 percent of the city's Brazilians had degrees from colleges or graduate schools, triple the number for some other nationalities from Latin America, such as Mexicans or Ecuadorians. Brazilians can afford to fly here legally on tourist visas, which require proof of jobs and savings accounts, then intentionally overstay them. Unable to transfer their credentials here, they work as housekeepers, shoeshine guys, go-go dancers, and limousine drivers, hoping to legalize themselves but knowing that in the meantime they will make far more money here than they could have as white-collar workers in Brazil.

"In Brazil you have quality of life, but here you have financial security," explained Jamiel Ramalho de Almeida, the neatly bearded owner of the Ipanema Beauty Salon on Thirty-sixth Avenue who holds a teaching degree from a Brazilian college. "When you get a taste of the good life, it's hard to go back to what you had before."

At least since Carmen Miranda, with a fruit bowl for a hat, chica-chica-boomed audiences out of some of their stodginess, Brazil has had a distinct mystique among Americans. Samba and bossa nova rhythms have shaped the music of Frank Sinatra and Manhattan's dance clubs. Movies such as *Black Orpheus,* with its alternately haunting, rollicking score, and *Dona Flor and Her Two Husbands,* with its antic story of the erotic pull of a dead husband for a remarried widow, have mixed magic, lust, and a Brazilian love of revelry to relax American restraints. Pelé ignited a romance with soccer that has become a ritual of suburban autumn weekends.

But the mystique has always been felt at arm's length. Very few Brazilians actually settled here. That has been changing. Brazil's often inflationary economy and unemployment that perennially hovers near 10 percent have driven professionals and merchants to find their fortunes elsewhere. The New York area—not just Astoria, but Newark's Ironbound and Danbury, Connecticut—has been a galvanic destination. Although the 2000 census counted 13,000 New York City residents of Brazilian ancestry, with 3,372 of them in Astoria, the Brazilian consulate thinks those are gross undercounts. José Alfredo Graça Lima, the consul general in New York, doubled those numbers, and Astoria officials believe there may be 15,000 Brazilians in the area.

So many, in fact, that Tatiana Pacheco told me, "I feel like I'm in a different Brazilian town instead of ten thousand miles away." She is a slender twenty-eight-year-old woman with long brown hair who in many ways typifies the Brazilian New Yorker. She went to college in Brazil, then came here in the late 1990s and took a job as an au pair. By the time I met her she was working as a counselor to immigrants from all over the world, not just Brazil, at Immigration Advocacy Services, a nonprofit group near the mosque on Steinway Street.

The Brazilians are scattered among Astoria's not always charming apartment buildings and row houses, with the most visible concentration on Thirty-sixth Avenue near the Thirty-first Street N train line. There Brazilians can have a compatriot cut their hair or wax their legs and crotch bikini style. They can buy Brazilian mango juice and the smoked pork parts used for feijoada, a fatty bean stew so heavy that it is typically followed by a nap. On Friday and Saturday nights, Brazilians, who seem to have a national joie de vivre, crowd several nightclubs to dance and drink and seduce. The Malagueta restaurant on Thirty-sixth Avenue at Twenty-eighth Street was one of thirteen Queens restaurants chosen for inclusion in the first Michelin restaurant guide for New York. There is also a smaller cluster of Braziliana on Thirtieth Avenue, with two restaurants, Sabor Tropical and Churrascaria Tropical, specializing in *rodizio*, the juicy grilled meats brought to the table on a skewer.

Astoria has supplanted Manhattan's Little Brazil—Forty-sixth Street between Fifth and Seventh avenues—as the center of Brazilian life. The two midtown blocks once had 100 Brazilian shops that sold electronic goods to tourists at cheaper prices than in Brazil. When import taxes were reduced, the shops went out of business, and João de Matos, who organizes the annual Brazilian Day that draws hundreds of thousands to a carnival around Forty-sixth Street, said the street is down to three restaurants and three shops, including one that sells the string bikinis Brazilians call *fio dental* (dental floss).

Eloah Teixeira, a sixty-year-old woman who managed a light-fixtures shop in Porto Alegre in southern Brazil, has weathered the decline in status that comes with cleaning houses for many of her twenty years in America. She lives in a ground-floor apartment and exults in being able to afford tickets for musicals such as *Chitty Chitty Bang Bang,* and sampling restaurants such as Malagueta. But housecleaning, she adds, "is a hard job, especially when you're sixty." The owner of Malagueta, Herbet Gomes, has a degree from a two-year Brazilian technical college and in Brazil was a skilled mechanic who repaired mining machines. But he earned just $700 a month in 1990 and dreaded losing a finger to a machine. He risked immigration and found work as a dishwasher.

"It was a shame considering what I did in Brazil," he said. "All these years I work to be a dishwasher? Wow, what have I done wrong? After two weeks, I loosen up."

He worked his way up to the position of cook at other restaurants, and, in 1999, married another Brazilian, Alda Teixeira, who worked as a housekeeper. Four years ago, they opened Malagueta, a fourteen-table spot serving shrimp stew and *pudim de leite* (flan). Not surprisingly, one waitress, Monica Araújo, has a bachelor's degree in international relations from Pontificia Universidade Católica in Rio de Janeiro.

Even the Brazilian shoe shiners around Grand Central are slumming in New York. Ricardo Stefano spends eleven hours a day, five days a week, brushing the scuffed oxfords and dusty loafers of businessmen near Grand Central Terminal, something he has been doing since arriving from Brazil fifteen years ago. Shining shoes was a step down from fixing glasses in his father's eyeglass shop, particularly for someone with a year of college. But trailblazing compatriots told him he could make far more money shining shoes in New York than he could fixing glasses in Brazil, and the rumors turned out to be true. At age forty-three, he makes $500 a week, half of which he sends back to his estranged wife and three children in the state of Minas Gerais. He has not seen his children since he left. But Stefano does not regret his decision.

"When you come to this country, you know what kind of job you will find—because you don't have language, you don't have papers," he told me as he polished a pair of shoes someone had left. "That's the price you pay."

The price he and other Brazilians pay for their supposedly enhanced life is even higher than Stefano admits. Dr. Maxine L. Margolis, a professor of anthropology at the University of Florida in Gainesville who has studied New York's Brazilians, told me most Brazilians have an incurable case of *saudades,* the longing for home, and so come to the United States as sojourners, not settlers, intending to return someday. Most of the Brazilians I interviewed told me wistfully of plans to retire there or return once they had made their fortune. Araújo, the Malagueta waitress, spoke of pining for a place where she is surrounded by the Brazilian zest for life.

"Here, you just think about your job, about making money," she said. "You don't think about life."

THE GREEKS, WHO JUST a decade ago made up half of Astoria's population, are leaving for other places. Many immigrants made enough money in coffee shops, diners, and construction to afford homes in more spacious Bayside and Whitestone in Queens or Roslyn on Long Island. Children who grew up in Astoria did so well in the area's schools that many now work as lawyers and engineers, and they too are seeking fresher terrain. "What's happening is what happened to every other immigrant group," said Harilaos Daskalothanassis, managing editor of the Greek-language newspaper *The National Herald*, which has a tristate circulation of 40,000. "They came here and found jobs and inexpensive homes and eventually they wanted bigger houses and yards. Now their children or they themselves when they make some more money want houses in less urban areas—and new immigrants move into their space."

But these new immigrants are no longer Greeks. Greece is such a prospering member of the European Union that Greeks no longer feel the need to leave their homeland, as they did in the late 1960s and 1970s, when they came to the United States at a rate of 15,000 a year and a neighborhood like Astoria could support a movie theater, the Ditmars, that showed only Greek movies. "Greece is not a poor country," Harry, as everybody calls him, put it. Until two decades ago, Greeks stayed put in Astoria, preferring its two-family brick houses (sometimes with three families inside them) to taller apartment houses. "Nobody really moved," said Tina Kiamos, the executive assistant at the Hellenic American Neighborhood Action Committee, a social service agency, who grew up near Thirtieth Avenue and Thirty-seventh Street in the 1950s but left Astoria thirty-five years ago for Bayside. They liked visiting a doctor who spoke Greek on Astoria's "Doctors' Row" on Thirty-sixth Street at Thirtieth Avenue. They were proud of St. Demetrios School, whose uniforms of blue jackets and gray trousers or skirts were marks of prestige and where one year thirty-nine of its forty-one graduates passed the tests for selective Stuyvesant and Bronx Science high schools. These children of furriers and street vendors would hang out on corners, or go to dances at the church or at their parents' Hellenic societies, or, when they were older, to the nightclubs that featured the springing, foot-dragging circle dances popularized by *Zorba the Greek*. "The guys always had cars, the girls didn't, and the girls always tried to get the guys to take them to a dance," Kiamos remembered.

If such flirtations led to marriage, the couple expected to live in an Astoria row house. But somewhere along the way, the guys started dating girls who weren't Greek and the girls started going out with guys who weren't Greek. Many had already stopped going to after-school programs that taught them Greek, so they stopped speaking Greek to one another as adults. Unlike their parents, they chose to go to college, to campuses such as St. John's or Queens College. If they became professionals, the next stop was not Astoria but perhaps Manhasset on Long Island. And if they married and had a "big fat Greek wedding," complete with clueless non-Greek in-laws, they seldom returned to Astoria.

At seventy-five-year-old St. Demetrios Cathedral, the heart of the parish, adorned with Orthodox saints in radiant gold halos, I spoke in 2002 with Father Panagiotis Lekkas, an Athenian, who told me that there were 374 baptisms in 1981 but just 160 in 2001; 150 weddings in 1981 but just 88 in 2001. Perhaps three out of four of Astoria's weddings are between Greeks and non-Greeks, according to Stephanopoulos, whose son is married to a non-Greek. Delis, the manager of Community Board 1, a wiry native of Salonika who has wavy black hair and a mustache and who smokes slim cigars, pointed out with a Groucho Marx impishness that some of the Greeks are hitching up with Latin American women. "Off the record, Latin girls are very cute," he said. Tom Kourtesis, who runs Hellas Radio, told me that "the old, old-fashioned Greeks, they are very mad" about the intermarriages. "Sometimes the first few months they don't even talk to the kids."

The losses have left the remaining Greeks with a sense of, to use a word of Greek origin, melancholy, an emptiness that aches beneath the traditional bravado. They miss the intimacy of a neighborhood where everyone speaks the same language. Fotini Kessissoglou and her husband, Stavros, moved to Astoria from Athens in 1986 and within two months opened Kesso Foods on Twenty-first Avenue, which sells a thick, tart, strained Greek yogurt that they top with cherry preserves or stewed fruit and must be what the ambrosia of the Greek gods tasted like. "We didn't like the yogurts here," Mrs. Kessissoglou said. "Stavros is picky. He wants to make everything perfect. This is what we argue about." The couple was delighted to live in a bustling city near the sea, just like Athens. But the joy of their success has been tempered by the Greek decline. "When I first came I said to myself, 'The Greeks are very clever. They choose the best places to live,'" said Mrs. Kessissoglou. "So I am sad when I see all the Greeks go to other places."

The decline should not be overblown. Astoria, named after the fur merchant John Jacob Astor, whose farm embraced the neighborhood, may still have the largest Greek population in one spot outside Greece, and there is still a robust Greek accent in the stretch between Ditmars Boulevard and Broadway. The sidewalks are dotted with more than 100 social clubs, where Cretans, Cypriots, Minoans, Thessalians, Ithacans, Macedonians, Cycladians, and émigrés from other regions in Greece play cards, eat Greek delicacies, and talk exuberantly late into the night. Athens Square Park, with statues of Socrates and Athena and three ionic columns, is a lively new social center. Ditmars Boulevard, one of three main drags, has shops that trumpet Greek gods and heroes— Venus Jewelry, Hermes Laundromat, and Hippocrates Health Center— and nooks sell Greek CDs, newspapers, ikons, and jewelry. Even the Amtrak overpasses are painted blue and white.

The Greeks still conduct their ceremonies the old way. On my visit to Astoria I had a lunch of lamb and potatoes at Stamatis on Twenty-third Avenue. Most of the restaurant was occupied by a long table of mourners who had just come from a funeral. Almost all the women were dressed in black, some with black lace over their hair. Many men were in black too, and when they stood, all seemed to hold their shoulders squared, their heads high, their feet planted firmly on the ground. It seemed a way of carrying themselves that bespoke their confidence in their manhood, a Mediterranean affectation. Although they had just buried a relative and friend, the mourners were avidly consuming a sizable feast—succulent roasted baby lamb, lemon-infused potatoes, moussaka, hummus, grilled octopus, and *skordalia* (a garlic and potato dip). The talk became loud and excited. There was even laughter. I could only guess that the person who died had been very old.

George Alexiou joined me for lunch. He is a short, sinewy realtor who came in 1972 to follow a brother studying hotel management, obeying an impulse for wandering the earth that he suggests is wired into Greek genes. "We Greeks are always with two suitcases, like the Jews," he said. His résumé reads like those of many Greeks, with sweaty jobs in restaurants and hotels followed by work as a manager at the St. Moritz Hotel and a captain at Maxwell's Plum, then his own coffee shop on the Upper East Side. "I worked seven days a week, fifteen hours a day," he said. He saved his money to buy houses, owning so many that he is president of the Greek-American Homeowners Association, which lobbies for lower taxes. Astoria's Greeks, he told me, still own many of the row houses rented by newer immigrants, but they are now splurging on grander $500,000 houses for themselves in more suburban locales in Queens. "They work hard; they deserve it," he said, as if I had questioned their right to such comfort. "The problem is we don't have new blood. The problem is Greeks are well off, they don't come over here."

And then the Greeks here are to blame as well, he said, with a touch of prideful irony. "They make their money in diners and coffee shops, but they want their sons and daughters to get a degree—that's a fact." He knows the neighborhood's trends because he rents apartments to young Manhattanites attracted by Astoria's polyglot character. These young people like jogging in Astoria Park and using its swimming pool, the city's biggest. "They love the variety," he said. "They want Greek, they want Balkan, they want Chinese. They love it." Our conversation continued blithely along these lines, and then there was that stunning moment that shatters a reporter's detachment. Alexiou revealed that his twenty-two-year-old son had been killed in a car accident. "Life stinks sometimes," he said. "You make money and then you lose the thing you love most."

After we paid the bill, Alexiou drove me around and we stopped at the shop of Philippos Markakis, a grizzled poet who sports a flamboyant handlebar mustache that virtually merges with his bushy sideburns. He claims to have written 4,000 poems about "love, work, sadness, nature, the sea." But that's not how he makes his living. He operates perhaps the only combination coin laundry and barbershop in creation, cutting hair on one side of a partition for $8 and letting people do their laundry on the other side. He sometimes laments the neighborhood changes.

"People, when they say hello, they don't understand each other and they're more a little apart," he said in accented English that testifies to his odyssey almost fifty years ago from the Aegean island of Fournoi. "Among Greeks you walk up, you say hello, and everybody knows each other. These new people you keep your hands at your side. They're nice people, but they have different habits."

Still, he said, "I'm going to die here because I love Astoria."

There is a sprinkling of young Greeks who choose to live in Astoria, and one is Amalia Kalogridakis, a staff writer for Hellas Radio. She moved to Astoria from Bay Ridge, Brooklyn, in 2002 when she was twenty-four. What she likes about Astoria is that she can talk the night away—sometimes until 3 a.m.—and then go home and feel safe and surrounded by her compatriots. "Greeks and late nights are the same words," she said.

The neighborhood, after all, includes some of the city's tastiest Greek restaurants, such as Elias Corner, which is a few blocks from Stamatis below the shadows of the el on Thirty-first Street. At Elias, you can pick out your red snapper or sea bass at the counter on your left as you enter and then eat it grilled, its skin crisp, in the back or on an outdoor patio. Hangouts such as Lefkos Pirgos on Thirty-first Street and Omonia and Galaxy on Broadway serve the city's best baklava and galaktobourekos. Markets such as Mediterranean Foods and Titan Foods on Thirty-first Street offer a half dozen kinds of feta cheese marinating in a barrel of salt water, a dozen varieties of black and green olives, the flaky spinach pies known as spanakopita, the Greek salami called *aero*, and the small metal pots for brewing Greek coffee. Kalogridakis notices that Greeks who have left for other neighborhoods return every few months to stock up on stuffed grape leaves. "They come back to Astoria when they need their Greek dose," is the way she puts it.

On one of my visits, I joined members of the Minos Club, natives of Crete, three of them owners of suburban diners, for a lavish lunch under a lush grape arbor with the sun glinting through. We ate grilled red snapper, stewed lamb, and tomatoes with basil flown in from Crete, and drank a homemade brown Cretan wine. They stared eagerly, waiting for my reaction, whether I too felt their Greek specialties were unrivaled. As we drank more of the wine, the president, Aristides Garganourakis, a spirited man with a thick mustache, reminisced about coming to America in 1974 to work as a dishwasher. "We came here because we had no choice," he said. "We had to survive." He learned the restaurant trade, then opened a coffee shop in East Harlem, a pizza shop in Yonkers, and finally a diner in Dobbs Ferry, where he now lives. His children helped out but are now forsaking the business. "We put them to work, twelve, thirteen years old, and they say good-bye." His son John is studying medicine at the State University of New York at Binghamton. Garganourakis hopes that John will still come to Astoria to nourish his Cretan roots, so the Minos Club works hard to make sure their children sustain their culture, providing lessons in Greek language and folk dances. Unlike other Hellenic societies, they still have a substantial membership of young people—142. With John they are succeeding; he travels to Greece every summer and he comes to Minos Society dances.

But the likelihood that the children will live in Astoria is increasingly far-fetched. Alexiou, the realtor, put it hauntingly to me: "Little by little, if we don't have new blood coming in, it's starting to die."

ASTORIA

...

WHERE TO GO

Al-Iman Mosque (ASTORIA'S LARGEST MUSLIM HOUSE OF WORSHIP)
24-30 STEINWAY STREET; *(718) 626-6633*

Kaufman Astoria Studios (WHERE *SESAME STREET* AND OTHER
PRODUCTIONS ARE MADE) 34-12 36TH STREET; *(718) 392-5600*

Museum of the Moving Image (EXHIBITS ON ART, HISTORY, AND
TECHNOLOGY OF FILM AND TELEVISION) 35TH AVENUE AT THE
CORNER OF 36TH STREET; WWW.MOVINGIMAGE.US

St. Demetrios Cathedral (GREEK ORTHODOX) 30-11 30TH DRIVE;
(718) 728-1718

Steinway & Sons (FACTORY OFFERS TOURS OF HOW PIANOS ARE
MADE) 1 STEINWAY PLACE; *(718) 721-2600*

WHERE TO EAT

Churrascaria Tropical (BRAZILIAN) 36-08 30TH AVENUE;
(718) 777-8171

Elias Corner (GREEK SEAFOOD) 24-02 31ST STREET; *(718) 932-1510*

Kabab Café (EGYPTIAN RESTAURANT) 25-12 STEINWAY STREET;
(718) 728-9858

Kesso Foods (GREEK YOGURT SHOP) 77-20 21ST AVENUE;
(718) 777-5303

Laziza of New York (JORDANIAN BAKERY, SPECIALIZING IN KONAFA,
A WARM CHEESE PIE RICH WITH SWEET SYRUP AND PISTACHIOS)
25-78 STEINWAY STREET; *(718) 777-7676*

Malagueta (BRAZILIAN RESTAURANT) 25-35 36TH AVENUE;
(718) 937-4821

Mombar (SOUTHERN EGYPTIAN CUISINE) 25-22 STEINWAY STREET;
(718) 726-2356

Stamatis Restaurant (GREEK) 29-12 23RD AVENUE; *(718) 932-8596*

Taverna Kyclades (GREEK SEAFOOD) 33-07 DITMARS BOULEVARD;
(718) 545-8666

Chapter 2

Melting Together in Ditmas Park

. . .

Astoria, and other neighborhoods like it, where greeks cluster in one section, Brazilians in another, and Arabs in a third, illustrate the mosaic theory of ethnic integration. New York, that theory holds, is really an arrangement of different-colored ethnic tiles often coexisting amicably but separated by the sturdy grout of chauvinism and suspicion. And so, the theory continues, the fabled melting pot is a fanciful myth, never true for the immigrant Jews, Italians, and Irish in its own time and even less true since the ethnic identity movement of the 1960s made ethnic aloofness a virtue.

But in some places in New York City cultures do seem to melt into one another, suggesting ever so tentatively that Americans are more ready to get along today than ever before. Indeed, in New York the amount of actual mingling that now takes place in so many places is striking. Perhaps no neighborhood better showed me this quite radical shift than Brooklyn's Ditmas Park. Even many seasoned New Yorkers have never heard of it, at best confusing it with the rest of Flatbush, but it is there, among the graceful Victorian houses and stout apartment blocks south of Prospect Park, that I saw the new face of New York taking shape.

Whites, blacks, Asians, and Latinos share this softly shaded patch, and no one ethnic or racial group is dominant. Moreover, the neighborhood's population of 8,243 is not cut up into discrete ethnic swatches but is significantly interwoven. Residents such as Fred Siegel, urban affairs professor at Cooper Union, like to stand on their verandas and proudly reel off the races and nationalities that flank their porches and backyards.

"The people two doors down are Guyanese Indian," Siegel told me when I visited. "The woman diagonally behind us is from Grenada. The people in that brown house are from Yugoslavia. There's a family nearby that are Moroccan Jews from Israel. Then we have a former ambassador from Grenada four or five houses down."

The variety of ethnic groups and economic classes is immediately evident on a stroll down Cortelyou Road, the shopping spine, where within seconds I passed a black man with cornrows, a Muslim woman with a head scarf, a white mother in Birkenstocks, and a man wearing a skullcap. The street's car service is Mex Express, but the nail salon promises a European pedicure. The canopy at R & R Meats advertises "Productos Mexicanos" as well as "West Indian Products." The Associated supermarket, owned by a Polish Jew, has a heaping Mexican section. Cinco de Mayo is a restaurant where diners include not only yuppie and boomer foodies but lots of actual Mexican construction workers as well. The neighborhood tavern, the Cornerstone, is rough-and-tumble, but its blue-collar regulars are black and white. "We generally all get along," said Matthew McLean, a neighborhood resident and teacher at Edward R. Murrow High School. Vladimir Popov, the sixty-seven-year-old clerk at the video store, can wax effusive on the varying tastes in film of his West Indian, Chinese, Russian, and southern black customers, even if his generalizations—for example, which ethnic groups prefer triple-X-rated films—should be taken with a grain of salt.

I rambled the well-shaded side streets with evocative English names such as Westminster, Argyle, Buckingham, Rugby, and Marlborough roads and saw lovely gabled Victorians and Queen Annes, some with colonnaded porches, looking especially beautiful on a spring day when fallen cherry blossoms dusted the ground and crimson and yellow tulips were blossoming in front yards. Here and there were also sturdy white- and redbrick apartment buildings. Westminster Road could have been a street in an old Westchester suburb like Pelham. But immediately I was struck by how many different kinds of faces I saw. There were young Chinese men playing basketball at a driveway hoop, a blond woman talking to her Pakistani neighbor, and Professor Siegel.

As I talked to residents, I was struck not just by how many different cultures were living in those houses and apartments but also by how

many cross-cultural friendships there were, so many that they had become run-of-the-mill, suggesting that the diversity was not merely cos-
metic. A prime example was Mavis Theodore and Hynda Lessman
Schneiweiss, apartment dwellers who have been friends for more than
ten years, though their backgrounds could not be more dissimilar.
Schneiweiss, a woman in her early eighties, is a Chicago-born Jew, the
daughter of a men's pattern maker who lost his job in the Depression
and was forced to move to Brooklyn for work. Until she retired she was
an engineering assistant at the company that sold heating and cooling
equipment to the World Trade Center. She has lived in the neighborhood since 1942, for many years with her husband, Saul, a handball
player and swimmer, on East Eighteenth Street. Theodore, who is single and in her fifties, is a black Trinidadian, the daughter of a builder
who taught her the importance of community service by helping village
women earn money selling their crocheting and pottery. A single
woman, she moved into the neighborhood twenty-five years ago and
since 2001 has worked at Wiley, the publisher, granting licenses to colleges and hospitals for online access to the company's scientific and
medical journals.

Schneiweiss and Theodore met through community work. When
muggings and drug dealing sent many old-timers packing, Schneiweiss
stayed put. "I always had hope," she said. "I wasn't going to move. I don't
like to be pushed, and I pushed back." She joined the Seventieth
Precinct Council and the community board and forcefully let the police
know crime was eroding the neighborhood's viability. When the city finally appointed police commissioners who deployed patrols effectively,
the neighborhood reaped the benefits. "Crime in this neighborhood has
gone down to practically nothing," she said.

Theodore, meanwhile, was busy keeping the neighborhood flame
alive from her own angle. She recalls a time when Ditmas Park was
largely filled with Jews, Italians, and blacks who carved out their own
turfs, and when she felt the sting of that checkerboard isolation. "If
black people came into the area, people used to ask you where are you
going," she recalled. But she got involved in community work too, and it
was at a meeting of the Newkirk Area Neighborhood Association that
she met Schneiweiss, its president. She convinced the organization to

get involved in providing packages of school supplies to children in homeless shelters, some of whom wind up in Ditmas Park schools. In 2005 she, Schneiweiss, and helpers gave out 1,200 packages to fourteen shelters. But they socialize outside as well, going together to concerts at Carnegie Hall. Indeed, Theodore calls Schneiweiss "my dearest friend."

"Everybody has to learn and live together, and you can't learn to be in a democracy if you live in Borough Park," says Schneiweiss, referring to an overwhelmingly Hasidic enclave in Brooklyn. Mavis replies, "This neighborhood is going to demonstrate what Rodney King said, 'Can't we all get along?' "

Friendships like these are also common among younger people in Ditmas Park. Daniel Shaw, who is white and was a Cornell University senior when we spoke, went to the neighborhood's public schools and Midwood High School and has been friends since kindergarten with Miguel Valiente, a Panamanian, Etan Marciano, a Moroccan, and Elizabeth Hui, a Chinese. "When my friends and I walk down the street, we look like a UN summit meeting, no joke," he said. In high school, they hung out at his house on Friday afternoons. Miguel, whose father is a building superintendent, and Etan, whose father is a real estate developer, helped Daniel, whose father is a psychoanalyst, move into Cornell. "As soon as I moved to Ithaca it was painfully apparent—I had never seen so many white people before," Daniel said. Daniel and Etan went on spring break to Myrtle Beach. While Daniel told of some unpleasant consequences in the mix of rich and poor—he has been robbed at knifepoint and his father was beaten by young men trying to steal a briefcase—he was glad he had been raised there.

"I've been thankful even for the muggings," he said. "It keeps me in check because as much as I grew up in a comfortable house, I know I'm lucky. I can't get too cocky."

Karali Pitzele, a history teacher at the School of the Future in Manhattan, is in her mid-thirties and white, the daughter of a Jew and a Christian who raised her as a Buddhist in New Paltz, New York. She chose the neighborhood ten years ago in part because her boyfriend then was Jamaican and as an interracial couple they would not stand out. Now one of her friends is Dawn Eddy, a twenty-five-year-old Trinidadian teacher, and she has a warm relationship with her Pakistani neighbor. The neighbor borrowed her dining room table for an evening's entertainment and she borrowed masala spices back. For the Muslim holiday of Eid ul-Fitr, which ends the Ramadan fast, Pitzele left a bag of chocolates dangling from her neighbor's doorknob, and the following Christmas the neighbor gave her bracelets and a Pakistani dress and scarf. Typically, though, she worries that "white people like myself may idealize" the ethnic harmony "from our position of privilege in the mix."

Many residents remark on the number of interracial couples or families in the neighborhood, for example, Joe Wong, a twenty-eight-year-old grandson of Chinese immigrants, his wife, Ellen Moncure Wong, a native of Virginia, and their blond-haired toddler, Yates. Wong, a systems analyst for New York University, grew up in Ditmas Park and went to Public School 139. Now he lives in the top two floors of his parents' house. "As you're growing up you're getting exposed to the diversity and this becomes second nature," he said. "You wouldn't choose to move here if you weren't interested in that type of diversity."

The two census tracts that make up Ditmas Park are remarkable for their ethnic palette. In 2000, the racial breakdown was 40 percent black (almost half from the Caribbean), 23 percent white, 17 percent Hispanic, and 16 percent Asian. There are third- and fourth-generation Irish and Italians, Jews who were born in Russia and others who moved over from Park Slope, and significant smatterings of Bangladeshis, Mexicans, Pakistanis, Chinese, Tibetans, and Nepalese. In a neighborhood where in 2000 the median household income was $37,670—and a fourth of residents live below the poverty line—there are houses owned by well-heeled lawyers and executives.

"The reason why this works is there's no majority of one—there's a majority of many," Susan Miller told me. She is a mother of four who lives on a block of Victorians with neighbors of Indian, Pakistani, Polish, Italian, Jamaican, and Orthodox Jewish backgrounds as well as a discrete group she identifies as "Caucasian left-wingers."

Others speculate that Ditmas Park works as a neighborhood because it is wedged among more monotone enclaves: Caribbean East Flatbush, Jewish Midwood and Borough Park, Chinese and Latino Sunset Park, the South Asian pockets along Coney Island Avenue, and the neighborhoods of professionals surrounding Prospect Park. People from each of these distinct enclaves spill over and mix in Ditmas Park. "This area belongs to no one, so you have a lot of everyone," said Siegel. "This is very much diversity by accident."

The outlook for such neighborhoods, according to a Department of City Planning analysis, is bullish. The 2000 census indicates there were 220 melting-pot tracts among the city's 2,217, or one of ten; in 1970 there were only 70 such tracts. According to the Department of City Planning, a "melting pot" contains at least three racial groups, each with more than 20 percent of the population and none with more than 50 percent. In 2000, melting pots were also found in Elmhurst, Jackson Heights, and Flushing in Queens. For decent, convenient housing, middle-class New Yorkers are far more willing to live next to projects, seedy tenements, and drug dens than they were twenty years ago. That means that rich and poor, black and white, native and immigrant, have grown accustomed to one another's faces and races in ways unprecedented in American history.

"People are living side by side in a way that a hundred years from now we may take for granted," said Joseph J. Salvo, director of the planning department's population division in a speech at New York University's Wagner Graduate School of Public Service that inspired my visit to Ditmas Park. New Yorkers, he added, are more ready to say, "I'm going to live next to the guy even though he's five shades different than me."

In part, this openness to mixing is the result of the post-1965 wave of immigrants that reshaped the city. The city's liberal tradition, and the sheer habit of encountering different cultures, has also made New Yorkers more open.

"Anybody who rides the subway is going to have a multicultural experience," said John H. Mollenkopf, director of the Center for Urban Research at the City University of New York. "One senses that people who can't handle that sort of thing moved out of New York, or don't move in in the first place. All these people may not love each other, but they certainly have found ways to tolerate each other."

Ditmas Park is part of Victorian Flatbush, which extends from Prospect Park down to the Long Island Rail Road tracks on the south.

By some estimates, Flatbush contains the largest concentration of free-standing Victorians in the United States. These are roomy, rambling houses, almost mansions, with broad, covered porches and plenty of gables and turrets on the outside, and fireplaces, parquet floors, oak wainscoting, deep window seats, and stained-glass windows on the inside. Some of these homes were built for such prosperous businessmen as the owners of Carter Ink and Ex-Lax and such movie stars as Mary Pickford. A house at 101 Rugby Road was the Pink Palace in the movie *Sophie's Choice*, the rooming house owned by Yetta Zimmerman where Sophie and Nathan meet and die in such heartrending fashion.

The cornerstone of Victorian Flatbush is Ditmas Park. Until the twentieth century, it was farmland owned by the Dutch-rooted Ditmas family. Then the subway line (now the Q) came along and the neighborhood sprouted Victorians along with London planes, Norway maples, and linden. In some streets, traffic medians were put in and landscaped, giving the area a parklike feel. In 1981, the eastern half of Ditmas was designated a historic district by the Landmarks Preservation Commission.

Most residents use words like "utopia" in describing Ditmas Park, but the harmoniousness shouldn't be overhyped. Friendships, I also discovered in talking to dozens of residents, seldom extend across class lines. Indeed, while outsiders may be dazzled by the diversity, the neighborhood abounds with cynics or at least agnostics.

"I notice that the people who live in the apartments and rent and are of a lower income tend to keep to themselves and the homeowners who live in the albeit diverse community of homeowners also tend to be exclusive," was the gingerly observation of Claire Beckman, a forty-four-year-old actress.

Neil DeMause, a *Village Voice* writer, said, "Homeowners relate to other homeowners, white Slope [Park Slope, a nearby upscale brownstone neighborhood] refugees hang out with other Slope refugees, East Indians with other East Indians. I doubt this is any more pronounced here than in other parts of the city but it's an indication of the degree to which you don't create a melting pot just by dumping a bunch of disparate groups in the same geographical area." Pitzele put it this way: "I think we're mostly cohabiting in this neighborhood and not melting. Most people are friendly with people of their own ethnicity and social class."

Gideon Levy, a young employee at a bohemian coffee shop called Vox Pop, notices that when schoolchildren walk home "you tend to see the races, cultures, skin tones, falling into their economic separations, which sadly often correspond to traditional racial stereotypes." Louise Moed, a white fifty-one-year-old lawyer for the city's corporation counsel's office, also pointed out that friendships occur when there are professional commonalities, like the relation between her and her husband and two black couples on her block. At least one spouse in each family is involved in law. Moed thinks the insularity is particularly striking among recent immigrants. She told of a Pakistani woman whose daughters wanted to play with her twin girls, but the mother was reluctant, "even though it was obvious her girls were having lots of fun with mine."

Paul Feldman, a website editor, contends that the "diversity works against a strong sense of community." He and his actress wife, Christine Siracusa, have a three-year-old son, Sam, and have lived in Ditmas Park for five years. "Maybe there is such a thing as too much diversity," he said. "Or too much too soon for one neighborhood to accommodate without splitting into microneighborhoods. A mix is happening, but there's no personality that is asserting itself."

Then too, the neighborhood is fairly self-selected, drawing people such as Beckman and Wong, who are willing to grapple with discomforts that might arise out of cultural differences. Beckman, who has had parts in Hollywood movies such as *The Door in the Floor,* said, "I think the multicultural friendships are very real, but I seek them out." She observed that the kind of misfits and unconventional types who in the 1950s were drawn to Greenwich Village are now drawn to Victorian Flatbush. She might know, since she grew up on the Village's Bank Street in the 1960s. She had lived for a time among the brownstones of Carroll Gardens but found the neighborhood had become "too white" and shifted to Ditmas Park, first into a rental on East Sixteenth Street, then into a rambling Victorian on Westminster Road that she and her husband bought with another couple. Flatbush, though, represented a return to her roots, since her grandfather was a Russian immigrant who settled in Flatbush in the early 1900s. She thirsts for intimacy with other cultures, and her best friend on the block is a Jamaican nurse.

Graham and Chelsi Meyerson moved into an 1890 vintage Victorian on Glenwood Avenue after the birth of their daughter, Olivia, who was twenty months old when I interviewed them. "When Chelsi and I had Olivia," Meyerson said, "we wanted her to know a lot of different people." Meyerson, who is Jewish, grew up in Forest Hills, where most of the people he would see on his walks were Jewish. A former cook at the chic Union Square Cafe, Meyerson in 2004 opened the Picket Fence restaurant on Cortelyou, and now when he walks to work, "I get to see white, black, Chinese, tall, short. Even in Park Slope and the Upper West Side you don't get to see the diversity that this city is famous for." He is happy that the children at the school Olivia will attend, PS 217, speak thirty-five languages.

But even if the neighborhood is self-selected, it did not just fall out of an idealist's dreamscape. Neighbors work hard at sustaining its distinctive alloy. Around Christmastime, the neighborhood holds what they call, with no double entendre intended, progressive dinners. Courses are served at a succession of homes chosen because they represent a spectrum of ethnicities. On Thanksgiving, a black minister holds an open house and serves a breakfast of flapjacks and bacon for all comers. Dan Shapiro, a Jewish data consultant who has lived in a fifteen-room Victorian for twenty-five years, said every neighbor is invited for weddings, funerals, and bar mitzvahs. "When Dennis Mooreman, Melba Moore's brother, died, the funeral was held in the black church and everyone showed up," said Shapiro. "When I had my bar mitzvahs for my son and daughters, I invited everyone on the block and everyone showed up. And that's very common."

Beckman runs a dramatic company, Brave New World Repertory Theatre, out of the ground floor of her home, and in September 2005 she put on a production of *To Kill a Mockingbird* using her porch and five of her neighbors' porches as the stage. Her daughter, Taylor, eight, played the impressionable southern youngster of the film, Scout; Beckman played the narrator, the grown-up Scout; and her husband, John Morgan, played Bob Ewell, the father of the young white woman who falsely accuses a black worker of rape. The rest of the cast was made up of professional actors and volunteer neighbors. On a later summer night, a thousand people crowded the sidewalks and roadway of Westminster Road to see the show, and most were exhilarated by the experience. "In a quarter-century of theater-going in New York, never have I seen an audience as integrated as the one that took their folding seats on Sunday: black and white, old and very young, with a healthy sprinkling of neighborhood teenagers," wrote one freelance reviewer. "This was street theater, people's theater, of the highest order."

A four-year-old organization, Friends of Cortelyou, sponsors ethnic tastings and pairs recent immigrants with fluent English speakers as "conversation partners." At Picket Fence, Meyerson intentionally hires a diverse staff, including Justin Alexander, a waiter from Trinidad, and Dana Nagler, a Jewish cook from Long Island, to prepare and serve his cheeseburgers on brioche, crab cakes, and pear gorgonzola bread pudding.

Vox Pop, the idiosyncratic combination coffeehouse, bookstore, and print shop, holds open-mike evenings, where rappers, poets, or political activists express their views. The crowd at one evening of poetry organized to raise money for a women's shelter was filled with black and South Asian women. With its blunt motto—"Books, Coffee, Democracy"—it's the kind of place where women feel comfortable breastfeeding their babies as they drink their lattes and eat their organic turkey baguettes. Vox Pop's earnest owner, Sander Hicks, whose goatee makes him look like a young Trotsky, styles himself a "rebel bookseller" who fights the chain stores and offers a "voice to people who don't have one." But whatever the ideological trappings, in his coffee shop people of different stripes rub up against one another in ways that are sure to leave some lasting influences on the neighborhood.

There are some who worry that a diverse Ditmas Park may be fleeting, that the motley place I wandered into was a snapshot frozen in time that was sure to be a very different place if I visited five or ten years from now. It is true that the history of Ditmas Park, unlike, say, Bensonhurst or Howard Beach, is one of perennial change. The 1970 census showed a neighborhood that was 95 percent white; Rugby Road was known as Doctors' Row. But when that count was taken, the tectonic plates under the neighborhood were already shifting. There were vacancies in some large apartment buildings—created by people who had moved up in the world or fled—and the city, struggling with a mushrooming and clamorous welfare population, filled those vacancies with broken families. Some of these families introduced drugs and muggings. White homeowners began selling, and middle-class blacks, not as put off by welfare families, bought up Victorians at fire-sale prices, effectively integrating even the neighborhood's affluent parts.

The upsurge of crime throughout the city in the 1970s and 1980s and a shaky economy meant more departures. Neighborhood-improvement groups such as the Flatbush Development Corporation and the Flatbush Tenants Council, led by Marty Markowitz, now the Brooklyn borough president (who lived at 400 Rugby Road), managed and repaired hard-pressed buildings and evicted troublesome tenants. Young whites starting families, such as Shapiro and his wife, Ruth, a junior high school teacher, were able to afford a fifteen-room Edwardian-era house for $53,000. Other pioneers included Geoffrey Stokes, another writer for *The Village Voice*, and the jazz pianist Kenny Barron. Orthodox Jews overflowed from Borough Park and Pakistanis from the area around the mosque on Coney Island Avenue.

But crime was still festering and almost no one would have chosen Ditmas Park as an example of congenial ethnic relations. In fact, they were more likely to write about ethnic tensions, for instance, an ugly boycott in 1990 by black residents of a Korean market on Church Avenue not too far from Ditmas. A Haitian woman had claimed she was pummeled trying to buy some plantains and peppers. The grocers claimed she had tried to leave without paying. The protest featured a gauntlet of pickets led by the provocateur Sonny Carson and the Reverend Al Sharpton. Demonstrators shouted threats and spit at anyone trying to patronize the store. Leaflets urged people to avoid shopping "with people who do not look like us." Mayor David Dinkins did little to intervene, and the neighborhood was stigmatized—not that it was all that attractive. The sidewalks in front of apartment houses on Rugby Road were littered with crack vials, houses were routinely burglarized, and drainpipes were removed for their copper.

"In the early nineties, this neighborhood was going to go," said Siegel. "A stolen car was dumped right in front. A guy came and stripped the car and then vultures came for the cheaper items, and you were afraid they would try your house. A Russian woman was mugged. Someone told her, 'What do you expect if you live in a neighborhood like this?' "

But things began to turn around, and Siegel believes much of the credit belongs to Mayor Rudolph Giuliani's commitment to stronger enforcement. Siegel was a policy adviser for Giuliani's 1993 election campaign and wrote a book about his administration called *Prince of the City.* Throughout the period, parents worked with the local school board to maintain classroom quality and fought successfully against a plan to eliminate gifted programs. They cajoled the parks department to turn a burned-out lot on Cortelyou into a playground called the Cortelyou Totlot that became an ethnic meeting ground. Black, white, and Asian families grew close in the process.

Siegel's wife, Jan Rosenberg, a sociologist at Long Island University and local real estate broker, deserves credit for helping revive seven-block-long Cortelyou Road by attracting restaurants—a decade ago it didn't have a single sit-down spot—and upscale shops such as Cortelyou Vintage, an antiques store with mid-twentieth-century furniture. In 2006, the Farm on Adderley restaurant, started by a South African, opened and received a warm review from *The Times.* Rosenberg is still trying to attract a bank. She's also sponsored events for getting cultures to know one another such as "Cortelyou Is Cooking," where residents from Mexico, Pakistan, China, Israel, and the Caribbean sample one another's cuisines.

The patchwork of efforts has been so successful that artists with children from gentrifying Greenpoint and Williamsburg are turning to this once-genteel and bourgeois corner of Brooklyn, stimulated by its variety. "It's always artists and liberals who are drawn to these communities," said Beckman. But now, with prices of some homes surpassing $1 million, Beckman and people like her fear that only well-heeled buyers will consider the neighborhood and that Ditmas Park's multicultural character could dissolve—meaning that in a decade the neighborhood's snapshot may be very different.

"What's scary," Beckman said, "is that it could change."

DITMAS PARK

...

WHERE TO GO

Pink Palace (SITE OF *SOPHIE'S CHOICE*) 101 RUGBY ROAD

Victorian and Queen Anne houses (ONE OF GREATEST
CONCENTRATIONS IN THE UNITED STATES) WESTMINSTER,
BUCKINGHAM, ARGYLE, RUGBY, AND MARLBOROUGH ROADS

Vox Pop (BOOKSTORE, COFFEEHOUSE, AND BOHEMIAN GATHERING
SPOT) 1022 CORTELYOU ROAD; *(718) 940-2084*

WHERE TO EAT

Cinco de Mayo (MEXICAN) 1202 CORTELYOU ROAD; *(718) 693-1022*

The Farm on Adderley (AMERICAN BISTRO) 1108 CORTELYOU ROAD;
(718) 287-3101

Picket Fence (ECLECTIC) 1310 CORTELYOU ROAD; *(718) 282-6661*

Chapter 3

Clinging and Rebounding in East Harlem

. . .

FOR FIFTY-SEVEN YEARS, CLAUDIO CAPONIGRO HAS WATCHED through the window of his barbershop as Italian Harlem has changed around him, but he and his shop have hardly changed at all. He still has the same three barber's chairs of peppermint green porcelain and faded brown leather that he had when he came to work in the shop in 1950 as a young greenhorn from the south of Italy.

"If I got this chair and it's a good chair and it can last one hundred years, why I got to put up another chair?" was his matter-of-fact explanation when I dropped in one day.

When hygiene codes demanded he use disposable razors, he submitted. But he still has his straightedge and a worn leather strop dangling from the arm of a chair, "just in case" (his euphemism for when health authorities aren't looking). Dusty bottles of Jeris Hair Tonic and Pinaud Eau de Portugal and pictures of his three daughters and two grandchildren guard the mirrored counter, but there is no telephone. Caponigro has never seen a need to have one, and customers cannot call him to make appointments. If there is an emergency, his wife has to call the bread bakery down the block.

"When you have a telephone, people, they call you," he explained, with the slightest edge of a complaint. "So-and-so call, 'Is Petey there? Could you see if he's outside?' Then I got to leave the customer. That's no good."

He takes customers in the order they walk in, and even regulars wait their turn silently, in shabby armchairs patched together with masking tape, while he lets those in the barber's chair—and with his lusty baritone, those waiting as well—know his thoughts about the Old World values he holds dear, values such as loyalty and respect. All the while, he takes slow, tender snips at each customer's hair, surveying his handiwork for balance and composition like an artist. You go to him not just for the haircut but for the world seen through one deeply experienced man's eyes, a man who has you imprisoned in a chair for fifteen minutes and knows there's not much else for you to do but listen. But you also go to Caponigro because he is a relic of a neighborhood that is hardly there anymore.

I came across Caponigro because I was looking for remnants of the old Italian neighborhood in East Harlem the way some Jews go back to the Bronx looking for the telltale Stars of David on Pentecostal churches. They want to remind themselves of the flourishing neighborhood they once lived in. In East Harlem, a neighborhood I first visited as a young man in the 1960s, I was surprised not by how little Italian flavor was left but that there was any left at all. The enclave in which Caponigro lived for his first two decades in this country and in which he still works had 80,000 Italians into the 1930s, extending from the famous—Fiorello H. La Guardia—to the infamous—mobster Frank Costello—but mostly embracing the carpenters, bakers, doctors, undertakers, housewives, and grandmothers who keep a culture vital. The neighborhood, which extends from Third Avenue to the East River between Ninety-sixth and 120th streets, shrunk dramatically after World War II, although an Italian village still thrived along the East River into the 1970s, surrounded on three sides by the neighborhood Puerto Ricans call El Barrio, their heartland.

But largely as a result of New York City's accelerating ethnic mobility, Italian East Harlem is down to a relative handful of Italians, a sprinkling of Italian stores, and a Roman Catholic Church, Our Lady of Mount Carmel. Ask one of the worshipers, Gena Bolino, a woman who was born in the neighborhood, how many Italians are left, and she will respond with exasperated simplicity: "You can count them."

Now that all the Italians of means and vigor have left, Italian East Harlem is in its slowly decaying finale, a hospice phase where those who loved the neighborhood gather round and wait for it to breathe its last breath. Claudio's Barber Shop, in its tumbledown shack on 116th Street near First Avenue, is thus an artifact of a bygone civilization, its fusty customs and etiquette a Rosetta stone to a place that barely can be said to exist, with Caponigro the cicerone who can serve as a guide to this vanishing civilization.

I was also taken with the crusty, charming, tenacious Caponigro because he exemplifies another theme of contemporary New York, what the journalist Pete Hamill observed in a recent book is the "New York version of nostalgia": "an almost fatalistic acceptance of the permanent presence of loss." In the rapid changes of the twenty-first century, Caponigro and veteran New Yorkers like him cling even more fiercely to simpler memories of the way we were, and that yields a set of bittersweet, paradoxical emotions.

"You are a New Yorker when what was there before is more real and solid than what is here now," the novelist Colson Whitehead has famously written, and ethnic wistfulness makes up a large part of that longing. Caponigro has watched as Italian East Harlem has been replaced by a new Spanish Harlem, filled not just with longtime Puerto Rican residents, who settled mainly after World War II, but increasingly with Mexicans and Dominicans, and, as I discovered, a whole new breed of middle-class Puerto Ricans. Puerto Ricans have been here so long they have seen compatriots leave for greener pastures—in the suburbs; Orlando, Florida; and Puerto Rico itself—and feel their turf imperiled. During the 1990s, the number of Puerto Ricans in East Harlem dropped to 34,626 from 42,816. They are now only 31.6 percent of the neighborhood compared to 45.3 percent in 1960. Mexicans have climbed to 9.4 percent and increasingly own the bodegas and have replaced *cuchifritos* luncheonettes with taco stands.

Yet the wonder of restless, protean New York is that, as many Puerto Ricans are leaving, others are returning. Puerto Ricans who grew up in the tenements and housing projects of El Barrio but moved away during the 1970s and 1980s, when crime, drugs, and housing abandonment were rampant, are moving back, now as professionals, artists, and intellectuals drawn by an authenticity they miss. They are moving in among the busboys and housekeepers and speak of down-at-the-heels East Harlem with the fervor of the early Zionists who dreamed of a Jewish restoration in Palestine. Their movement, the returnees say, is a philosophical crusade to keep Spanish Harlem Puerto Rican.

"Puerto Ricans are coming back to the neighborhood," said Dylcia Pagán, an esteemed Puerto Rican nationalist whom I met at a local artists' hangout. She grew up on 110th Street in the 1950s, and became such a champion of Puerto Rican independence that she was convicted in a bombing plot and spent nineteen years in federal prison. She was granted clemency by President Bill Clinton and now works in information technology in San Juan. When I met her, she was in the neighborhood to look at a brownstone she wanted to buy. "Many of us got our education, got better jobs, and now are saying we want to come back to our community," she told me.

YOU GO TO CLAUDIO CAPONIGRO, as Peter Guaragno, eighty-five years old, has once a week for half a century (as long as there are no horse races that day), because life goes on in his shop the way it always has, retaining its appeal to those who shrug off the siren songs of modernity. "He's the only one I trust," says Guaragno.

Caponigro is a tall, sturdily built silver-haired man who wears gold-rimmed bifocals for his nearsightedness. "I was born with a smile," he told me. He is so devoted to those whose hair he cuts that he keeps two hundred mass cards for the funerals of dead customers he has attended. He charges his customers $8 a haircut even though one mile south, on the Upper East Side, prices of $30 are common. I took one of his $8 haircuts.

"I believe that eight dollars for this neighborhood is plenty," Caponigro said as he trimmed my hair. "A lot of people here are on SSI, government assistance. They poor people. How can I charge more? Those guys charge twenty or thirty dollars; today they're here, tomorrow they're out of business. Me, a reasonable price, I'm still here."

For the same survival reasons, he never discusses politics. "You want to stay in business all your life, one thing you cannot talk about is politics or religion, because before you know it you get into an argument," he said. But he nevertheless told me stories about the politicians whose hair he cut, or didn't cut—Carmine DeSapio, the legendary Tammany Hall leader ("a great, great, great gentleman"), and Vito Marcantonio, the legendary left-wing congressman who represented Italian Harlem for seven terms between 1934 and 1950. Marcantonio used another barber, but Caponigro's ethics are such that he never held it against him.

"He was my friend, but he was not my customer," Caponigro said. "Because he never double-crossed his barber on Second Avenue. He was loyal to Mr. Louie Lambarelli. I was proud of him that he was loyal. Couple of people say he was this and that. He was a socialist. He was a communist. To me, he was a lovely man, especially for the poor people. He died broke. He was generous. He couldn't see people suffer."

Only once, he said, did he make an exception to his rule that customers wait their turn. Frank G. Rossetti, another Tammany Hall leader, was in Mount Sinai Medical Center and needed a shave and a haircut. Caponigro kept six customers waiting while he hurried to the hospital to tend to the old boss. As a result, Rossetti's son Frank S. Rossetti, now a State Supreme Court justice, has a special regard for the last barber of East 116th Street. "The son always have respect for me," Caponigro said proudly.

As East Harlem's Italians told me of the rueful ache they feel at seeing the sepia-tinted neighborhood of their childhood fade into oblivion, I recognized their emotions as familiar. I lived on the Grand Concourse a few blocks north of Yankee Stadium from the mid-1950s through the late 1960s, from the age of ten until I was twenty-one, and I saw the streets off that boulevard transformed seemingly overnight. During the years I grew up there, the Concourse neighborhood was a sharply defined swath of New York where the rituals of life seemed immutable. Jewish, Irish, and Italian children played punchball in the alleyways squeezed between the Art Deco and redbrick apartment houses. On Sunday mornings, families dispatched couriers to the neighborhood's bakeries to pick up rye breads and Danishes for breakfasts that assumed the sacredness of a Communion meal. On any sunny day, gray-haired and middle-aged idlers sat out on aluminum beach chairs sizing up the comings and goings of their buildings' residents with the understandable condescension of those newly arrived in the middle class toward those—the immigrants—who hadn't yet made it. On weekend mornings, fathers and mothers in their best off-the-rack suits and dresses wheeled baby carriages and dragged small children on the way to synagogue or church for some spiritual refreshment.

There were colorful barbers in that neighborhood too who, like Claudio Caponigro, stayed long after their ethnic brethren had fled. In my gossamer memories, there were two refugees named Bernie and Boris, with Bernie the good-humored bear to Boris' more dour wraith. It was always a deep pleasure to go into their shop, the air sweet and sharp with the fragrance of hair tonics and aftershave, the sunlight fragmented by the talcum powder dust, the hubbub of kibitzing customers certifying that you had been admitted into a male sanctum sanctorum. Bernie and Boris would spend at least a quarter hour tending with efficiency but tenderness to the confidential needs of your scalp. High-spirited Bernie was something of a gallant and had a smiling, carefree, open-armed way of shrugging off the world's problems. Boris was quieter, more dyspeptic and turmoiled. His plump, peroxide-blond wife would sometimes come into the shop and sit on the plastic-backed chairs with the waiting kibitzers in what seemed to a young boy a violation of the shop's decorum. But whatever their foibles, both Bernie and Boris knew what synagogue and schools you went to and how well you were doing in school. They asked whether you were diligently studying for your bar mitzvah or had decided on a college—a question not many neighborhood tradesmen asked. Your father was their customer too, after all, and they knew all that he had gone through during the European war they shared.

Many years later, I passed the shop; Bernie had died, but Boris was still there. He seemed to have gained a whole new spring of confidence in his step, was more talkative than I remembered. He was his own man now in his own shop. But I could see by the dingy, cracked walls that the shop was going to seed. Only a handful of his aging Jewish customers remained, and he was giving haircuts mostly to black and Puerto Rican men. Without Bernie and his old customers, Boris, it seemed, would not keep the shop open much longer. He showed me the heavy lock he now had to keep on his shop so local thieves wouldn't break in and a metal cylinder he slipped over his candy-striped barber's pole so malicious teenagers wouldn't crack its glass. What a contrast he was to the optimistic Caponigro.

In Caponigro's shop, it was nice to be surrounded by such an Old World Italian paragon and his friends and their throwback mannerisms—

the gesturing hand with the uplifted palm, the repeated allusions to loyalty, the unambiguous opinions, the undeniable warmth. But the longer I got to know his shop, the more apparent it became that most of Caponigro's respectfully silent customers, when they spoke, spoke Spanish. And that was as it should be. Puerto Ricans, seeking better futures than they could hope for in the chronically ailing economy of their hardscrabble island, began moving into East Harlem in significant numbers in the 1920s, when most of the neighborhood was Jewish and Italian; then in the late 1940s, another economic crisis on the island and the lure of postwar jobs here brought a major stream of migrants and Puerto Ricans.

One reason was that the Italians were forsaking the neighborhood's tenement and brownstone apartments. The Italians had started immigrating to the United States at the end of the nineteenth century, built the subways and skyscrapers, and moved to Harlem because it was a step up from the seedy congestion of the Lower East Side. But now they were departing East Harlem for sweeter prospects, ready to live on the leafier fringes of Brooklyn and Queens or in suburban homes with patches of grass, two-car garages, and driveways with basketball nets. And they could afford to do so now that they held jobs that required more brains than brawn. As a result, the neighborhood is down to a few Italian outposts. These include the 115-year-old Morrone Bakery, makers of a superbly crusty-on-the-outside and chewy-on-the-inside loaf of sesame-sprinkled bread; the hyperexclusive Rao's restaurant, which draws the limousines of the city's power brokers as long as they are steady friends of the owner; Patsy's pizza parlor, where lines of blue-collar aficionados wait to pick up its thin, spicy pizzas; three funeral homes; and Our Lady of Mount Carmel, where a few elderly neighborhood residents go to say their novenas.

I asked Rosa Morrone, an Italian immigrant who is the wife of the owner of the eponymous bakery, what happened to the Italians, and she told me as she showed me her timeworn dough-mixing machine. "My kids married; they all live on Long Island, except one son who's not married, he lives with us," she said. "They don't want to live on this street; they want to live on Long Island. I don't like Long Island. I like this place. I like to walk to all the stores. I don't drive. Where am I going to go?"

. . .

BY THE 1950S PUERTO RICANS began to put their stamp on the flavor and beat of the gritty neighborhood, with their bodegas and botanicas, sidewalk domino players and blaring salsa rhythms. The neighborhood became known more as Spanish Harlem, certified as that by the 1961 Ben E. King song, written by two Jewish guys, Jerry Leiber and Phil Spector, both enchanted and unsettled by the novel, slightly dangerous, no longer sedately European culture arriving at New York City's doorstep.

Much of that community is now Mexican and Dominican. Still, Puerto Ricans are coming back because they have tasted suburban life, found it a touch too bland, and sought to regain something remembered they could not let go of. Like many Puerto Rican strivers, David and Betty Cutié had forsaken the jostling streets of Spanish Harlem for the suburbs fifteen years ago, settling in a split-level ranch in Rockland County. But when their daughter, Nina, was grown and they were thinking about retirement, the Cutiés—David was a principal, Betty a guidance counselor—realized they missed the sounds and smells of the old neighborhood. Several years ago, they moved back, fixing up a brownstone on East 118th Street and finding that the streets retained much of the coarse, festive mix they cherished: gaudy murals, coconut-ice vendors, hole-in-the-wall luncheonettes with Tito Puente rhythms, ragged tenements next to fussed-over gardens. The neighborhood was on an upswing, with much less of the crime and drug dealing that had driven them out. But the upswing also meant that this quintessential Latino quarter was gradually losing the accent and influence that had defined it. Besides contributing the sheer enhancing presence of his family, David Cutié serves on Community Board 11, which plays an advisory role in city zoning, housing, and budgetary policies. "We felt the neighborhood needed us, that we had things we could contribute," he told me.

Puerto Rican exiles are pumping new life into the neighborhood, sprucing up once-decaying buildings and enlivening the area's cultural life with art galleries and theater troupes. The city and the city's big landlords, however political or mercenary their motives, are pitching in. Starting in the mid-1980s, the city sponsored the construction or rehabilitation of at least 10,000 homes, and town houses and apartment buildings are blossoming where there were empty lots, often right next door to the mammoth housing projects built for the neighborhood's poor. As a result of these relatively upscale returning Puerto Ricans, the median income for Hispanics in the neighborhood grew by almost 18 percent during the 1990s to $18,313.

Many of those who return are coming back as a result of calculated efforts by individuals and organizations that are trying to sustain a cultural Puerto Rican core in East Harlem. One such organization is the Taller Boricua Gallery, which collects and exhibits contemporary Puerto Rican art but also helps artists buy neighborhood properties. The neighborhood, according to Fernando Salicrup, the gallery's director, now counts more than 1,000 artists and theater people, including many with international reputations, among them José Morales, Diógenes Ballester, and Antonio Martorell (whose works have been exhibited at the Whitney Biennial and who lives at 106th Street and Lexington Avenue). Together, these homecomers have introduced an upscale Puerto Rican spice that belies stereotypes of superintendents and doormen. On Thursday nights, the Taller Boricua Gallery holds Julia's Jam—a chance for Puerto Rican poets and short-story writers, for musicians who play the folk music of *bombas* and *plenas,* to strut their stuff.

One of the resident writers is Nicholasa Mohr, who capered on the streets of East Harlem of the 1940s. "No matter where you lived, even if people lived in Brooklyn or the Bronx, they always came here," she said. "They came to La Marqueta [the legendary market under the Metro-North tracks that at its peak was home to 200 vendors selling avocados, yucca, plantains, and folk remedies but has shrunken to a handful of merchants], or they would come to see relatives, or go to church at St. Cecilia's. This was the capital, the heart of the Puerto Rican community."

In 2001, Mohr, by then a successful writer of novels for adults and teenagers about life as a Nuyorican—a New York–reared son or daughter of Puerto Rican parents—decided to return to her childhood streets. She bought a duplex condo in a converted school on East 108th Street. It is a breathtaking two-level loft furnished in elegant bohemian, with tastefully spaced shelves of books and an eclectic collection of eye-catching paintings. But the chance to live in the handsome apartment is not entirely what drew her back to El Barrio. The rough-edged streets had more to do with her decision. "It's very pleasant being in a Latino community," she said. "There's a warmth I'd forgotten about. There's a warmth about being greeted in the morning and hearing both English and Spanish being spoken."

Another charter member of the art community, Mario César Romero, a freelance curator who never quite left the neighborhood, tried to give me a sense of why these streets are so revered by walking me around the blocks off 106th Street. On our tour, he took pride in what he called the carnival street scene—the colorful semi-illegal community gardens, the Mexican flower sellers, and the flamboyant murals that in some places strike a visitor as folk art but in other places seem more like malicious graffiti. Salsa, he reminded me, was born in El Barrio. Don Pedro Albizu Campos, the thwarted Simón Bolívar of Puerto Rican independence, came to El Barrio when he was released from jail. He called the neighborhood the "symbol of the Puerto Rican diaspora."

Romero is a gregarious man, and his wit barely conceals the anger born of seeing people who came here brimming with hope only to find themselves diminished. "When Puerto Ricans come here they bring all of their politeness and humility," he said. "We call it 'always bent.' They come to New York and get their asses kicked one at a time. Our people have changed and become more aggressive because it's the only way to exist."

The returning Puerto Ricans are actually the vanguard of a wider gentrification that is changing the face of East Harlem just as it has changed Harlem to the west and Fort Greene, Bushwick, and East New York in Brooklyn. Whites and Asians too, mostly singles, are crossing the once Berlin Wall–like demarcation of East Ninety-sixth Street and taking up apartments next to housing projects and bodegas, drawn by cheaper housing prices. Tall apartment buildings are replacing tenements and rubble-strewn lots above Ninety-sixth Street. Voguish restaurants and cafés have popped up on ramshackle blocks, including La Fonda Boricua, Dinerbar, and, briefly but significantly, SpaHa (a SoHo-like coinage for Spanish Harlem). This once-bedraggled neighborhood now has a Blockbuster and a Duane Reade pharmacy. Two-bedroom apartments that might have been had in the mid-1990s for $600 a month were going for triple and quadruple that amount a decade later.

Brownstones that in the 1960s could be purchased for $10,000 were going for $500,000. Brokers underplay the Spanish Harlem name and casually speak of the neighborhood as the Upper Upper East Side or Upper Yorkville. And the truth is, as a result of the influx of Puerto Rican professionals and young whites and Asians, the neighborhood's median household income climbed almost 10 percent during the 1990s, and will probably rise even more sharply in this new century.

Among the white pioneers I met were the tenants in Esther Sirol's two renovated rooming houses on 101st Street. Sirol bought the buildings in 1995 when they were filled with welfare families and has spent hundreds of thousands restoring the buildings' original early-twentieth-century touches. She has installed antiques throughout, as well as a whirlpool and sauna. Her buildings have the feel of country inns. Among her sixteen tenants, she boasts doctors from Mount Sinai Medical Center, directly on the other side of the Metro-North tracks, professors at nearby Columbia University, a vice president at Morgan Stanley, and some lawyers. One tenant I met was Julie Feuerstein, the daughter of Lutheran missionaries from the Midwest. Another was Muriel Sainato, a twenty-six-year-old actress from Florida whose two children are being taken care of by her former mother-in-law. "I was afraid you couldn't walk down the road without someone shouting a vulgarity, but it's been fine," Sainato told me.

Not for everybody, however, because pioneering requires the grit to wait out the rough early years. Ian Bell, a twentysomething publicist, moved with his friend Jackie Fritz, a twenty-two-year-old choreographer from St. Louis, from a cramped one-bedroom in Chelsea into a two-bedroom loft on East 108th Street for which they paid $2,000 a month. But the apartment is in the middle of East Harlem, directly across the street from a low-income housing project. They thought they could conquer their fears about safety by taking taxis at night. "We figured that the amount of money we spent on taxis would equal our rent in Chelsea," he said. But when I ran into them one year later they told me it was hard to find fresh fruits and vegetables, hard to see a movie, hard to get friends to visit them, and a longer commute. They've had an unpleasant encounter—some young men said to them, "Look at you silly white people." When we last spoke, they were moving out.

Aurora Flores, a journalist, counts herself as one of the pioneers in the Puerto Rican homecoming movement, having moved fifteen years ago from the Upper West Side to an apartment on 107th Street off Fifth Avenue when fellow Puerto Ricans—those who had been the first in their families to go to college and get decent jobs—were leaving. "They acquired a middle-class status for themselves and the first thing they did was move out of El Barrio," she said. While she grew up on the Lower East Side, she had always been enchanted by Spanish Harlem as a young girl when her mother did her shopping there. By the time she was in high school, she was drawing up posters and writing screeds for the Young Lords, the sometimes feared Puerto Rican street gang that turned into a revolutionary cadre until it fizzled out in the 1970s under police attack and its own infighting. As a single mother, she now runs a public relations business that centers on Spanish Harlem and promotes Latin concerts, including the weekly Julia's Jam.

She explained her decision to move in by a desire to firm up her son's ethnic pride, telling about an incident that happened when her son, Abran, was a student at highly selective Hunter College Elementary School on the Upper East Side. Classmates had been urging him to quit speaking Spanish because, in Flores' account, that was the language of the "people who clean their houses." She decided she would "not let my son get whitewashed when he has these deep roots," and she transplanted herself to Spanish Harlem.

In 1996, Tanya Torres, who was born in Puerto Rico and lived as a teenager in Queens, decided with her teacher husband, Carlos, to buy a four-story row house on Lexington Avenue for $118,000. The building had recently housed a brothel. "We used to receive customers for a year afterward," Torres told me. "People had keys to the front door. Finally we changed the locks." On the ground floor she and her husband set up the Mixta Gallery, whose paintings and sculptures have drawn mainstream reviewers. During our talk, she told me of drug addicts in a tenantless building nearby, the taint of sidewalk garbage, and the cluster of drunks hanging out to loud music across the street.

"It's dirty, and it's not the most beautiful place in the world," she said. "Yet, there's a real sense of community. People know what's going on in your life, and you kind of know what's going on in their lives. We get so involved in everything here we forget there's a world outside there. Sometimes we used to go out and say, 'We can breathe again!' because we had not been outside of the Barrio for a month."

The epicenter of the Puerto Rican resurgence is 106th Street, a corridor that roughly connects several pivotal institutions, including the nationally known El Museo del Barrio on Fifth Avenue and the Julia de Burgos Cultural Center on Lexington Avenue, a former school building named after the Puerto Rican poetess and nationalist who died on the streets of East Harlem. The center now houses the Taller Boricua Gallery as well as theater and dance organizations. On that block too is the movement's Rick's Café, La Fonda Boricua, a restaurant started by a City University–trained psychologist, Jorge Ayala, and his brother Roberto. It is known both for authentic home-cooked chicken and goat curry, each served with rice and beans and fried sweet bananas, as well as for its walls displaying works by the neighborhood's artists. One night a week, the owner jams on a small stage with jazz musicians. La Fonda is where the Latino professionals meet to make deals and connections— people such as Pagán, the Puerto Rican nationalist, and Romero, who grew up in East Harlem and has become something of its informal promoter. "There is an intelligentsia, a bohemia that has moved in," Romero told me.

But he also voiced a theme that is trembling just under the surface of the hopeful changes—that the skyrocketing rents will drive out the low-wage earners: cooks, busboys, and housekeepers, many of them Puerto Rican but also Mexicans and Ecuadorians. "There is an incredible renaissance here," Romero said. "On the one hand it's a blessing, but on the other hand a lot of Puerto Ricans are forced to move. Sometimes the political leaders don't fight hard enough for the poor. I don't object to charging more rent, but not at the expense of people who have historically lived in the community."

Some returnees worry that the neighborhood will get so prettified that the very flavors that drew them back will fade. Salicrup, the gallery director, is not one of the worried ones. "What protects this area are the housing projects," he said. "If you're thinking of moving to El Barrio, you might end up with a project next to you. The poor are always going to be there."

. . .

ONE CAN ARGUE that a saving remnant of Italians will also always be there. Beyond Caponigro, a few lingering Italians have learned to accommodate to the neighborhood's shifting ethnicity. They illuminate another everlasting theme about New York, one that is the flip side of its mutability—its adaptability. In a stately former bank building not too many doors down 116th Street from Claudio's Barber Shop is Farenga Brothers funeral home. It dates back to the turn of the century and at its peak performed 200 Italian funerals a year. It might be wistful to think that Salvatore Farenga is keeping the business founded by his great-grandfather going until the last of his compatriots die, but he cannot afford to be that sentimental. He has been able to stay in business by learning how to accommodate Puerto Ricans and other Latinos. Farenga, a decorous, silver-haired man in his mid-fifties, tried to explain to me how different the business was when he was a youngster. "In those days, it was an ethnic business," he said. "The Irish went to the Irish funeral home, the blacks to the blacks, the Sicilians went to the Sicilians, and the Calabrese went to the Calabrese. There was loyalty to your fellow townsmen. You wanted them to do well."

But with New York's increasingly shifting ethnic boundaries, he predicted that the funeral industry would shift "from ethnicity to service and location, and I was right." Yes, he does get the odd Italian suburbanites who when death strikes like to return to the old neighborhood, to the streets where their kin played stickball, worshiped, fell in love, brought up children, and made the old friends who now will mourn them. But 90 percent of Farenga's funerals are for Puerto Ricans and other Spanish speakers. Farenga Brothers has had to learn that the floral arrangements at Latino funerals need ribbons adorned with the names of the givers, and that a grieving family likes the funeral home to collect the ribbons so it can express its thanks. And while many Italian families put family photographs inside the coffin, Latinos consider doing so akin to a curse. Italians like to see the coffin aboveground when they leave the cemetery; Latino families like to have the coffin lowered while everybody is still at the graveside.

Caponigro, the barber, never saw a need to adapt, even though his customers are increasingly Spanish speaking. I got a glimpse into why when he told me his life story—one that took so many bounces when he was younger that keeping his life as steady as possible became essential. He was born in 1931 into a family of barbers in the town of Campania in the province of Salerno. His father and his brother Emilio were barbers. He was in the Salerno area when the Nazis seized power from Mussolini's Fascists. He saw Jews being rounded up for deportation and later saw American bombs falling on his town. "I saw the whole battle, saw people die in front of me with the bombing," he said. "What I saw in that war, forget about it." At war's end, at just fourteen, he started his own barbershop, but by twenty he was so wearied by the oppressive poverty around him that he took an opportunity to travel to New York. (Three of his sisters still live in Italy and so did his mother until she died a few years ago.) "I find a lot of pleasure, a lot of beautiful people in this neighborhood," he told me. "I find a second Salerno here."

In his early days, he remembers, perhaps through the distorting lens of nostalgia, doctors, lawyers, and politicians occupied the handsome brownstones, with small green awnings over each window along 116th Street, and there were two or three barbers on every commercial block. The gravel-voiced comedian Jimmy Durante, a compadre from Salerno, used to drop in at his shop. "It was a pleasure just when he opened his mouth," Caponigro remembered. He used to say to me, 'Hey, Claudio.' " Frank Rossetti, the future judge, and Guy J. Velella, the future state senator, played ball on the block.

When the Italian population began declining as the younger generation sought homes in the suburbs, and crime and drugs lapped at the streets, Caponigro stayed put. He even shunned extra security contraptions. "Everybody's got a rolling gate," he said. "I don't need a rolling gate. I don't have no enemies. Everybody's got respect."

Instead, he let his shop accumulate an attic's load of tchotchkes—a bullhorn, a bicycle with one large wheel and one small wheel, pictures of John Wayne and Durante, a 110-year-old shoeshine box. So charmingly quaint was his ramshackle shop that Jennifer Lopez made a music video there. With shifting cultures, he grew into something of an Italian chauvinist. A sign in his store says the following:

MICHELANGELO, DANTE, VIRGIL, DAVINCI, GALILEO, RAPHAEL, VERDI, FERMI, BOTTICELLI, TOSCANINI, CELLINI, BOCCACCIO, CICERO, CARUSO, MARCONI, VESPUCCI, BERNINI, MARCO POLO, TITIAN, THOMAS AQUINAS, VIVALDI, PETRARCH, AND COLUMBUS. NO OTHER PEOPLE CAN MAKE THAT STATEMENT.

He lived for many years right across the street; then, when the neighborhood got rougher around 1969, he moved his wife and three daughters to the Bronx. But he saw no need to move his shop. Puerto Rican and Mexican men do not need their hair trimmed all that differently from Italians, so he continued to make a living. And over the years, he has learned enough Spanish to converse with gusto. "You pick up a little today, a little tomorrow, soon you speaking the language," he said.

He caters to many Puerto Rican families whose hair he has cut for three generations. Fifty-eight-year-old Frank Estrada was waiting patiently one day for his turn under the scissors, and recalled his years as Caponigro's customer. "I brought my son when he was small," Estrada said. "Now he brings his children here." Caponigro takes pride in such pedigree. "Three generations, they sit on that chair," he told me, pointing to one of the peppermint green chairs. "The grandfather, the father, the baby."

Now that there are glimmers of new affluence, Caponigro, who might have once worried about losing his shop to the waves of surrounding poverty, should probably be worried about losing his shop to developers. The last time I looked, land had been cleared a block or two to the east along the East River for a Home Depot and a Costco. But Caponigro seems to have shrugged off both the forces of decline and those of resurgence.

"If I got to go away from here, I retire," Caponigro told me. "I don't be a barber no more. The Spanish people, they say, 'Claudio, you got to stay forever.' There was a lovely, beautiful girl with three kids. I told her she have to wait, but she said, 'I don't go to another barber. There's only one Claudio.' She makes me proud when she said there's only one Claudio. Those words I never forget."

EAST HARLEM

...

WHERE TO GO

Claudio's Barber Shop (NO TELEPHONE, NO RESERVATIONS)
360 EAST 116TH STREET

Farenga Brothers Funeral Home (MULTICULTURAL FAREWELLS)
204 EAST 116TH STREET; *(212) 534-3700*

El Museo del Barrio (THE MET OF PUERTO RICAN ART AND CULTURE)
1230 FIFTH AVENUE; *(212) 831-7272*; WWW.ELMUSEO.ORG

La Marqueta (A FORLORN ETHNIC MARKET UNDER THE COMMUTER
TRACKS) 116TH STREET AND PARK AVENUE

National Museum of Catholic Art and History (ECLECTIC
EXHIBITS ON CATHOLIC HISTORY AND CULTURE) 443 EAST 115TH
STREET; *(212) 828-5209*; WWW.NMCAH.ORG

Our Lady of Mount Carmel (120-YEAR-OLD CENTER OF ITALIAN
COMMUNITY, WITH A SHRINE TO THE VIRGIN THAT HAS BEEN
BLESSED BY PAPAL AUTHORITY AND A FEAST ON JULY 16)
448 EAST 166TH STREET; *(212) 534-0681*

Taller Boricua at the Julia De Burgos Latino Cultural Center
(CONTEMPORARY PUERTO RICAN ART, MUSIC, AND POETRY)
1680 LEXINGTON AVENUE; *(212) 831-4333*

WHERE TO EAT

Dinerbar (AMERICAN RESTAURANT) 1569 LEXINGTON AVENUE;
(212) 348-0200

La Fonda Boricua (PUERTO RICAN RESTAURANT)
169 EAST 106TH STREET; *(212) 410-7292*

Morrone Bakery (ITALIAN) 324 EAST 116TH STREET; *(212) 722-2972*

Patsy's (THE ORIGINAL, WITH THIN, COAL-FIRED PIZZA)
2287-91 FIRST AVENUE; *(212) 534-9783*

Rao's (SOUTHERN ITALIAN RESTAURANT, BUT RESERVATIONS ONLY FOR
THE WELL CONNECTED) 455 EAST 114TH STREET; *(212) 722-6709*

Chapter 4

The Cobbler of Chinatown

. . .

AMONG THE CHURNING SIDEWALKS OF CHINATOWN, ZHONG WEN Jiang has found his niche. From morning until sundown, he squats on a makeshift stool planted on a sliver of pavement alongside the steps of an old school building, and i   n that nook he mends worn shoes. Crowds of people surge by on narrow Bayard Street, but with his sturdy back against the stoop of the building and his bony legs straddling a homemade cobbler's last, he slices off a piece of rubber or leather, swabs on a yellowish glue, pounds in a few nails, and files the rough edges off a fresh heel or sole until it is ready for walking.

Sometimes he takes a break for a filtered Chinese cigarette or for a rice gruel carried from the home in Brooklyn he shares with his wife. But otherwise, he fixes shoes seven days a week, in the swampy days of summer or the frigid bite of winter, deterred only by a blizzard or a downpour. Why does he work so diligently at what is plainly an illegal job? I asked him. "If I don't come here, what's going to happen to all the people who need their shoes fixed?" he replied.

Zhong would be a charming curiosity, an intriguing twist on the immigrant peddlers who have long been a fixture of the city's commercial hubs, except that he is not alone. Just around the corner on Mulberry Street are two other shopless cobblers, one with a Honda generator that runs the grinder he uses to file off leather edges. And nearby are two watch repairmen who fix delicate mechanisms while standing at umbrella-shaded booths out on the sidewalk. Not too far away is a fortune-teller, Madame Gong, whose customers sit on small plastic umbrella-shaded stools on the sidewalk as she reads their palms and faces, communicates with their ancestors, or advises them on what day of the week it would be most propitious to marry or start a business.

And these shopless craftsmen and servicepeople are not confined to Chinatown. Along Roosevelt Avenue in Jackson Heights, Carlos Roldan, a forty-seven-year-old immigrant from Colombia who sports a Hawaiian shirt and Groucho Marx eyebrows, washes shopkeepers' windows out of a shopping cart that holds his squeegees, rags, and cleaning agents. Customers can reach him only by beeper because he not only does not have a shop but also does not have a home, spending nights sleeping on the floor of a taco stand on the avenue. On Third Avenue in the East Bronx, men with nicknames like Country and Mouse repair alternators or do lube jobs and tune-ups right on the street, jacking cars up as traffic whizzes by while keeping an eye on the passing police cars that could give them tickets for working illegally. They get their parts from avenue auto-parts shops, which have bought into this symbiotic relationship, however illicit, because it assures them a steady stream of customers.

Across the city, migrants from Asia, Latin America, and the Caribbean, accustomed to such street workshops in their homelands, have set them up on New York's sidewalks as well, and changed the commerce and look of whole neighborhoods, among them Chinatown and Jackson Heights. Scholars told me the phenomenon reflects not just the variety of the immigrant influx but also the city's rising costs of doing business. "If you can have a store without paying the rent, you do it," said Dr. William B. Helmreich, an urban ethnographer at the City University of New York.

Since this has always been a city with a soft spot for an ingenious or enterprising way of scratching out a living at a cut-rate price, these rogue businessmen more than survive. Cynthia Lee, a curator at the Museum of Chinese in the Americas, housed in the onetime school that is the backdrop for Zhong's business, explained to me why these workmen are so embraced, even if they pose competition to some struggling shopkeepers. "It's the spirit of entrepreneurship in the Chinese American community," she told me. "If you can find a way to make a living, you do it."

There is often a line of people waiting to hand their shoes to the cobbler of Bayard Street, largely because his prices—$15 for a leather sole and heel—are about half those of the rent-paying, shop-owning shoemaker a few blocks away. And the authorities seem to leave him alone even though he is in a spot flooded with all manner of authorities. The jail cells of the Manhattan House of Detention, the notorious Tombs, and the offices of the district attorney of Manhattan are across a small park from his stand, and the Fifth Precinct of the police department is a few blocks away on Elizabeth Street.

"What about the police; don't they hassle you?" I asked him as we spoke through an interpreter provided by the museum.

"The police officers are my customers," he replied.

Zhong enchanted me not just because he was a novel variety of peddler but very specifically because he fixed shoes. My father did too, for many years. Indeed, without his talent for shoemaking I might not be writing this book in the United States or anywhere at all. Like Zhong, my father was raised as a farm boy, in his case in the Galicia region in what was then southeastern Poland. He was not yet twenty years old when the Nazis attacked on September 1, 1939, but he avoided the horrors of the occupation because of a fortuitous accident of geography. His village was in a Ukrainian-speaking part of Poland that was absorbed into the Soviet Union as part of Stalin's infamous nonaggression pact with Hitler. My father was drafted into the Soviet army and after a year or so in the cavalry he was dispatched to the Ural Mountains, where he was assigned to a military factory that manufactured soldiers' boots. That work sustained not just him through the war but also my mother, an undernourished and despondent refugee with whom he fell in love. Indeed, my father had become what was regarded among the bedraggled refugees, with the barest tongue in cheek, as a wealthy man. He was illicitly making extra pairs of boots for the officers, boots they especially needed for the Russian winter, and they expressed their gratitude by slipping him cans of pork and beans or bottles of vodka that he traded for food. My mother was so grateful for his affection and, in no small part, the food he provided that she married him in December 1943.

He continued fashioning shoes until the war ended and for a year afterward, until he and my mother and their infant—me—made our way to Poland, where they learned with finality that his parents and six sisters and her parents and six of her brothers and sisters had been slaughtered. Like other refugees, they settled in the displaced persons camps in occupied Germany and waited for visas to the United States. In March 1950 they brought his last and other cobbler tools with them to New York and stored them under the bathtub in our first apartment on Manhattan's West Side.

My younger brother and I would sometimes slide the tools out and, after shaking off the balls of dust, examine them as if they were sacramental objects: the last, which looked like a bony leg with an upside-down foot at one end, the blade sheathed in black leather, which served as its only handle, his thick, coarse file, a pair of cast-iron pliers, which I knew by its Yiddish name, a *tsvang*. We were beguiled by these artifacts from the grimy world of working stiffs and the cunning arts my father had acquired and that we too might absorb when we grew up.

Every once in a while, my father actually fixed a shoe. He would slip the shoe over the sculpted foot and clamp the last firmly between his knees. I would see him take a swatch of leather and shave it with his calloused but deft fingers until it matched the worn sole. The work was so frustratingly precise that he kept his pink tongue gripped between his teeth to control his tension. He would brush glue on the new sole from a metal jar whose sweet bovine smell was intoxicating. Then he slipped some brads between his lips—I marveled how he never swallowed them—and pounded them in one at a time along the rim of the sole to fasten it to the shoe's upper half. This work was the best proof of my father's competence, and in a world where an immigrant like him had few other ways to assert his significance, it was inexpressively important to me. My mother had her own way of showing her competence and earning a livelihood. She was masterful with a sewing machine. Hunched over our old black Singer with its gold lettering, she would hem our pants, make her own dresses, and for most of my years growing up take seasonal jobs trimming the edges of straw hats. You didn't need English for such jobs and could support yourself at least until you put your children through school and they could accomplish the dreams you never could.

Now a man from a remote Chinese village was surviving in the same wily ways, doing what he deemed necessary to scratch out his living, just like my parents, just like the Italian, Irish, and Jewish immigrants of a century ago. Many of the city's Chinese, who with a population of 261,551 constitute the second largest of the city's immigrant groups (after Dominicans), can be found in the illegal sweatshops among the 600 Chinese-owned garment factories in Chinatown, the Garment District, or Sunset Park, Brooklyn. They are the busboys and dishwashers at the 1,400 Chinese restaurants in New York City. And they constitute a large share of the new breed of unlicensed food peddlers, who prepare foods at home and sell them on the street right out of shopping bags and homemade carts that don't come under the scrutiny of the health department inspectors. Such ways of earning a living may explain why the per capita income for Chinese Americans is a woeful $16,700, much lower than the $22,402 for the city as a whole, according to a 2004 study by the Asian American Federation of New York. Despite the Chinese reputation as a "model minority" and the achievements of such Chinese as Dr. David Ho, the AIDS pioneer, cellist Yo-Yo Ma, and designer Vera Wang, most Chinese come here with limited schooling, with one-third of adults having no more than a ninth-grade education.

Chinatown, where Zhong works, is still the great thumping heart of the city's Chinese community. The maze of narrow tenement-lined streets is filled with more than 200 restaurants, teahouses, and dim-sum shops; Buddhist pagodas and pagoda-roofed banks and telephone booths; gift shops displaying silk kimonos, fans, lanterns, porcelain, and other novelties; apothecaries with arcane herbs and roots; newsstands selling four daily and a dozen weekly newspapers for readers whose sympathies are either with mainland China, or Taiwan, or Hong Kong; food stores with roasted ducks strung up as if they had been hung for capital crimes, bins of exotic mollusks (one store had twenty-one varieties of fresh shrimp when I last visited) and tanks of live fish, esoteric dried mushrooms, fresh litchi nuts on the stem, and all sorts of oddball green vegetables.

Although there are furtive changes—yuppies are moving in to some of those tenements and paying high rents—Chinatown is still the mecca where Chinese from the five boroughs and the region come on days off, usually Sundays or Mondays, to refill on Chinese provisions, tend to business and immigration matters, and check in with their mutual aid societies (*feng* or *fong*) or their clan associations, both of which provide medical care, burials, and legal assistance.

It is fitting perhaps that Zhong, though married, is a solitary male worker. Chinatown was a bachelor society until the Second World War because the Chinese Exclusion Act of 1882, repealed by Franklin Delano Roosevelt, prevented most workers from having their wives and families join them. Chinese roots in New York, by some accounts, go back to the 1850s, when a merchant named Ah Kam opened a tobacco shop on Park Row and a grocery on Pell and took an apartment on Mott Street. The Wo Kee store opened in 1872 at 34 Mott Street, followed by fish markets and vegetable stands. Mott Street gradually became the spine of a Chinese shopping area. ("And tell me what street / Compares with Mott Street / In July," Rodgers and Hart wrote in "Manhattan" in 1925.) Chinese immigrant men working in hand laundries or rolling cigars could go to Mott Street to stock up on food and clothing and often find a home-cooked meal. When the Chinese, most of them Cantonese, realized that Americans were intrigued by homespun dishes such as chop suey ("bits and pieces"), they consciously sought out a tourist trade, and thus was born the lively Chinatown of the guidebooks.

To get in touch with Chinatown's past, I visited the Museum of Chinese in the Americas just above Zhong's workshop. Among the intimate detritus, much of it salvaged from dumpsters, are pressing irons used by the ubiquitous launderers, a crimson silk robe used by Chinese opera troupes, a photograph of a Chinese baseball team, a newspaper's tray of Chinese characters in lead type, a lion's-head mask used in a Chinese New Year celebration, a picture of Miss Chinatown 1971, and some artifacts that recall a Chinatown that until the 1930s was pocked with gambling, sex, and opium dens and was the battleground of Mafia-like bloody turf wars fought by rival *tongs*. Eventually, the Chinese branched out, and the museum displays the remnants of a cramped Chinese laundry in the Bronx of the 1950s, complete with shirts wrapped in brown paper, those familiar pink, green, and yellow numbered tickets, and a touching photograph of the family who lived behind the store. There is a poignant letter written by a wife in Hong Kong to her husband stranded in Chinatown, feelingly telling him, "With all these years in the foreign land, you are just work for others, slaved yourself for the sake of others."

Until 1965, Chinatown occupied only a seven-block-long quarter along streets like Pell, Mott, Doyer, and Bayard and had a population of 20,000. But the 1965 immigration law changed all that. With immigrants streaming in from once barely represented provinces such as Fujian, Chinatown quickly gobbled up Little Italy, large swaths of the Lower East Side, and the blocks north of City Hall, becoming the largest center of Chinese population in the Western Hemisphere. But Chinatown faced new problems too. A young *New York Times* reporter, Yilu Zhao, wrote movingly in an article in 2002 about how newcomers from Fujian are bewildered by a world set up for Cantonese and Mandarin speakers. (Fujianese is as different from those languages as Yiddish is from German.) She told of how Renhui Tian, a Fujianese immigrant, wept in 2001 at Kennedy International Airport as he greeted two of his sons for the first time since they were infants. Xiaoxian and Xiaoqin, then five and seven, were born in Chinatown. But as infants Tian had sent them back to their home province in southeastern China to be raised by their grandparents so he and his wife could work longer hours to pay back the smugglers who charged them $40,000 for getting into the country. The Tian boys came into the city's schools already lagging academically because their doting grandparents hadn't bothered to teach them how to count or read letters.

However central Chinatown is, Chinese have also for three decades now been leaving its bleak tenements for new frontiers outside Manhattan including Flushing, Elmhurst, Sunset Park, and Bensonhurst. There the solid brick row houses and attached homes are proof of their clambering up the social ladder just as they were for the Italians, Irish, and Jews of a half century ago. Indeed, by the 1980s only 30 percent of the city's Chinese lived in Chinatown. The Chinese usually follow the D, F, J, and Q subway lines so they can get back to Chinatown easily. Zhong, for example, no longer lives in the railroad apartments of Chinatown; he takes the J train to his two-bedroom flat in Brooklyn, for which he pays a rent of $1,000 a month. Poignantly, he said he did not know the name of his neighborhood but got off at a stop he recognized by its first two letters, *Cr*, which means it is probably Crescent Street in Cypress Hills along the Queens border with Brooklyn.

Sunset Park was a neighborhood I had never visited, though reading some census studies told me it was among the city's most polyglot, with 49.2 percent of its 120,464 residents born abroad, 19,451 of those in China. So with an explorer's relish I took the subway there and walked around streets that I soon discovered were fragrant with the smells and flavors of Latino products on the west and Chinese products on the east. In that eastern half, among the pastry shops, fruit stores, and fish shops along Eighth Avenue, I found Maggie Leung's cluttered and narrow uniform shop. It is practically a directory to the kinds of jobs the neighborhood's residents hold. A refugee from Chinatown, she sells burgundy vests for waiters, smocks with orange piping for beauticians, pink aprons for manicurists, blue tunics for supermarket cashiers, and heavy cotton coats for meat handlers and noodle factory workers. Those heavy cotton coats are even suitable for the neighborhood's growing cadre of doctors. And Leung, who has known for a long time that Chinese garment sweatshops have been closing and that laid-off women need uniforms for such next-rung jobs as home health aides, sells white dresses for nurses' aides as well. "The customers teach you what you should carry," Leung, a slim, dark-haired woman of forty-eight, told me, smiling at the cleverness of the thought. "They ask for it and you know you can sell it."

Leung, a native of Hong Kong, got into this odd business by canny calculation. She was selling handmade tea bags in her father-in-law's kitchenware shop in Chinatown and noticed how many restaurant owners were asking whether the shop sold chef's aprons and white shirts for kitchen workers. "They didn't have in the store," she said. "So, I think, I should make it!"

The business did so well that she decided to start her own shop near her home in Sunset Park. Fortune Restaurant Uniform and Supplies Inc., on Eighth Avenue at Fifty-second Street, is a shining example of immigrant resourcefulness, the kind that spots an unfilled niche created by the influx of fellow newcomers and makes profitable hay. So well known has Leung become that she now gets orders from as far away as Nebraska and Wyoming, often from Sunset Park residents seeking their fortunes in the hinterland. "No matter where, there's always a Chinese restaurant," she said, her eyes glinting merrily.

The business, which includes a small factory in the nearby Fort

Hamilton neighborhood, is a family affair. Leung's sister Jenny sews and embroiders; another sister, Margaret, cuts fabric; a third sister, Connie, takes care of bookkeeping; and a fourth, Shirley, helps with packing. Leung's son, Lenny, twenty-five, a student at New York City College of Technology, arranges shipping on a computer, and her daughter, Angela, twenty-four, a student at Brooklyn College, has put customers' contact information in a database. Leung's eighty-seven-year-old father, Yukyuen Lam, occasionally drops by for a few hours to wrap finished uniforms in plastic. "Even if we don't make a lot of money, I enjoy it so much because the family works together," Leung said.

By contrast, Zhong mends shoes on his own. He is a poised, slender man with once-delicate fingers blackened by his work. He is diligent and rigorous, not the shiftless kind of person who often ends up in such seat-of-the-pants work and that the pushcart-era peddlers of the Lower East Side might have called a luftmensch—literally a person who lives off air. He was sixty-six years old when I spoke with him, yet he worked seven days a week from nine or so in the morning until seven at night.

Zhong had spent most of his working life as a farmer in a village near Canton. His wife, Zu Zhoa Ho, had relatives who had immigrated to the United States, and, pining for them, she eventually joined them here. In March 1997 Zhong came here to live with his wife and took a first job of pressing clothes in a sweatshop. One day he noticed a very old man fixing shoes on the sidewalk near the corner of Bayard and Mulberry streets, just across from the neighborhood's merciful patch of green called Columbus Park. The spot is alongside a 112-year-old building built as a public school that today houses cultural and social groups whose officials do not seem to mind the peddlers on their doorstep. (By contrast, the neighborhood's storeowners often charge peddlers on their doorstep for sidewalk space—a presumably illegal rent for an illegal tenant.) He asked the old man, Chou Szeto, whether he needed help, and after a few such entreaties, Chou took him on as an apprentice. A year later, Chou turned the business over to Zhong, though when I last saw Chou he was eighty-six years old and still dropping by to give his student postgraduate pointers.

The Hans Christian Andersen of Chinatown carries his entire enterprise in a two-foot-long wooden box bound to a portable luggage caddy.

Every night he drops off the box, decorated with sketches of a panda and a goose that he drew himself, at a relative's on Elizabeth Street before taking the subway home. As he mends shoes, some customers sit on a second makeshift stool and wait while others just drop their shoes off. His clients are not just local Chinese, but whites and blacks who work in the nearby courts and jails. On one of my visits his customers included the chauffeur of a passing limousine and a smartly dressed professional woman. Zhong, speaking with me in Cantonese through Keith Chong, a guide from the Museum of Chinese in the Americas, told me how he patched forty to fifty pairs of shoes a day, charging, for example, $2 to replace a small heel on a woman's pump and $15 for a leather heel and sole on a man's shoe. He said he averaged $180 a day in income, all of which he keeps.

"Basically, there's no cost of doing business," he said.

Zhong told me his wife worked five days a week as a dishwasher a three-hour-drive away in the Foxwoods Resort Casino in Connecticut. She sleeps over there during the week and he stays in touch with her with a silver cell phone holstered to his belt. He spends the few hours at home alone reading a Chinese newspaper or watching television, absorbed by the filmed clips on news shows even though he does not know English. But mostly, he said, he gets pleasure just fixing shoes seven days a week. "I'm old," he said. "I can't do anything else. But I can fix shoes."

It is one of the harsh prices of immigration that the couple are separated by great distances from their three grown children, all of whom live around Taishan, China, and can afford to stay in their homeland. Their son, Zhong Siao Pang, is a taxi driver; another son, Zhong Zhung Yi, is a fishmonger; and a daughter, Zhong Siao Nei, is married to a harbor official. The Zhongs take one trip a year home, usually during the Chinese New Year or at a Chinese memorial day in the spring. Zhong told me that he doesn't want to return to China to live with his children because he couldn't get as good a job there. By the standards of life in China, he feels flush here. "I'm not really prosperous," he said, "but a two-bedroom apartment is prosperous." When he is too old to work, he said, he may return to China for good.

When I first met Zhong, his business location had one crucial feature to recommend it. It was covered by scaffolding, and had been for the past ten years, because the old school building has been undergoing exterior repairs. The scaffolding acted as an umbrella in winter and a shade tree in summer, and provided one less reason for Zhong to actually buy his shop. When I returned to visit Zhong in the summer of 2005, the scaffolding was gone. The city had finally pointed the cracked masonry and sandblasted the building, leaving a stately redbrick castle for all to see. The museum was happy that tourists and passersby would no longer neglect it, thinking its home was under construction, but Zhong was not pleased by the loss of his roof. Still, he did not spend his time grousing. He bought a beach umbrella for $18 to shade him against the summer sun and augmented that with a black rain umbrella that he strapped to a banister of the stoop. For a finishing flourish, he planted a white straw sombrero on his head, looking quite the dude. He did not think wintery weather would deter him, except for the most brutal snowstorms and downpours. A propane-fired heater helps ward off the chill of the coldest days.

"If it's a heavy snowstorm or rain, the customers won't come anyway," he told me, smiling.

Like most peddlers, Zhong does not have the required $200-a-year city license, but he does not seem to have incurred the wrath of the cobbler at Get Sun Shoes on Elizabeth Street, a man in his mid-fifties named Ma Wenwei, who owns a legitimate shop equipped with antiquated sewing and polishing machines and who pays $2,000 a month in rent as well as taxes. "It doesn't affect business," Ma, who came here twenty years ago from Canton, told me genially. "We're using a machine and they're using hands, so it's not as good."

But Zhong said he thought it was the machines that were not as good, and he does not charge as much as Get Sun's $28 for replacing a leather sole and heel. Of course, the shoes in the Elizabeth Street shop await their owners neatly arrayed in designated cubbyholes. But Zhong, whose customers' shoes are kept in plastic bags or scattered on the sidewalk, does not think he has to be that organized.

"If it's not your own shoes, you won't take it," he said.

CHINATOWN
...

WHERE TO GO

Columbus Park (CHINESE CHESS, TAI CHI, AND A FLOWER MARKET)
MULBERRY AND BAYARD STREETS

Mahayana Buddhist Temple (SIXTEEN-FOOT BUDDHA)
133 CANAL STREET AND MANHATTAN BRIDGE PLAZA

Museum of Chinese in the Americas (ARTIFACTS OF CHINESE
AMERICAN LIFE AND HISTORY) 70 MULBERRY STREET;
(212) 619-4785; WWW.MOCA-NYC.ORG

WHERE TO EAT

Chinatown Ice Cream Factory (GREEN TEA, AVOCADO,
BLACK SESAME) 65 BAYARD STREET; *(212) 608-4170*

Mei Lai Wah Coffee House (TRY THE EGG CUSTARDS AND STEAMED
RICE BEEF NOODLE) 64 BAYARD STREET; *(212) 925-5435*

Moon House (UNASSUMING BUT DELICIOUS RESTAURANT)
67 BAYARD STREET; *(212) 766-9399*

Chapter 5

Signs of the Times in Douglaston–Little Neck

. . .

WITH ITS BOUILLABAISSE OF NATIONALITIES AND ETHNICITIES AND its 8 million ambitious, sometimes clawing personalities squeezed into a rather cramped 309-square-mile patch, New York is a city in perpetual conflict. The big surprise is that there isn't more open warfare. So whenever someone waxes lyrical about how well such a Babel of peoples gets along, raise an eyebrow or two, because there are more than a few exceptions.

Take the prosperous, overwhelmingly white neighborhoods of Douglaston and Little Neck in eastern Queens. The number of Asians living there has more than doubled in fifteen years as the city's Korean and Chinese immigrants become doctors, bankers, hospital administrators, and entrepreneurs and leave their original beachheads in Chinatown or Flushing. A visitor to these parts can hear many tales of how the American mill of assimilation is working its special grace. I discovered a champion ballroom dancer from Seoul who is giving tango and rumba lessons to the neighborhood's longtime white residents. I found a Fujianese immigrant who opened a kosher Chinese vegetarian restaurant, availing himself of the help of Jewish neighbors in getting a rabbinical certificate. I learned that on Sunday afternoons, the area's leading Episcopal church rents its sanctuary to a small Korean congregation. I learned of a nine-year-old Chinese violinist, Aaron Huang, who has performed at the White House and in front of the pope and is being taught by Anna Heifetz, a distant relative of Jascha, who was himself an immigrant. Yes, I thought at one point, inhaling these delicious whiffs, America's melting pot is bubbling briskly.

But it would have been wrong to conclude that there weren't any substantial lumps in that bubbling gruel. This area of graceful old homes on a serene bay of Long Island Sound scalloped by golden marshes is being rattled over something unimaginably mundane, the kind of small but viscerally crucial matters that make up the web of daily survival in New York. Many of the established white residents told me they no longer feel welcome in most of the stores along Northern Boulevard, the boulevard they have strolled along and shopped on for generations. The stores there were once owned by people like them—Irish, Italian, German, and Jewish merchants. But those merchants flourished so well that they sent their children off to colleges and graduate schools, where they were launched toward careers as professionals, not shopkeepers. The aging merchants had to sell their shops to the highest bidders, and these turned out to be the latest flock of newcomers with a knack for mercantile trade—Koreans, who now own most of the shops along this stretch of Northern Boulevard.

What chafes at the old-timers is that the Korean storeowners are not beholden to the venerable rules of retailing, particularly now that an increasing number of the new buyers of those graceful houses on Long Island Sound are also Korean professionals and businesspeople. The signs the Korean merchants have been putting up above their stores are in large Korean ideograms that non-Koreans do not understand—in many cases with no hint in English of what is being sold. Walk down several blocks of Northern Boulevard between Douglaston Parkway and the eastern boundary that divides Queens from Long Island's Nassau County and you'll think you're in the city's newest Koreatown, not along the spine of what into the 1950s used to be an exclusive WASP enclave on the northern side and a Jewish-Italian-Irish preserve on the southern. Take a typical example, the Little Neck Janchi Maeu, a grocery store on the corner of Glenwood Street, right near the Nassau County line. Its signs have lots of blue, red, green, and orange lettering in Korean, but except for a single line with the store's name in English, there is nothing to inform an English-speaking passerby what it sells, which should not be surprising since its stock—products such as cabbage kimchi, eel, sea mustard soup—is aimed at Korean tastes.

"The perception is that these businesses are serving their own people," Paula Gerber told me as we sat schmoozing in a real estate office on Northern Boulevard. "They're not realizing that when you're on the street you're supposed to be serving everyone." She is the office manager of an agency that employs four Korean agents, but she shows the changed neighborhood to a broad spectrum of home buyers.

Sol Winder, who for forty-five years has owned Scobee Grill, a diner popular with residents of both Little Neck as well as ritzier Great Neck, was even more blunt in letting me know how older neighborhood residents felt toward the Korean newcomers. "They feel they're taking over the area," he told me.

It is a not uncommon irony that Winder is an immigrant himself, for some of the most ardent complaints often come from immigrants who feel they worked their way up by sticking to the old rules and wonder why the newcomers shouldn't do the same. His aggravation demonstrates a hard and paradoxical truth about American assimilation: An immigrant past gives one no special sympathy for a newcomer's blunderings. Born in Lvov, Winder came here as a teenager in 1948 after an odyssey that entailed fleeing the Nazis for frigid Siberia and spending two years in the displaced persons camps in Germany. He graduated from a technical college, opened a coffee shop, and was thirty in the 1960s when his father-in-law helped him and two partners start Scobee Grill, which was named after a rough approximation of his father-in-law's Polish hometown. Even though his encyclopedic menu includes matzo ball soup and gefilte fish, he wanted to build an American diner, and the cuisine is standard diner fare of hamburgers and eggs over easy. He can chronicle what happened to Little Neck and Douglaston better than a sociologist. "Forty-five years ago, they were young people raising families," he said. "Now they raised their families; their children married and moved away. The children aren't looking in Little Neck. They're looking in Westchester and on the Island. The older folks are going to Florida or dying out."

The new Koreans in the neighborhood stop in at his diner on weekends. Some even enjoy the matzo ball soup. "They're hardworking people—you have to give them that," he said. But he knows the neighborhood he has worked in and been an iconic part of for forty-five years will never again be what it was.

Underneath much of the ferment about the signs is a feeling that Koreans are somehow defying the bedrock American imperative to blend in. The United States, as a nation built by immigrants beginning with the Mayflower Pilgrims and Jamestown settlers, has prided itself on displaying a more welcoming outlook toward foreigners than the rest of the world. But there has also been an unspoken bargain—that the newcomers adopt the ways of the country whether they want to or not. "We welcome everybody," Markian Duma, chair of a local civic group, the Little Neck Pines Association, told me. "This neighborhood is made up of a lot of ethnic groups. I happen to be Ukrainian. There are some Irish, some Italian in our group. We already have an ethnic mix. All we would like people to do is don't stand out. We try not to tell anyone to blend in, but we're one country."

While many of the dynamics are true of the cosmopolitan city as a whole, neighborhoods such as these in Little Neck and Douglaston are especially worth watching because they are laboratories for the second stage in the cycle of absorption set off by the immigration law of 1965. Asian and Latino strivers started out in crowded tenement ghettos working dawn-to-midnight jobs in restaurants and garment factories. Their first move up was to the more decorous apartment houses of neighborhoods such as Flushing. They are now doing well enough to penetrate the city's leafiest—and whitest—precincts.

Little Neck and Douglaston, on the eastern edge of Queens, are right across a small cove from Long Island's Great Neck, the model for F. Scott Fitzgerald's nouveau riche West Egg in *The Great Gatsby*. Douglaston could have served as either Egg because it too is rich—nouveau and old money. It is a peninsula where some houses can cost $4 million. The wealthiest section, Douglas Manor, is an enclave of 600 homes set among winding, hilly roads, including Queen Annes, colonials, Mediterraneans, Tudors, and arts and crafts creations by the cherished nineteenth-century designer Gustav Stickley. There is even a 600-year-old white oak on Arleigh Road that is among the city's oldest trees.

The area was Dutch farmland until the early half of the nineteenth century, when William Douglas carved out an estate crowned by a Greek Revival mansion that now houses the Douglaston Club. After the civil war, New Yorkers began transforming Queens from such large estates into almost suburban expanses of single-family houses stretching along a lengthening railroad that allowed them to travel quickly into Manhattan. By 1866, the railroad's tentacles extended from Flushing to Great Neck and the Douglas family donated a farm building to serve as a railroad depot, asking only that the station and the growing village around it be called Douglaston. By the first decade of the twentieth century, their estate was chopped up into what today would be called a development tract, luxurious as it is. Douglas Manor, designated as a city historic district, has such touches of elegance as its own cooperatively owned marina and playing fields right on the shore. That's why residents over the years have included Ginger Rogers, columnist Hedda Hopper, and pianist Claudio Arrau. As late as the 1950s it was a white Protestant bastion where Jews, Asians, and blacks were largely prevented from buying.

Little Neck, which straddles the Long Island Expressway, is more plebeian. Houses, sometimes attached, range in value from $300,000 to $850,000, and are arrayed on forty foot-wide lots. There are plenty of parks, particularly the glorious forty-two-acre wetland of reeds and marsh grasses called Udalls Cove Park. In short, it too is an attractive spot where residents appreciate the trappings of suburban tidiness—and real-estate taxes half of those in next-door Nassau County.

Asians have been drawn to Douglaston and Little Neck by these features but also, in stereotypical fashion, by schools that are ranked as the city's best. The neighborhood is in the heart of what used to be called District 26, where in the days of an otherwise lamentable decentralized system of thirty-two districts, more than 90 percent of students met the city's reading and math standards and 87 percent of teachers had a master's or higher degree. While all immigrants value schools, no groups seem to have put faith in their catapulting powers more than the Chinese, Koreans, and Indians, so District 26 is an irresistible magnet.

In 1990, just 11.6 percent of the two neighborhoods' 23,000 residents were Asian. By 2000, that had doubled to 23 percent. The U.S. Census counted 2,656 Koreans and 2,115 Chinese, but by 2006 no one doubted that there were many, many more. Even the population of once-exclusive Douglas Manor had become 10 percent Asian, according to Bernard Haber, a former president of the community board. Haber, long the neighborhood's civic sparkplug and a civil engineer who helped build the Throgs Neck Bridge and the Cross Bronx Expressway, drove me around to show me the neighborhood's increasing Asian cast, and informed me about one Asian source—wealthy exiles from Hong Kong who left the British colony before 1997 as it was about to be taken over by the Communist Chinese.

Yet, amid this breathtaking evidence of America's openness, there was also the uncomfortable brouhaha over the Korean signs. Along Northern Boulevard, the few Korean merchants I could find who spoke English made sure to tell me that Korean signs are not intended to offend anyone but reflect the reality that the customers are almost exclusively Korean. Young Kim, the owner of Ladykin Salon, a beauty parlor, told me in halting English that she tried to attract non-Koreans but ultimately her poor English requires American customers to show her magazine pictures of the hairstyles they want. "Our problem is English," she said.

Other shopkeepers said they would gladly put up English signs, but with each billboard or neon fixture costing an additional $500 or more, they would rather avoid the expense if what they sell is aimed mostly at Koreans.

I spoke to several Asian scholars to try to understand what was going on. Dr. Pyong Gap Min, a professor of sociology at Queens College and a Korean immigrant, believes that Koreans can more easily avoid mingling with Americans and marinating in American life because they "are too strongly tied to their ethnic network." Among Koreans, Christian churches are the center of Korean life as they are not among the Chinese, with 550 Korean churches in the New York area to choose from. Three out of every four Koreans go to church every week, and many attend twice a week. "So it's very difficult to get involved in American organizations," Dr. Min said.

Another barrier is the unifying Korean language. Chinese are fragmented by a wealth of incompatible dialects including Mandarin, Cantonese, and Fujianese. But Koreans speak the same congenial tongue—one whose grammar, pronunciation, and word order are even more different from English than are those of Chinese. Koreans are also better educated than average Chinese immigrants and, Min suggested, more comfortable in their own skins. Dr. Thomas Tam, director of an

Asian research institute at Queens College, added another factor: Koreans sense the narrow-mindedness and suspicion that more established Americans feel toward them. In response, he said, "there are people who try to assimilate as much as possible but some who try to be even more isolated."

By contrast, Chinese immigrants have been more willing to wade into the American mainstream. In addition to language, Chinese are separated from one another by geographical and political origins; they hail from either Taiwan, or Communist China, or Hong Kong and are influenced by the bitter legacies of those divisions. The forces compelling them to meld with other Chinese are thus weaker and more splintered than they are for Koreans. Moreover, the Chinese are a more established immigrant group, and many Chinese who do well enough to make it to such places as Douglaston and Little Neck are already second- or third-generation Americans. One descendant of Chinese immigrants, Sandra K. Lee, an insurance broker in Great Neck whose grandparents emigrated from China to Chinatown, told me that Chinese Americans tended to be more eager to fit in, sometimes to a deferential and obsequious extent, whereas Koreans, as a cultural group, are "more assertive and outspoken."

Oddly enough, it was four Chinese American students driving in a Lexus along Douglaston Parkway who were the victims in the summer of 2006 of one of those special New York brews of youth, resentment, and racism, ending in the kind of beating that, as long as anyone can remember, had never occurred in this part of Queens. Two blue-collar white men, one a twenty-year-old resident of Little Neck, were quickly arrested for viciously punching and kicking two of the students, one of whom was hit with a Club steering wheel lock. They were heard using slurs against the Asian students in a beating reminiscent of attacks against blacks in Bensonhurst and Howard Beach.

Whatever the specific reasons, conflict of the sort between the Koreans and the longer-rooted descendants of white European immigrants crops up not only in New York but even more heatedly in parts of the United States where the experience of assimilation is not built into the genome. Authorities in Fremont, California, in the seemingly enlightened San Francisco Bay area, tried to get Sikh teenagers to stop wearing little ceremonial swords around their necks; they compromised by requiring only that the swords be blunted and wired to their scabbards. In 2003 I visited the faded mill city of Lewiston in Maine, a state where 97 percent of the inhabitants are white. The small city of 36,000 had an unexpected immigration crisis, and some leaders at Bates College, the major institution there, thought my book *Displaced Persons,* which tells how Holocaust survivors like my family adapted to America, might offer lessons to help the city cope.

What was the problem? More than a thousand Somalis from Africa had suddenly moved in over two years, finding their way up north from Atlanta, where they had been settled as political refugees by federal immigration authorities. Lewiston's fraying downtown was sprouting Somali women in colorful head scarves, but hardened Lewistonians did not seem to appreciate this exotic touch in their midst. Moreover, jobless Somalis were straining welfare services and schools.

Lewiston's mayor at the time composed what was at best an insensitive letter to the Somali community, pleading with them to ask compatriots in Atlanta to stop coming. "Please pass the word," he wrote. "We have been overwhelmed and have responded valiantly. Now we need breathing room. Our city is maxed-out financially, physically, and emotionally." Jim Spencer, a former 7-Eleven employee and petition-circulator interviewed by my colleague *New York Times* correspondent Pam Belluck, sounded like some Little Neck residents when he warned that the Somalis think "they're basically going to take over our city." Somali elders called the mayor's letter bigotry, and they pointed out that Somalis were patronizing struggling stores and occupying apartments that would otherwise be vacant.

Even the distress triggered by foreign-language signs is not peculiar to Little Neck. Palisades Park, New Jersey, responded to the signs posted by its Asian shopkeepers with a law insisting that half the space of any sign displaying words in a foreign language be in English.

In Douglaston and Little Neck, there are non-Korean shopkeepers who think the Koreans are largely misunderstood. Jacques Amar, who runs a small French café on the boulevard, stocks four brands of Korean vodka because many customers are Korean. "They're hardworking people; they're ambitious," he told me.

Quite contrary to what people may think, they like life. They are not as dull as people perceive them. They're charming. If you remember, in New York every new group comes to this country and puts signs up in their language. That's because they identify their business to their own people. If a Korean did not see Korean writing, he doesn't know that the store is Korean. And maybe he's looking for a Korean place. It gives him a certain comfort to go in. Like any group, they want to be with their own people. They have no animosity toward Americans. If you love them, they will love you. If you don't love them, they won't love you, which is absolutely natural. They do have a hard time trying to mix, so it will take a long time and effort from both sides.

But Amar is relatively new to the boulevard. For the old-time merchants and residents, who cling wistfully to sepia-tinged pictures of the neighborhood, Northern Boulevard's transformation has been especially upsetting. Frank Mockler, seventy-five when we spoke in 2003, owned Patrick's Pub, a restaurant that specialized in corned beef and shepherd's pie, and the Claddagh Shop next door, which carried Aran sweaters, Donegal shawls, Dublin kilts, lace, crystal, and other Irish imports. In the mid-1960s, when he started out, half the neighborhood was, as he put it, "Irish and English," mottled with police officers and firefighters. In Douglaston, the residents included an Irish Catholic former air force officer, John McEnroe, who was single-mindedly preparing his hot-tempered son, John Jr., to be a tennis champion.

In his salad days, Mockler used to sell 5,000 Irish coffees a week and 1,400 pounds of corned beef on St. Patrick's Day. But the Irish moved on to fancier suburbs—his own daughter lives in Huntington, Long Island. When I interviewed him, he was selling fewer than 1,000 Irish coffees a week. "You don't get the local people," he said. "The people coming into the neighborhood are not assimilating into the society." He allowed that eventually the Koreans would adapt and learn American ways. Maybe they would even patronize his pub. But he ran out of time. Two years after we spoke, the pub closed, and not too long after so did the Claddagh Shop.

Paradoxically, the neighborhood's whites have been more than willing to sell their homes to middle-class Koreans and other Asians and have not scorned them as neighbors. Indeed, whatever misgivings the longtime residents feel seem to crystallize around the picayune everyday issues of getting along, which may barely smolder but can emit lots of smoke. Parking, for example, is another source of neighborhood tension. Korean churches have been popping up all over the neighborhood, and their strikingly fervent members fill the pews on Sunday, gobbling up parking spaces and making it difficult for families who live near a church to invite friends over for, say, a barbecue. When I visited the neighborhood, Eun Hae Presbyterian, a congregation that had worshiped in Flushing for fourteen years but had outgrown its sanctuary, was trying to build its new home in Little Neck. It had plans for a sanctuary that could hold 494 worshipers. What disturbed neighbors-to-be was that the church fathers had designed an adjoining parking lot with just thirty-two spaces. Michael W. Song, the church's lawyer, played down the everyday impact on parking, arguing that the church was filled mostly on Sundays and was not "the hub of the immigrant population." Still, he said, to appease its neighbors, the church was trying to negotiate a lease for an additional fifty spaces at a nearby mall.

Despite these conflicts, there are many wisps of congeniality between old-timers and newcomers. White Protestants have been a shrinking presence in northern Queens (even the once-exclusive Douglaston Club now counts Jewish and Asian members), and that explains why mainline Protestant churches rent space to Korean Protestants or sometimes change over entirely. Douglaston's Zion Episcopal Church rents its sanctuary on Sunday afternoons to a Korean Presbyterian congregation of perhaps forty families, the Great Commission Church, for $12,000 to $14,000 a year. A footnote at the bottom of Zion's signboards alerts passersby that a Korean congregation is "also worshiping here." The Reverend Patrick J. Holtkamp, Zion's rector, told me that the church rejected the Korean group's request for a separate sign in Korean. Zion wanted to project the image of a congregation on the rise, as it stubbornly is, rather than one that is biding its time before selling out to its Korean tenants. Indeed, Zion's congregation has doubled in twelve years to 200 families, largely as the result of programs that appeal to young Episcopal families. It has tried a number of approaches to embrace its

Korean tenants, even holding several joint services. But in our chat Father Holtkamp admitted that such overtures were inadequate in overcoming the language barrier and had produced little social interaction.

A more charming illustration of ethnic bridging was Yihung Li's restaurant on Northern Boulevard. Li, who is known by all as Charlie, immigrated from China's Fujian Province in 1978 and opened a Chinese restaurant in the Ridgewood neighborhood along the Queens-Brooklyn border, and by the late 1990s he and his wife and three children had done well enough to buy a house in Little Neck. They were attracted by the neighborhood's safety and tidiness, and by such schools as PS 221, where 100 percent of the students meet the math standards and where their youngest son Peter would go. (A daughter, Mei, was in medical school; another son, Shing, at Cornell.) Li found that his neighbors, many of whom turned out to be Jewish, were quite cordial, if not quite intimate. "Our block is very friendly," he told me. "If my alarm goes off, they call me, which is nice. We help each other." In 2001, at the age of forty-three, he decided to open a Chinese restaurant nearer his home. As a Buddhist worried about high cholesterol, he decided to make it vegetarian and called it Zen Pavilion. He also had a brainstorm. Northeastern Queens still has many Jewish residents, and he figured that making his restaurant kosher would lure many of them from rival Chinese restaurants. (Jews historically have had a particular affinity to Chinese food, not only because dishes such as wonton soup have their Jewish counterparts—chicken soup and meat-filled dumplings known in Yiddish as kreplach—but because in their immigrant days a Chinese restaurant was one place they might be treated with respect, Cynthia Lee at the Museum of Chinese in the Americas told me.) So when he needed the information, it was Charlie Li's Jewish neighbors who told him where he could find kosher suppliers and a rabbi willing to certify a restaurant that stays open on the Sabbath. Now his Jewish neighbors enjoy his meatless Sesame Veggie Chicken, Moo Shu Fantasia, and Chunked Veggie Lamb Stewed in Casserole. So immersed is he in the American ethnic blender that in the summer of 2002 the restaurant played host to a Jewish naming party for a Chinese baby girl adopted by two gay men.

Despite such shimmering stories, the American Mixmaster goes only so far. Most of Li's friends are Chinese, immigrants like him who may live in Flushing and Chinatown. His American friendships are still rather superficial, extending no farther than the occasional chat. "We get together, talk to each other; it does not really go deeper," Li acknowledged. But he is not downhearted about this state of things. "If you help each other when you need it, that is good enough," he said.

In 2002, Sehyoung Jang, a Korean, opened a dance hall, Tri-State Hall, in what had been a Northern Boulevard furniture store, to teach neighborhood residents everything from the fox-trot to the tango to salsa. He and his dance partner, Evelyn Basak, are a striking tale of assimilation all by themselves. She is a fetching young Polish immigrant who met Jang in a Manhattan dance school and became Jang's partner and fiancée. Jang, twenty-eight years old when we spoke, is a tall, slender man who grew up in Seoul. As a young man, he was taken under the wings of a Puerto Rican ballroom dancer and her Chinese dancer husband. They legally adopted him and helped shape him into the dancer he is. When I visited, I was treated to Jang and Basak gliding across the hall's hardwood floor, embracing in a steamy clutch, jaggedly breaking off, pirouetting like a top, then showing off their individual flourishes. This pair often enters top-flight amateur competitions where the entry fees are more than $1,000 and the costumes cost $3,000—and sometimes take top titles. They could probably make a full-time career out of competition, but Jang devotes much of his energies toward the dance hall. They teach the gracious forms of ballroom to the old-timers' children and Korean children and on Sunday morning organize a dance club for Koreans and longer-rooted Americans between the ages of eighteen and twenty-five. "I want to put Korean and American people together," Jang told me. "If they can dance together and hold hands there will be more relationships. When you dance you don't care about country or culture."

Many neighborhood residents think it's a matter of time and conditioning before Koreans are woven into the area's fabric just as Jews, Irish, and Italians were decades ago. "We're simply not used to dealing with a wave of immigrants because it hasn't happened in our lifetime in this area," Eliott Socci, a retired software consultant who is president of the Douglaston Civic Association, told me.

And Sam Furgang, owner of a cluttered antiques shop on Northern Boulevard, predicted that even the tempest over the signs, which at bottom he said was silly, would pass as future generations adapt and blend in, just as his Yiddish-speaking parents did. "My father came here and settled on the Lower East Side," Furgang said. "I see pictures of that time and the signs were all in Yiddish. But the Jews got out of there. So go find me a Yiddish sign there now."

LITTLE NECK

...

WHERE TO GO

Douglaston Club (GREEK REVIVAL MANSION AND COURTS WHERE JOHN MCENROE LEARNED TENNIS) 600 WEST DRIVE; *(718) 229-3900*

Tri-State Hall (BALLROOM AND DANCE LESSONS BY A KOREAN-POLISH TEAM) 254-18 NORTHERN BOULEVARD; *(718) 631-8080*

Zion Episcopal Church (AMERICAN AND KOREAN SERVICES) 243-01 NORTHERN BOULEVARD; *(718) 225-0466*

WHERE TO EAT

Giardino Ristorante (CLASSY ITALIAN) 44-37 DOUGLASTON PARKWAY; *(718) 428-1090*

Scobee Grill (DINER WITH A JEWISH SPECIALTY OR TWO) 252-29 NORTHERN BOULEVARD; *(718) 428-5777*

Chapter 6

From Russia with Longing in Brighton Beach

. . .

IN RUSSIA, THERE IS A CHERISHED EXPRESSION, SAYS ANATOLY ALTER, furrier to the women of Brooklyn's Brighton Beach: "We're not so rich that we can buy cheap merchandise." This thought, he says, helps explain why when winter clamps its salt-edged chill on Brighton Beach's incongruous streets, even Russian women of modest income must drape themselves in fur. Walk along bustling Brighton Beach Avenue, the flavorful spine of the neighborhood that stretches underneath an elevated subway line, and you will see fur worn not just by nouveau riche housewives who come back to the old neighborhood to shop but also by Russian grandmothers laden with plastic supermarket bags and by willowy coeds. What they wear are not synthetics or mere collars, but often full coats of lush and flowing mink or at least muskrat, beaver, rabbit, or raccoon. Even ermine, chinchilla, and sable can be spotted—just as some of the more successful apparatchiks wore them in Moscow and St. Petersburg. In fifteen minutes one frosty morning on this plebeian avenue, half the women I counted were wearing fur, more furs than I ever saw in an hour along ritzy Park Avenue.

"We're hardworking and we make money and we can buy the same things as rich people," Victoria Goldenstein, a robust, dark-eyed, dark-haired businesswoman, told me as she cheerfully swaddled herself in mink in Alter's store. Already sporting a lustrous mahogany mink from Bloomingdale's, she was in Alter's shop with a mink-clad friend to drop off a Persian lamb coat for repair. While there, she could not resist trying on Alter's minks. This woman emigrated from Moldova fifteen years ago—hardly long enough to make a fortune here—but she seemed surprised, even a tad insulted, that someone would think her imprudent or question her wearing something so extravagant.

Call them ostentatious or vulgar or recklessly spendthrift, but Goldenstein and Brighton Beach's other fur wearers reveal something essential about immigrants, something that has always reshaped the look and spirit of the city's neighborhoods and is doing so now with unusual ferocity. Immigrants who make the decision to settle here do so with more than a frisson of remorse or self-questioning. It's not that they don't take pleasure in what this country has to offer. It's just that such life-altering decisions are never made with unalloyed conviction. Those who make them always look back.

And when they look back they want the trappings, totems, and touchstones of home, even if home was a frightening, corrupt, and stinting police state. For Russian women, whatever money they and their husbands make, they want to wrap themselves not just in the warmth of a fur coat but also in the plush feel of whatever it was that constituted luxury, when it was available.

Entire city blocks in neighborhoods such as Brighton Beach are remaking themselves to satisfy lusts for such throwbacks—not just for furs but for food and other products of home. Dozens of Russian food shops line Brighton Beach Avenue, in the somber shadows of the elevated B and Q train lines. At M&I International Foods, for instance, there are Zabar's-like arrays not only of canned and jarred former Soviet Union products, but also of cuts of fresh meat, smoked and marinated herrings, varieties of odd fresh fish, sausages, cheeses, caviar, and black breads flown in from those countries overnight. Buxom peroxided blond salesclerks stare at customers in bored silence or Brezhnev-era suspicion, rarely smiling. In some places customers line up Soviet-style to pay cash or food stamps before getting their groceries. There are dozens of new restaurants serving blini and pirogen and a half dozen sprawling nightclubs with Russian rock bands on stage and smoked sable and vodka on the tables. The newspaper stands are crowded not with the *Daily News* but with *Izvestia* and two or three dozen other newspapers either flown in from Russia or Ukraine or published right in New York. There are at least two Russian bookstores and other shops that stock Russian tapes and videos. English signs are translated into the Cyrillic alphabet (or vice versa). And most of the conversations along the street are in Russian.

Visiting Brighton Beach, wrote travel writer Vitaly Vitaliev, "is a unique opportunity to visit the country that doesn't exist anymore—the Union of Soviet Socialist Republics. . . . An American, arriving there by accident, stands out and gets stared at—like an Eskimo in the streets of Abu Dhabi." My colleague *New York Times* reporter Sabrina Tavernise, who spent many years in the Soviet Union, wrote of Brighton Beach as a community "frozen in time" that newer immigrants brought up in an eagerly capitalist Russia dismiss as a museum, a "cartoon of Russia." "In the traditional arc of the immigrant experience, the first ethnic outposts, like Little Italy or the Lower East Side, can often become anachronisms, resembling, at least to later arrivals, an exaggerated version of home that has become badly dated," she eloquently wrote.

Brighton Beach was born as an anachronism. It was developed right after the civil war by businessmen who wanted to give it the cachet of the English Channel resort. In addition to an ornate hotel with Victorian turrets and broad verandas, it boasted a boardwalk for fashionable promenading, a racetrack, and, by 1907, the fifteen-acre Brighton Beach Bath and Racquet Club. Jews of those earlier immigrations would leave tenements and shabby wood-frames of East New York and Brownsville and head not very far away to this spot that must have reminded more than a few of the Black Sea and other beach resorts they knew as children in czarist Russia. Even for those born here, Brighton Beach, with its closely packed apartment houses and summer bungalows, had the same bracing briny air and the same endless sandy beach as its more popular neighbor, Coney Island. Those who moved to Brighton found they could have a free summer vacation by the sea every year while living only a subway ride from work.

Scrappy strivers that they were, these newcomers held what they considered classy diversions at the baths—knish-eating contests, one-wall handball tournaments, mahjong matches, marine escapades in the three swimming pools. Milton Berle and Lionel Hampton entertained them. This was the animated but sweetly homespun Brighton Beach of Eugene Morris Jerome, Neil Simon's aspiring writer in *Brighton Beach Memoirs,* who lived in overcrowded splendor just off the beach and lusted after his shapely cousin. It was the Brighton Beach of Neil Sedaka (his last name, his real one, is a version of *tzedaka*, the Hebrew word for "charity"), the pop star of the 1950s and 1960s famous for "Calendar Girl" and "Breaking Up Is Hard to Do." Ten Sedakas were crammed into his parents' two-bedroom apartment on Coney Island Avenue and distracted themselves with his mother's Victrola by playing 78s of the Barry Sisters singing such schmaltz-dripping Yiddish warhorses as "My Yiddishe Mamme," "Shein Vi Di L'Vone" ("Pretty As the Moon"), and "Mein Shtetele Belz" ("My Village of Belz"). That explains why in 2004 I saw Sedaka give a Yiddish concert at Carnegie Hall in which he had the joint jumping. It seemed more than just coincidence when he told me that he spent his first royalties on a "Hadassah tallis"— a mink stole—for his mother. Fur was magic even then.

By the 1960s, the Brighton Beach Baths had 13,000 members. But that era may have been its deceptive apex. Those knish-eating, mahjong-playing Jews were getting grayer and frailer, and their children hankered after suburban backyards. Apartments of the dead and retired went begging, so the city began filling them with welfare tenants. The neighborhood, like much of the rest of the city, went into a tailspin of drugs, violence, and squalor that in its case turned out to be mercifully short.

Rescue came in the 1970s from a most unlikely source—international diplomacy. Soviet Jews were demanding to leave their despotic country and American Jews were clamoring on their behalf. The Soviets, eager to broaden contact with the West and sign trade and disarmament treaties, used Russian refugees as bribes and barter. When the refugees came here, most of them headed to places that looked just like home. Brighton Beach became a magnet for Jews from the Black Sea port of Odessa and for other Russians as well. The neighborhood seemed to metamorphose overnight, with such cafés as Gastronom Moscow and Tatiana Restaurant serving borscht, pirozhki (fried meat pies), *vatrushki* (cheese pies), and kvass (a mildly alcoholic tea-colored drink made from fermented bread often flavored with strawberries or mint) right on the boardwalk, and shops selling Russian clothes, books, and bric-a-brac. In the early 1990s, when the Soviet Union splintered apart, another flood of immigrants poured in, though now many were settling in such neighborhoods as Bensonhurst and Midwood in Brooklyn, Pelham Parkway in the Bronx, and Rego Park in Queens. In 2000, the last time an official count was taken, the New York area had 236,163 immigrants from the former Soviet Union.

I should not have been surprised by the prevalence of fur in Brighton Beach in winter. When my parents came to this country, they took deep pleasure whenever they could connect with a taste of home—a schmaltz herring from a local dairy store, a rye bread, or sour cream. They would dispatch us on quests for just the right rye bread. My mother was frugal in many respects—she never took a taxi, almost never ate in a restaurant. But she would treat herself to a fine cloth coat from Levine & Smith, a discounter of fashionable coats down on the Lower East Side, because the right coat was important for showing off her accomplishments during a *shpatzir*—a weekend stroll—along Broadway or Riverside Drive, which echoed a custom imported from Warsaw. And she would make sure my father had a handsome gray topcoat as well. A reckless purchase was a porcelain ballerina or baroque chess players that reminded them of the luxuries of home. "Europe" became a word I associated with quality.

Most of the Russian, Ukrainian, and Moldovan professionals who came over in the early 1970s worked as taxi drivers, nannies, or beauticians until they qualified here to work again as doctors and professors. Now some have been here long enough to feel secure; more than a few have been able to buy some of the 850 condos in the Oceana—the development that replaced the leveled Baths—at prices starting at $500,000 and rising to $2 million for a sea-view penthouse. Others have moved to the neighborhood next door, Manhattan Beach, tearing down the wooden cottages and run-down stuccos and building gated mansions on the same small lots, the bulk and glitz offending their American neighbors. Take Alex Puzaitzer. As a teenager twenty-five years ago in Communist Odessa, Puzaitzer shared a cramped two-room apartment with his mother and older sister, sleeping on a sofa bed. But as a successful entrepreneur, he bought a small house in Manhattan Beach, razed it, and built himself a stately beige Mediterranean—with a veranda, tall metal gates, and terra-cotta roof tiles—a house that reminded him of houses he had glimpsed on visits to the Riviera. The home is spacious enough for his college-age daughter and teenage son to have their own bathrooms and for twenty relatives to dine together on holidays. But not all of Puzaitzer's neighbors in this once-unassuming suburban-like neighborhood are happy about his hard-won elbow room.

"Each one is outdoing the other to show how big a house they can build, showing their wealth to an extreme degree, and it just doesn't fit in," Phil Metling, a retired optometrist who has lived in Manhattan Beach since the 1950s, told me.

What Metling missed is that often the scale of the houses reflects a family's yearning to declare that after years of scratching out a living they have arrived. Alter the furrier understands this principle of human psychology in his bones, because it's the same reason so many of his customers buy expensive furs.

"They want people to recognize them," he told me. "It's a little, maybe, show-off, but maybe not. Fur is glamour, and when you make the first step in life you want a nice car, nice clothing, nice jewelry, and fur is part of that. People here, the second, third generation, they stop showing off what they achieve. They don't have to."

In his early sixties, Alter has chiseled good looks, the erect bearing of a Cossack (a comparison he wouldn't appreciate, given the Cossack cavalrymen's pogrom-laden history), and the brazen flair of a Seventh Avenue designer. His one concession to flashing success is his diamond pinky ring. Alter, like me, is the son of Polish Jews who fled the Nazis and found refuge in the Soviet Union. His mother was originally from Lublin and ended up in Kiev, where he was born in 1941. His father, Boris Alter, operated a small government fur shop in Russia and taught Alter the ropes of the trade. The younger Alter and his wife, Raya, came here from Kiev in 1978. On his third day in New York, he found a job as a machine operator in Manhattan's fur district. Barely two years later, he opened his first fur shop in what had been a laundry on Brighton Beach Avenue. Then, ten years ago he opened a second shop a few blocks away, eventually buying the entire building. Classic Furs now carries 2,000 furs priced from as low as $500 all the way up to $40,000, and it draws buyers from Switzerland, Sweden, and Mother Russia herself. We chatted on the second floor of his emporium as Tamara Zapolotsky, a saleswoman, helped customers try on furs nearby.

American women, he told me, waste their money on a variety of winter coats—perhaps a tweed overcoat for work, a parka for shopping and weekend walks, a camel hair for the opera. But Russians, he told me, "look to fur like everyday necessity." They like "to look their best" when they leave the house—no parka, jeans, and sneakers for them. "In the summertime, they can show off everything else," he said, with a twinkle in his eye. "In the wintertime they can't."

"American women, they have closets with lots of garbage—another *shmatte* for two hundred or three hundred dollars," he said. "If a woman go to Anne Klein, a cloth coat can cost three thousand dollars. For three thousand dollars, she can buy a magnificent mink coat. If a woman wear an Anne Klein coat and another woman wear a mink, who's going to get more attention?"

He believes Jewish women in America carry some of their Russian inclinations in their genes. "Every Jewish woman has to have a fur coat, and when they go to synagogue they have to wear fur. Historically, they are born with that love. Only the czar and high society in their countries were able to wear fur—mink, sable, ermine."

I was to learn that he had the deeply experienced insights of a veteran anthropologist. When I went to actual academics, they simply confirmed in more intellectually dense phrases what Alter had told me. Richard Alba, a distinguished professor of sociology at the State University of New York at Albany who specializes in ethnic studies, said that wearing fur may be flashy, but it is understandable given the struggle of gaining a foothold in this country and the need for some acknowledgment. "The ways of demonstrating that they have been able to maintain or enhance status are really very critical for immigrants," he told me. "For the Russians, it may be having an expensive fur they couldn't afford in the Soviet Union. For the Italians, it was owning property."

To cater to this Russian passion for fur, the shopping district along eight blocks of Brighton Beach Avenue and along intersecting Coney Island Avenue boasts three fur shops, a number that would be striking even in an affluent part of Manhattan. Ordinary clothing stores stock a rack of furs, and even one electronics and import store had a sizable selection, though Alter and another fur shop owner, Irene Perchonok, told me furs in such places are of low quality. "We specialize in fur," Perchonok told me. "Mentally if you're going to buy underwear, you're not going to buy it in a fur store."

Perhaps it's something of a conceit, but it occurred to me as I strolled the neighborhood that fur is a historically immigrant business. Much of the New World was settled by fur trappers who were willing to penetrate the pristine interior of the country in search of mammals whose pelts would safeguard them against winter. The trading posts they set up to sell their fur and buy provisions for their trade grew into some of the great American cities. But given the Soviet Union's fabled winter, fur is particularly talismanic for women born there. It embraces them in the homeland they never stop missing, no matter how deep their affection for this country.

Russians who grew up in this country and, hungry to fit in, despised furs as their parents' musty baggage from the Old Country often find as they grow older that they long to wear fur. "I never thought I would wear fur," Alter's daughter, Regina, a corporate lawyer at Dreier & Baritz on Park Avenue, told me. "When I was a kid, Russians tended to wear furs and Americans didn't. Now that I'm all grown up, I see them differently. They're beautiful, they're light, they're warm, and they're back in style."

Diana Daniloff, a twenty-two-year-old New York University law student and immigrant from the Caucasus region, told me as she looked with her mother for a long mink in Alter's shop, "It's warm, it looks beautiful, it makes the woman look gorgeous."

Russians don't have the Puritan American ethos of sin and its accompanying sense of guilt and are not as easily swayed by animal-rights activists who protest the wearing of fur. Nor do Russians have the same ethic of thrift. "When you live in a country like Russia, where you are not allowed to have lots of money and everything is taken care of for you, whatever money you have, you want to spend it" is the way Alter explained the Soviet mentality. Communism discouraged people from saving since there wasn't much they could buy with their nest eggs, and it encouraged a culture of what can charitably be called an oblique approach to the law. Raya Alter told me that in such a system, signposts of prestige were important. Ordinary Russians would wear thickly lined cloth coats, while wives of government officials often wore Persian lamb coats with blue mink collars.

"People want to get in America what they couldn't get in Russia," she said.

Moreover Russians here finally feel secure. "They feel themselves in their own country, their own place," Alter said. "And they're not worried about tomorrow. Tomorrow they can buy a Chevrolet. Today they want a Mercedes. They want to live today." So Russians are more likely to spend their spare cash and not worry about squirreling money away for retirement or for their children.

Perchonok, owner of Majestic Furs on Coney Island Avenue, articulated the difference between the Russian and American philosophies of life pithily. She is an immigrant from St. Petersburg who has been here since 1975, yet is typically Russian in many ways, as evidenced by her insistence on close family ties. Her adult son calls her every day.

"American people like to put money in a bank; Russian people like to live—go on a good vacation, have good houses," she said. "American people believe they're going to leave a will for their children, so the children have to wait for the parents to die. Russian people, they give their children today. If I have it, let them enjoy it.

"Show me a woman who does not like a fur coat or diamonds. I never met one. If you can afford mink, you buy mink. If not, you wear rabbit or sheepskin. In Russia we believe you better buy one, but a good one. In Russia we always say, 'We are not that rich to buy cheap things.' "

Oh, yes, I had heard that expression before.

IN MY TRAVELS around Brooklyn, I also discovered another totem of home that has infused Russian life in New York. Immigrants from the former Soviet Union, I learned, have opened a dozen ballroom-dancing schools and studios where hundreds of children, in flouncing skirts or flashy sports shorts, learn how to dance sambas, waltzes, mambos, and jive dances while their ambitious mothers fret in the waiting rooms. For Americans, ballroom dancing may be archaic, reeking of royalty and the czarist balls, but in Russia it is still an emblem of cultivation, and immigrants want to sustain it here. Indeed, imported Soviet-bred dancers are reviving the art of ballroom dancing not just in New York and not just for Russians, but for Americans across large parts of the United States.

A telling result is that in New York, New Jersey, and Connecticut, immigrants from the former Soviet Union now own eleven of the twenty-three Fred Astaire dance studios, the chain of franchises that Astaire, the icon of suave, founded in 1947 to spread his terpsichorean grace through the American populace.

There are ballroom dance studios in Brighton Beach, but for variety's sake I took the subway four stops north in Brooklyn to Midwood. There, new Soviet immigrants who can't find apartments in crowded Brighton Beach are settling in apartment houses scattered among single-family homes occupied by Orthodox Jews and by longer-settled Russians who are prospering well enough to afford Midwood's houses. On Quentin Road, I found the King's Ballroom and DanceSport Center, an island of elegance among the neighborhood's helter-skelter sidewalks. It had a bright room the size of a basketball court and with the same light hardwood floor. In the narrow reception room, I came across the brothers Atanasov—Dimitre, fourteen, Vladimir, twelve, and Alex, nine. We talked for a half hour about their interest in dance and they told me in unaccented and smoothly vernacular English that they had to take up to five hours a week of dance lessons after school, grumbling like typical American boys. Dimitre suggested that the afternoon dance lessons are so uncool, he hides them from his friends at Dyker Heights Intermediate School. "I'm there 24/7," he complained. "I spend more time there than at home."

I particularly enjoyed talking to them, with their immigrant parents alongside, because they reminded me of my family whenever we used to encounter Americans. While our parents sometimes mangled the language, my brother and I, and later my sister, conversed with a slangy authority, our European roots barely audible on our lips. But we too immersed ourselves in traditions our parents needed to cling to—in our case the Orthodox yeshiva world our parents had been raised in. There were more than a few times that my brother and I also thought that inherited world fusty and uncool.

Yet, while the Atanasovs whine like typical American boys, the three brothers do not dance like typical American boys. While I was there, they spun three stylish girls across the gleaming floor, doing a rumba to the music of "Skylark" and a jive dance to Duke Ellington's "Take the A

Train." The couples were not just counting steps but doing splits and raising legs in the air with masterly panache.

It is dancing like theirs that has allowed Russians and other émigrés from the former Soviet Union to dominate American dancing competition. In the last decade, exquisitely trained dancers looking for American-sized paydays have immigrated to the United States and become the luminaries of professional and amateur ballroom. They have elevated the quality of showmanship, executing their rumbas and waltzes with a flourish and precision rarely seen here since the nimble tread of the feet of Fred Astaire. They have dressed up their moves with Fosse-like angling of the hips and shoulders, giving dance more of a postmodern edge and athleticism. In the process, the Russians have spurred something of a revival of cheek-to-cheek dancing. Archie C. Hazelwood, the former president of the United States Amateur Ballroom Dancers Association, told me that "ballroom dancing has increased in popularity and a big factor are immigrants."

Russians teach dance to earn money for the costumes and entry fees they need to compete or simply to earn a living. At Brooklyn College in Midwood, Sergei Nabatov, a forty-eight-year-old Ukrainian and one-time international champion, offers four different one-credit courses in ballroom dancing. At eight o'clock one morning—not exactly waltz time—I saw Nabatov put thirty-seven smartly dressed but often gawky students from the Dominican Republic, Israel, and Colombia, as well as garden-variety Americans, through a series of swirling rumbas and Lindies. It was their finals, and Nabatov was grading them. The students seemed to relish the test in a way they would not have had it been in organic chemistry. One immigrant from Vietnam, Julia Mach, told me that she was once "a girl who sat out dances." "Now I enjoy it so much, the feeling you get when you can match the mood and the music," she said. "I love it!"

The Russians here were practically born to dance. In Moscow, for instance, every public school offers ballroom dancing and children start taking lessons in the first grade and continue at least through the fourth. After school, many parents send children for private lessons. Just as it did for gymnastics, the Soviet Union set up rigorous dance programs for the most promising young people so they could shine in international competition. Even now, dance contests are often broadcast on television, something that until recently was rare in the United States.

The tradition of ballroom dancing, of course, extends at least as far back as the great czarist balls. But in more recent decades, dancing became an expression of what Dr. Anna Shternshis, an assistant professor at the University of Toronto who studies popular Russian culture, called "culturedness." Once, you were considered cultured if your house had such simple possessions as a lamp, books, a tablecloth. Later on, you were considered cultured if you gave your children music and dance lessons. The interest in dancing was especially strong among Jews, who in New York compose a majority of the Russians. Since in the Soviet Union they were commonly barred from religious expression, they adopted secular expressions of their identity.

"They had to invent things that made them Jewish," she said. "It was a hidden Jewish identity because there was no other way to develop a Jewish identity. So the children do ballroom dancing and study music and try to do well in school because they think this is what their parents think it means to be Jewish."

Here, the parents are often too burdened carving out new lives to spend money on dance lessons for themselves. But they enroll their children in schools in Brooklyn or in dance camps in the Catskills. The professionals, of course, make sure their offspring take their art seriously. Irina Atanasov, the mother of the dancing Atanasovs, is a professional dancer, and her Bulgarian-born husband, Dimitre, manages a Fred Astaire studio on East Forty-third Street in Manhattan. "In high school, when we had gathering, we didn't smoke, or do drugs—we danced," he said. "There is the erotic background—it's nice to feel a young girl's body next to you, to flirt. It gives some predisposition to dance." Dimitre wonders if the decline of dance in the United States was the result of the sexual revolution, which made it easier to have sex without dancing's foreplay.

Many of the Russian champions who came here, such as Taliat Tarsinov and his wife, Marina, intended to go back. "We will come to America, we will make money, we will get rich, and we will go back," he said of his thoughts in 1992. "When we left we were crying." But life here has proven too good to forsake. He owns the Astaire studio on East

Eighty-sixth Street in Manhattan. He does not just prepare people for weddings and bar mitzvahs, but refines the moves of champion dancers, so they express the music's inherent drama. "When I teach a couple ballroom dancing, I tell them it will be a reflection of life," he said. "I will teach you how to lead and follow, how to give each other space so everybody will feel comfortable, how to be next to each other but not in the way of each other. It's a conversation between two people, and it's all about man and woman and their relationship to the music. It's a very good sexual education. You learn how to respect your partner, if you're a man to see a woman in front of you."

While the Russians have much to teach, they are also learning much from Americans, particularly the capitalist skills of marketing and advertising needed to transform a notion into a thriving business. "We're learning how to be successful, how to make dance studio a hot spot," Tarsinov told me. "We Russians don't know how to sell, and we like to learn."

If they do win converts to ballroom dancing around the country, the Russians will have achieved a turnabout of sorts. In the 1957 hit musical *Silk Stockings,* Astaire played an American who wielded his elegant footwork to convert three comrades and a long-legged Ninotchka (Cyd Charisse) to the joys of capitalism. Now, in real life in the United States, the Russians seem to have turned the tables, wielding elegant footwork to take over the art Astaire is most identified with, and doing so in true capitalist style.

BRIGHTON BEACH

...

WHERE TO GO

Boardwalk (WALK ALONG THE ATLANTIC OCEAN ALL THE WAY TO CONEY ISLAND)

Brighton Beach Avenue (FROM OCEAN PARKWAY TO CONEY ISLAND AVENUE, A RUSSIAN BAZAAR)

Classic Furs (ONE OF THE CITY'S LARGEST FUR SHOPS AND AN ETHNIC TREAT) 221 BRIGHTON BEACH AVENUE; *(718) 332-5138*

King's Ballroom and DanceSport Center (DANCE LESSONS FIT FOR A CZAR'S CHILD) 1207 QUENTIN ROAD, MIDWOOD NEIGHBORHOOD OF BROOKLYN; *(718) 336-3627*

M&I International Foods (THE ZABAR'S OF BRIGHTON BEACH) 249 BRIGHTON BEACH AVENUE; *(718) 615-1011*

WHERE TO EAT

Café Arbat (STYLISH RUSSIAN BISTRO) 306 BRIGHTON BEACH AVENUE; *(718) 332-5050*

Café Tatiana (BORSCHT WITH A TROPICAL DÉCOR) 3145 BRIGHTON THIRD STREET, ON THE BOARDWALK; *(718) 646-7630*

Moscow Cafe (BORSCHT SERVED TO THE SOUND OF CLACKING DOMINOES AND OWNED BY THE WINTER GARDEN BANQUET HALL NEXT DOOR) 3152 BRIGHTON SIXTH STREET, ON THE BOARDWALK; *(718) 934-6666*

Chapter 7

Long Day's Journey from Bedford Park

. . .

Tʜᴇʀᴇ ᴀʀᴇ sᴏᴍᴇ sᴍᴀʟʟ ᴍᴇʀᴄɪᴇs ᴛᴏ ʟɪᴠɪɴɢ ᴀ ᴛᴡᴏ-ʜᴏᴜʀ ᴛʀᴇᴋ by subway and bus from a low-paying job.

In the morning, Intesar Museitef always gets a seat on the D train because her station is the second from the line's origin in an eclectic huddle of apartment houses in the northern Bronx known as Bedford Park. On the return trip home she always gets a seat on the E train because the station she gets on in the far reaches of Queens is at the beginning of that line. Otherwise, her four-hour round-trip, which takes her under virtually the full breadth of the city and includes the added torment of two fifteen-minute bus rides, is dull, achingly so.

"It's boring," Museitef (*Moo*-seh-tef) told me as we started her return trip one spring afternoon after she finished spending four hours caring for a frail widow. "To sit for two hours on a train is boring."

Sure, there are suburban commuters to New York from, say, Dutchess County or the Poconos who endure four-hour commutes, but usually they are drawn by Wall Street jobs with hefty bonuses or blue-collar jobs with ample wages and benefits. But there are workers in all corners of the city who are willing to travel breathtaking distances—sometimes for as many hours as they work—for few dollars and virtually no benefits. They do this because whatever small amount they make is essential to putting food on the table and self-respect in their souls, and they can't be choosy about where the job is. Museitef, a pretty, sad-eyed Palestinian immigrant who covers her long dark hair with a head scarf and greets the world with a genial, even garrulous manner, commutes four hours each workday just to work four hours a day and twenty hours a week. She gets paid $7 an hour, but if the time consumed commuting is factored in as part of her workday, she is actually getting paid $3.50 an hour, far below the minimum wage.

Most of the people in New York City who punish themselves with these long commutes for low-wage household jobs are, like Museitef, immigrants, and they often live in modest neighborhoods such as Bedford Park, far from the city's center, with no outstanding charms or attractions to recommend them other than that they are along a subway line and their remoteness makes their apartments relative bargains. These immigrants living in the city's low-rent fringes are willing to travel to distant jobs for work for the same reason that Willie Sutton robbed banks: That's where the money is.

Neighborhoods with still-affordable rents such as East New York in Brooklyn and Bedford Park in the Bronx are filling up with immigrants, but the places they work may be in Tribeca; Rye, New York; Oyster Bay, Long Island; or Teaneck, New Jersey. The reason for the disjunction between work and home is economic. The families who can afford babysitters and cleaning women live in Manhattan's plush heartland or in verdant pockets on the city's margins or suburbs. The people who work for them cannot afford the car needed to live in the suburbs, nor can they afford apartments close to midtown. So, many choose to live on the outskirts of the city reachable by subway, train, or bus, though not necessarily the same outskirts where the jobs are available.

Time is a flexible commodity for these workers; money is not. They throw away the precious time most of us demand for ourselves to give our lives some zest—time for eating dinner with the children, going to a movie, lunching with friends—so they can earn what they need to get by. Museitef, in her early thirties when I met her, is a divorcée who must work to feed and clothe herself and her seven-year-old son, Mouath, and pay the rent on their third-floor apartment on the upper end of the Grand Concourse, the legendary tree-lined boulevard of decorous apartment houses where I lived as a teenager. Even if there hadn't been that Concourse coincidence, I was drawn to Museitef's story because I had long thought about immigrants who have tiring treks to jobs few others want to do. For one thing, I have employed them. For fifteen years, my wife and I have lived in suburban Westchester County, and we have had a succession of nannies and cleaning ladies to tidy our home and keep an eye on our daughter, Annie, when she was young. Almost all of them traveled from Queens or Brooklyn, and not from just any parts of those boroughs, but often from the far end of those boroughs. Nazmoon, the Guyanese babysitter who took care of Annie when she was in grade school, journeyed to our house from Richmond Hill, Queens, enduring a forty-minute subway ride to Grand Central followed by a half-hour railroad commute. A cleaning lady we employed, a Colombian immigrant named Aura, came from just as far away in Jackson Heights, Queens. Like many working parents hoping to keep a lid on our roiling lives, we didn't ask too many questions about what such rides meant in terms of lost money, wasted time, and assaults on the spirit. We were happy to have found someone who was tender and conscientious with our child or took pride in an unblemished home.

Even before we hired Nazmoon, I knew in my marrow the price of those commutes, for my immigrant father was such a commuter. Within a few weeks of getting off the boat, he was told of a job in Newark, New Jersey, that paid $40 a week for a week that lasted from early Monday morning until midday Saturday. We were living in New York City then, on the West Side of Manhattan, an hour's commute from Newark. Later we moved even farther from his job—the Concourse, an hour and a half from Newark. My father was almost always out of the house by the time I awoke, but occasionally I opened my eyes in time to glimpse his gangly, black-haired figure rise at 5:45 a.m. or so, and sometimes I would get out of bed to watch him gobble down a piece of buttered rye bread for breakfast washed down with instant coffee. He would slap together a cheese sandwich for lunch and rush out of the house to catch the subway down to Canal Street, where he would still have to rendezvous with Sam and Leo, two co-workers who were driving from Brooklyn and would give him a lift through the fumes and traffic jams of the Holland Tunnel to the General Textile Company in Newark. The company made the asbestos-lined covers for ironing boards, and that hour-and-a-half commute was for the pleasure of crawling under sewing machines to oil or repair them and to make sure the Puerto Rican seamstresses had all the fabric and needles they needed.

I could not help noticing the imprint left by his work and long slog home. We would hear the key turning around 7:30 every night, and there would be my father, with a smile that confirmed his delight in seeing us but also a fog of weariness over his ebony eyes. Sometimes he surprised us with three small Van Houten bittersweet chocolates he would buy in the penny vending machines that in those years were ubiquitous in subway stations. Our pleasure—and the plate of food my mother would bring out for him—was his compensation for all that effort. My father was a shy, introverted man who carried the pain of losing his entire family in the Holocaust buried inside him, so that may explain why he and I talked so little during the years I grew up in his house. But the time stolen from his life by that job and that commute was partly to blame as well.

While factory grunt work has always been a big employer of immigrants, so has household work. The 2000 census, notoriously wide off the mark when it comes to jobs filled by illegal immigrants, counted more than 18,000 household workers in New York City—nannies, maids, cleaning people, home health aides—who endure daily trips of ninety minutes or more for jobs paying less than $25,000 a year. More than 90 percent are women, three out of every four were born outside the United States and do not speak English well, and most seem to hail from the West Indies or South America. Daniel Cornfield, a sociologist at Vanderbilt University who specializes in labor issues, told me that people who take these jobs come from terribly poor or unstable countries and are "desperately seeking work." "The transportation they take is often a reflection of an intense need to find any kind of job that will pay them," he said.

Even into the 1950s, unskilled immigrants could rely on manufacturing jobs clustered in a central location such as Manhattan's Garment District, but a large proportion of manufacturing jobs have evaporated, while much of the low-wage growth has been in household work and home health care. Even if those jobs are available close to home, landing them often requires submitting to an indignity or two. A *Times* colleague of mine, Nina Bernstein, reported in a 2005 article that immigrant women—Mexicans, Ecuadorians, and Poles—were lining up on an overpass of the Brooklyn-Queens Expressway in the Hasidic Williamsburg section of Brooklyn for $8-an-hour cleaning jobs. Most of them were hired on the spot by pious Jewish women who, burdened by eight or ten children, needed them to render their homes spotless for the Sabbath. While Americans are familiar with street-corner clusters of men seeking landscape or construction work, the photograph accompanying the article showed what on the docks used to be known as a shape-up, though this time it was made up of twelve women in jeans and T-shirts sitting on an overpass railing shaded from a sultry sun. If those cleaning jobs had any advantage, it was that they were not too far from some of these workers' homes. In many cases, though, it takes several years for immigrants to gain enough English, savvy, and contacts to find jobs closer to home.

When I decided to write about her in 2004, I met Museitef at her apartment in the regally christened but nondescript neighborhood of Bedford Park. The neighborhood, a collection of brick apartment houses that were built after the opening of the Jerome Avenue elevated subway line in 1917, was given the cachet of the name of a London suburb by early-twentieth-century developers. Like most unheralded Bronx neighborhoods, it has an array of modest shops and services—groceries, candy stores, beauty parlors, drugstores, travel agencies, shoe repairers, cell phone retailers, medical clinics, and churches. They may seem unremarkable to a visitor, but they contain insular worlds where the intimacies of clothes, body, diet, faith, and family are discreetly traded every day. Most of the neighborhood is tucked within the boundaries of the New York Botanical Gardens and Fordham University on the east, the Jerome Park Reservoir on the west, and tree-lined Mosholu Parkway on the north. The Grand Concourse is its spine. Some of the buildings have fire escapes braiding down their fronts and privet hedges concealing small rectangles of earth. Some have weathered decorative Tudor half-timbers that testify to the genteel ambitions of the people who built them. (One of the neighborhood's residents was William Fox, the Hungarian immigrant garment worker who bought a nickelodeon in Brooklyn for $1,666 and turned it into Twentieth Century Fox.) A few buildings have the faded charm of the Art Deco confections that once made the Grand Concourse so grand, with striped tan brick façades, wraparound corner windows, lobby murals, and sunken living rooms. Interspersed on the hilly side streets are Queen Anne–style cottages and wood-frame houses, many of which have been divided up into two or three apartments.

A large patch of the neighborhood to the west consists of acrid-smelling, cyclone-fenced yards for parking subway cars. But then comes its most famous institution, the Bronx High School of Science, a selective school that has produced seven Nobelists in physics, not to mention singer Bobby Darin and novelist E. L. Doctorow. I went to that school in the early 1960s and got off daily at Museitef's Bedford Park Boulevard station and walked a half dozen blocks among the Irish, Jewish, and Italian residents to the spare Bauhaus school building. I remember not a single shop or hangout that might have diverted me, though schoolmates were often drawn by the enchantments south of Bedford Park around Fordham Road—the long-gone ice cream parlors Jahn's and Krum's and the ornate movie palace of Loew's Paradise Theater, with its cavernous ceiling of twinkling stars.

Thirty years ago, Bedford Park's outlook seemed grim, as a plague of arson, drug dealing, and middle-class flight rolled up from the South Bronx across Fordham Road to its very doors. Neighbors organized, often led by Roman Catholic church groups surviving from the days when Bedford Park was heavily Irish (the Academy of Mount St. Ursula, the oldest continuous Catholic girls' high school in New York State, and St. Philip Neri Roman Catholic Church, where Rudolph Giuliani married his first wife, are still there). The enclave held on long enough to benefit from the influx of immigrant strivers, the product of the 1965 immigration reforms, who were by the 1980s ready to make their next step up the economic pyramid. They found the sometimes battered apartment buildings far more inviting than the dwellings they knew in their native lands and appreciated the choice of two subway lines to whisk them to work.

Today, the neighborhood is no longer defined by a dominant ethnic group. Instead, it is inhabited by a motley patchwork of ethnicities, including Dominicans, Puerto Ricans, West Africans, Bangladeshis, Koreans, Jamaicans, Cambodians, Vietnamese, Albanians, and Latin Americans. Museitef's census tract, number 413, has 7,515 residents, but only 21 percent are white, with a large proportion of those defined as elderly. More than 55 percent are Hispanic, 11 percent black, and 8 percent Asian. One of every three residents was born abroad, and only 20.6 percent finished college. The median household income in 2000 was a low $32,037—compared to more than $38,293 for the city as a whole. One of every six residents has no job.

Museitef fits right in to the neighborhood. With a handsome bronzed face and an engaging, even flirtatious tooth-filled smile, she is the daughter of an itinerant businessman, Fahmi Museitef, who for twenty years sold carpets door to door in Wisconsin, which may explain her ease with English and her midwestern conviviality. She was born in Ramallah in the West Bank, which Israel conquered from Jordan in the Six Days' War of 1967, four years before she was born. As if in contradiction of that territory's occupation, she was named Intesar, which means "victory." She grew up in Ramallah in a family of seven sisters and four brothers and married there as well. Museitef was seven months pregnant in 1997 when she was instructed by her husband to travel to New York to get them both residency papers so they could eventually immigrate. Museitef and her son, Mouath, stayed for a time with a sister, Hanan Khalil, who lives in the Bronx with six children. But the home was so crowded she moved to a shelter run by Women In Need and stayed for two years. The organization gave her two weeks of classes in working as a home health care aide, teaching her how to help elderly clients get in and out of bed, shower, dress, and walk safely. She also learned to do their cooking, shopping, and cleaning. Her job title barely existed forty years ago, but such jobs, often paid for by Medicare and Medicaid, have allowed more established working couples to provide care for their elderly parents.

Around 2003, Museitef was dismayed to learn that her husband had started a second family with another woman in the West Bank. She decided to remain in New York and see whether she could make it on her own. (She and her husband divorced in 2004.) The sparsely furnished apartment she lives in costs $995 a month, but all but $106 is paid for by federal Section 8 subsidies. With only $140 a week in part-time income, that $106 is hard to squirrel away, though she does receive food stamps, Medicaid, and a stipend from Women In Need for transportation and telephone. At the time I decided to tag along on one of her daily commutes, she worked for the Personal-Touch Home Care agency of

Queens, which would assign her for a few weeks or a few months to an elderly person's home. The clients usually lived in Brooklyn or Queens.

"I keep telling them to look for something in the Bronx," she told me. "They say, 'We're going to find for you.'"

Such mismatches are not uncommon for the 12,000 home care aides affiliated with the health care workers union, 1199SEIU. Jennifer Cunningham, executive vice president of 1199SEIU, explained that the union negotiates with large providers who monitor the patients but they subcontract the job of home care assignments to small agencies such as Personal-Touch. The union, she admitted, has "not done a very good job" pressuring the providers to compel Personal-Touch and other employers to match job sites more conveniently with the addresses of workers such as Museitef. Workers who are not attached to agencies or unions have it worse, since they rely on an informal word-of-mouth network, not on hard information about where jobs can be found.

"There has to be a more rational way," said Cunningham. "To be poor in this country and new to this country, there's a sense that you should be happy to have a job, period, and not question why you travel so long and get paid so little."

On the day I accompanied Museitef, she rose at 5:30 a.m. after a night of sleeping on her couch (she had given her bed to her visiting sister, Ola). She murmured her Muslim prayers, put on a stylish cream-and-tan striped jacket, and ate a breakfast of toast and butter accompanied by a cup of Arabic tea. She woke Mouath up at 7 a.m., watched the morning news shows, paying special attention to events in the Middle East and the reports on subway delays, then called her mother in Ramallah, a call that she could afford with a $2-an-hour phone card. While I waited for her to get ready, I looked around the tidy apartment, noticing a mix of the American and the Middle Eastern—prayer beads on a table, framed parchments with passages from the Koran, the kitschy touch of a telephone shaped like a basketball and inscribed with Michael Jordan's name. Like other American kids, the spirited Mouath, a lean straw of a boy with an impish smile, is a huge Michael Jordan fan. With Mouath in tow and myself tagging along with a notebook and pen, Museitef scrambled down three flights to the sidewalk and crossed the wide Concourse to meet Mouath's school bus, displaying in her darting dark eyes and quick smile an enchantment with the city's bustle. "I love walking," she told me.

At 8:23, she kissed Mouath good-bye and headed for the Bedford Park Boulevard station. Ten minutes later, the D train barreled in, with its gift of empty seats. Getting comfortable in a snug corner seat—"I always love sitting in the corner," she confided—she took out a sheaf of potential questions on the American citizenship test she was going to take the next day. As the train sped through dark tunnels and brightly lit stations, she tried to remember how many stars and stripes are in the flag, who is the vice president, how many amendments there are to the Constitution. Museitef told me she also passes the time on such commutes reading from the Koran and daydreaming about what future her Mouath will have in America.

On her subway trips, Museitef told me, she has seen people smoke, drink, brawl, and, even once, try to jump in front of a train. She is often wary of people who stare at the scarf wrapped trimly around her scalp and neck, a headdress she calls by its Arabic name, *mandeel*. "People ask me if I shave my head," she said. "I say, 'I'm not Jewish.'" If someone who seems threatening approaches, she said, she prays quietly in Arabic: "Allah, protect me from bad people." "I was not scared in Ramallah, even with the killings," she said. "Since I'm here, my mother worries about me. But you can't hide from death. Whatever happens, happens."

At 9:03, the D train pulled into the Seventh Avenue station in midtown Manhattan and she stepped off, skipping briskly downstairs to the next platform, only to watch a Queens-bound E train pull away. She would have to wait for the next train, which appeared a few minutes later. For much of this stretch of the ride, the car was largely empty and she got lost in her cocoon of thoughts. Scattered around the car were passengers listening to their iPods, studying textbooks, snoozing. The mechanical subway voice announced the names of the stations and warned riders in a singsong, "Stand clear of the closing doors."

Inevitably, she scanned the ads that ran like a banner across each side of the train. One was about lead poisoning, and it reminded her that she had once noticed her son displaying some of the symptoms and called her landlord, who quickly repainted the apartment. The many ads for business schools and technical colleges, though, prompted a twinge of remorse that she had not pursued more than a few courses toward a nursing assistant's degree. She took such courses at the Borough of Manhattan Community College but dropped them after the September 11 attacks partly because strangers on the downtown streets taunted her for being Muslim. Besides, she said, if she took courses, "Who is going to be with my son?"

Her inability to secure a better job weighs heavily on her, she told me in the rumbling din of the train, but she takes heart in what her mother has told her: "I'm proud of you. For an Arabic woman to do what you're doing."

Several times during our subway conversation, Museitef used the expression "inshallah," which means "if Allah wills it." It speaks of a fatalism underlying Muslim culture, and Museitef has much to be fatalistic about. She told me matter-of-factly, possibly suspecting that I was sympathetic to the Israeli side of the half-century-old quarrel, that working as a nurse's assistant in Ramallah, she had endured even longer commutes than she now has. When she needed to get from her village of Beiteen into Ramallah itself, she could spend hours clearing Israeli checkpoints.

"If you're lucky, they let you in," she said. "If you're not, they send you back home. That's why people come here."

She seemed to harbor no ill will toward Jews, though. She spoke affectionately of the Jewish woman in Brighton Beach she had cared for for three years before getting the job in Jamaica, Queens. They are still in touch. "Here we're friends and there we're enemies," she said. At 9:44, the E train pulled into Jamaica Center, the last stop. She climbed up to the street in time to be disappointed once again—the Q85 bus was pulling away. "Sometimes, I miss the bus, I have to wait twenty minutes," she said. "In winter, it's so cold." This time another drew up quickly, and soon it made its sputtering way along Merrick Boulevard, a major Queens artery that runs through a largely black neighborhood. She gazed out at passing storefront churches such as Abundant Life Deliverance, beauty parlors, hair-braiding shops, and fried chicken restaurants. At 10:05 the bus dropped her off at Rochdale Village, among the world's largest housing complexes, with twenty middle-income cooperative apartment buildings, each fourteen stories, built in 1960 on the site of the Jamaica Race Course. Most of its 25,000 residents were once Jewish, but the makeup changed there after 1970 just as it did in the surrounding South Jamaica neighborhood.

At 10:12, almost two hours after leaving her Bronx neighborhood, Museitef rang the doorbell of Mary Spencer's sixth-floor apartment. Spencer is a retired postal worker who has progressive supranuclear palsy, a Parkinson's-like disease that impairs walking, balance, and focus of one's eyes. To this stranger, the disease was most noticeable in Spencer's glazed, frozen-eyed expression. Spencer lives with her ninety-one-year-old mother, Elizabeth Riggs, in a well-kept apartment graced with plants whose lushness betrays Spencer's fussiness. Spencer's daughter lives too far away to care for her regularly, so for the past three months, it has been up to Museitef to feed and bathe Spencer, straighten her room, and dress her. This morning she tenderly buttoned Spencer's jacket and eased her legs into the footrests of a wheelchair before rolling her outside for a visit to the pharmacy.

"One day I'm going to be old," Museitef whispered to me. "If you take care of somebody well, it will come back to you."

When they returned, Spencer was fed and dressed and helped into bed to watch television. We spoke briefly, and it was clear how firmly aware she was of her caregivers' long commutes. "They should get paid well," she said. "They have to travel so far to take care of me."

Toward the end of the four-hour shift, Spencer, lying in her brass bed under her covers, and Museitef, in a chair alongside, were together watching a rerun of *The Cosby Show.* Soon it was two o'clock and time for the trip home. Museitef may have felt slightly self-conscious that she was not working at a job that was more taxing on her obviously nimble mind, because as she was about to leave, she told me, "If I leave this job I have nothing. So I'd rather take this job than do nothing."

At 2:14 the Q85 bus wheezed to a stop outside Rochdale Village and Museitef swiped her MetroCard in the fare box. The bus passed a Wonder Bread outlet and Museitef mused how much she loves fresh bread. "Sometimes I eat a whole loaf. I love bagels too." It occurred to me that she had not had lunch. She rarely does while working, though she sometimes nibbles on carrots and sips from a bottle of water.

By 2:34, she was on the E train heading toward midtown. She let me know that while she traveled, she often thought about her family on the West Bank. She is most worried about her mother, who has diabetes. She spoke of her sister Ola's visit and of how she enjoyed taking Ola to the local International House of Pancakes, though Ola disappointed her by her lukewarm response to New York. Someday, she said, she wants to return to Ramallah as a full-fledged nurse. As if to prove her merit, she remembered how her brother Ayman, who lives in the Bronx, once cut himself on a bologna slicer, and it was she who soothed it with a home-grown remedy of olive oil and salt. "Nursing is in my blood," she said.

Lulled by the train's rhythm, she was daydreaming again after a few minutes, sometimes anxiously pondering the citizenship exam. "I'm thinking about my test tomorrow," she said. "The whole week I'm not sleeping. I wait for this for seven years." (She passed the test the next day.)

At 3:14 she switched at Seventh Avenue for the D train, which was so crowded with rowdy homebound teenagers, she had to stand. She was not in a rush, because Mouath is in an after-school program, but she wanted to have enough time to prepare supper, say her prayers, and take Mouath to the playground. The D train emptied at 125th Street, and as she took a seat, she revealed to me that she had not had a paid vacation in three years. Union rules require that she complete 1,800 hours of work to qualify for one.

The way back seemed longer to her, but at 3:50 the train pulled into familiar Bedford Park, and a few minutes later she turned the key in her apartment door. Another two hours of commuting had passed, but this time she was home.

BEDFORD PARK

...

WHERE TO GO

Bronx High School of Science (ONCE THE NATION'S BEST PUBLIC
HIGH SCHOOL, PRODUCING SEVEN NOBEL PRIZE WINNERS, AND STILL
AMONG THE TOP) 75 WEST 205TH STREET; *(718) 817-7700;*
WWW.BXSCIENCE.EDU

Fordham University (A 160-YEAR-OLD JESUIT UNIVERSITY, THE FIRST
CATHOLIC COLLEGE IN THE NORTHEAST) 441 EAST FORDHAM ROAD;
(718) 817-1000; WWW.FORDHAM.EDU

New York Botanical Garden (ONE OF THE WORLD'S GREAT
COLLECTIONS OF PLANTS) BRONX RIVER PARKWAY AT FORDHAM
ROAD; *(718) 817-8700;* WWW.NYBG.ORG

St. Philip Neri Roman Catholic Church (GRACEFUL
NEIGHBORHOOD INSTITUTION WHERE RUDOLPH GIULIANI GOT
MARRIED FOR THE FIRST TIME) 3025 GRAND CONCOURSE;
(718) 733-3200

WHERE TO EAT

THERE'S NOT MUCH IN BEDFORD PARK, BUT THE ARTHUR AVENUE
ITALIAN DISTRICT IS ON THE OTHER SIDE OF FORDHAM.

Bedford Café Restaurant (GREEK DINER) 1 BEDFORD PARK
BOULEVARD EAST; *(718) 365-3446*

Dominick's (COMMUNAL TABLES) 2335 ARTHUR AVENUE;
(718) 733-2807

Roberto's (STELLAR ITALIAN) 603 CRESCENT AVENUE; *(718) 733-9503*

Chapter 8

Staying in Touch in Jackson Heights

. . .

JESUS L., A RUMPLED, BRAWNY CONSTRUCTION WORKER, IMMIGRATED to this country alone and illegally eleven years ago from the southern highlands of Ecuador and never returned. Just as he figured, he was able to support the wife and three children that he had left behind in more than tolerable style with regular wire transfers of cash. He even sent a daughter to college, something he could not have done had he remained in Ecuador with a shoemaker's earnings that barely put food on the table. But what he had not counted on was how much he pined for those three children. He had not seen his daughters mature into young women nor his son mushroom from an infant to a near teenager.

But just before New Year's 2005, there all three children were, or virtually so, conjured up in real time on a wall-mounted, flat-screen television by the hocus-pocus of the Internet. Jesus, sitting on a black leather couch in a storefront in the teeming immigrant quarter of Jackson Heights, Queens, could see his children seated together in a small room in Cuenca, his graceful sixteenth-century hometown city, and his children could see him. Television cameras on the walls in both rooms were beaming images from Queens to Cuenca and from Cuenca to Queens, and the images were displayed on corresponding television screens. Jesus could see his children giggling self-consciously in the way young people are prone to do in home movies. He gazed in wonder and delight as they spun around to show him how they had grown. He was not even annoyed when, in the eternal way of children, they asked him for a dog. And the children could see their father's face, read his expressions, calculate the meaning of his movements. They could sense his love and remorse coming through the ether, and the encounter diminished the fear that the man who gave birth to them—and could not visit them in Ecuador because he might never be able to reenter the United States—was becoming a stranger.

"You are so tall," Jesus was able to tell his son, Santiago. He had not laid eyes on Santiago since he was nine months old, but Santiago was now, Jesus could plainly see, a lean, dark-haired boy of twelve.

Maribel, twenty, and Nadia, seventeen, showed off their shapely figures, hands on hips in mock fashion-model style, and Jesus was spellbound. "You are so nice, very beautiful," he told his daughters.

Jesus' wife, Maria, was sitting next to him on the leather couch. She had joined her husband in New York two years before and had not seen the children since, leaving the younger boy under the eye of the older girls and other relatives. So she stood up in front of the camera to show them the latest family event: her bow-shaped belly.

"One more brother is coming up!" Maria, who works in a hat factory, informed them, although in truth she did not know then whether she was expecting a boy or a girl. The children were tickled to see their pregnant mother in her crimson maternity blouse, as Jesus and Maria could clearly see by their dazzled faces on the television screen.

This tender reunion, a small but significant salve for the heartbreak of severed families, took place the way it did because of the wizardry of videoconferencing. A technology first devised for business titans to communicate with their far-flung underlings has now been adopted by the hole-in-the-wall travel agencies and money-transfer offices that dot nearly every block in Jackson Heights and other immigrant neighborhoods like it. And that is not the only technology that has transformed the immigration experience and narrowed the chasm between immigrants and their homes and cultures.

Walk around Jackson Heights or heavily Asian Flushing next door, or Washington Heights in northern Manhattan, or Flatbush in Brooklyn, and televisions are tuned not to American soap operas and quiz shows but to foreign programs in a hodgepodge of languages. I stopped in randomly one morning at Jong Ro Barber Shop on Union Street, Flushing, and customers waiting there for the seventeen-dollar haircuts were watching soap operas on the orderly shop's Samsung television beamed not from Hollywood but from South Korea. They were riveted by melodramas with the same languid pace, low-rent sets, and over-wrought music that makes American soaps what they are, but in a language that let them feel at home. "I do watch American TV, but for an emotional outlet I need Korean TV," Soo Oh Choi, the shop's owner, told me, speaking with the help of a translator.

Hundreds of thousands of immigrants in New York and millions more across the United States receive these foreign channels—from the Philippines, the Middle East, Russia, Colombia, Ecuador, Italy, France, Poland, Greece, India, even Vietnam, because of the feverish competition between satellite and cable companies eager to expand markets. These immigrants can follow the same local catastrophes, laugh at the same homespun jokes, and revel in the same corny soap operas as their kin overseas. And if they want to discuss those shows with their relatives, a phone card makes doing so far cheaper than in the days when calls overseas had to be booked hours in advance and depleted a working family's budget.

And there is much more. Those scruffy, ubiquitous travel agencies offer incredibly cheap flights back home, so cheap that many Dominicans, Indians, Colombians, and Guyanese with kosher immigration documents can afford to fly home once or twice a year. These "shuttles" allow immigrants to straddle two worlds, work or operate businesses in two countries, and, in more than a few cases, raise children with different spouses in two countries. How different that is from the immigrants of a century or even a half century ago, who knew when they left their homeland that the decision was irrevocable and they would probably never have the money or free time to see their kin again. "Danny Boy" is a lament for such an Irish emigrant. Indeed, the Irish would hold a wake for someone departing for America, so like a death was the experience.

Now not only can immigrants keep in gossipy touch with their relatives, but other technologies make it simple to transfer money to their native cities and towns on a weekly or monthly basis, allowing poor immigrants here to subsidize their relatives back home. During the 2004 uprising against the government of Jean-Bertrand Aristide in Haiti, I went to the Flatbush section of Brooklyn to a shop called Boby Express, where Haitian men, most of them with the shopworn look of subsistence laborers, lined up to send small amounts of their earnings—$50 or $200—to their beleaguered relatives back home. Food deliveries had been disrupted by the violence in the poorest country in the Western Hemisphere, and prices had multiplied three and four times for whatever foods were available. "Everybody is desperate to send money," Marie Chery, who manages the threadbare office, told me. But money would be in the pockets of those relatives in the Caribbean within hours if not minutes so they could eat.

The totality of technologies has irrevocably transformed the look and commerce of the city's neighborhoods. While a typical American commercial drag caters to the needs of living here—eating, dry cleaning, cutting one's hair, furnishing a home—the stores along Roosevelt Avenue in Jackson Heights, and Dyckman Street in Washington Heights, and Flatbush Avenue in Flatbush seem to cater to the needs of living in foreign countries, or at least staying in touch with relatives who do. Not only do there seem to be more satellite TV antennas along the faces of apartment buildings, but the sidewalk storefronts have a preponderance of shops that handle or sell money transfers, travel arrangements, cell phones, phone cards, and overseas packages—sometimes all in one spot.

Not too long ago, I took a stroll on Roosevelt Avenue, the Broadway of Jackson Heights and a teeming but cheerful street peppered with flamboyant Spanish signs and overpowered by the shadows and rumble of the elevated tracks that carry the fabled number 7 line. It was this subway line that in the 1920s allowed Jewish and Italian immigrants from the overcrowded Lower East Side and middle-class WASP professionals looking for swanky but reasonably priced housing to settle in Jackson Heights. The neighborhood had pioneering "garden apartments," with Gramercy Park–like private parks hidden among the tall buildings, and many handsome two-family houses. Its residents have included comedians Don Rickles and John Leguizamo, photographer Alfred Eisenstadt, and Alfred Moshe Butts, the inventor of Scrabble.

But in the 1970s that subway line became known as the Orient Express and more recently the International Express, as first Asian and then Latino immigrants seeking a neighborhood on a more human scale than Manhattan began moving in. Along Roosevelt Avenue's bazaar, Little India on Seventy-fourth Street soon segues into a Little Ecuador and Little Colombia by the Eighties blocks, with sprinklings of Korean, Afghani, and Filipino along the way. With the exception of a few American franchises such as McDonald's, the shops are aimed mostly at immigrants in their own language, including Patel Brothers, a large Indian supermarket that sells snake gourds, porcupine-like cucumbers, and the knishlike dumplings known as samosas; Indian Sari Palace, with racks of wraparound silks in vivid magentas, sherbet orange, and robin's egg blue; Butala Emporium, where you can buy Hindu-English dictionaries and statues of Nataraj, the god of dance; Los Paisanos, a grocery stocked with Colombian, Peruvian, and Ecuadorian foods and produce; and El Indo Amazonico, a botanica that in addition to erotic herbs and love potions sells plastic statues of Jesus on crutches next to others of lovers entwined within a heart.

In the more Ecuadorian strip, I was not surprised to see groceries that sell frozen guinea pig or restaurants such as Barzola that sell a spectrum of *batidos*—fruit milkshakes—and seviche—marinated cocktails of octopus, shrimp, or tuna. But I was struck by the sheer number of global service offices, three or four or more to a block, that permit immigrants to call their relatives, sometimes videoconference, send packages, and arrange monthly giros—the wires of cash—to send back home. Delgado Travel, founded by an Ecuadorian immigrant and now boasting two dozen offices in the United States, has three branches on a mile-long stretch of Roosevelt Avenue alone. There are appliance showrooms—branches of such large Ecuadorian chains as Comandato and Créditos Económicos—where a flush immigrant construction worker can pick out a refrigerator and stove for his wife back in Quito and the same model will be shipped from an Ecuador warehouse right to her doorstep. One corner store allows a migrant here to pick out the style of house he wants built for his family in Ecuador.

Watching Jesus videoconferencing with his three children in Cuenca, I could not help but think how my immigrant parents had far fewer resources back in the 1950s. My mother's one remaining relative in Poland was an aunt who had survived the Nazis' occupation by hiding in the sewer. My mother certainly could not afford to visit her in Warsaw or call her by telephone, and the idea of watching the same television programs was an H. G. Wells fantasy. Their chief mode of contact was the airmail letter. My mother would write one every few months, and a flimsy envelope with an address in that aunt's spidery handwriting and some odd postmarked stamps would arrive a few weeks later. While the letter would contain news, it also usually contained a plea for money, which my mother would dutifully send. The cash would take weeks to arrive.

One day my mother's letter came back stamped "Deceased." My mother's English was not yet good enough to know what the word meant, so I had to explain to her that her aunt had died. That is how she learned. From a bureaucratic rubber stamp.

The methods of communication have changed, and wondrously so. At some of the immigrant storefronts, with their tattered awnings and windows saturated with gaudy posters for cheap flights and money transfers, Ecuadorians, Colombians, Pakistanis, Mexicans and others in the past two or three years are discovering what Jesus L. found: spanking small conversation rooms with computer-driven plasma televisions and video cameras. With a few clicks of a remote and at a relatively low cost—$1.50 per minute for Jesus L.—the setup takes them back to their hometowns and brings their hometowns here. When I asked an urban sociologist, Sharon Zukin of Brooklyn College, what was the significance of videoconferencing, she told me simply, "It reduces the emotional distance." Jesus puts it even more simply: "I can see their faces, I can see how they are, tall or small, so the emotion is very different," he said.

Videoconferencing cannot re-create the warmth of a relative's hug or the scent of a cherished child. Nevertheless, it is a qualitative leap in turning the experience of immigration into something less than a permanent break. Rather than being confined to memories and nostalgia, immigrants today can participate actively in the daily events and decisions of their native homes, guiding the schooling of the children they left behind or having a voice in whether to rent or buy a home. The conversations are often emotionally excruciating, testimony to the toll that living abroad alone for so many years can take on marriages and family life. At Austro Financial Services on Roosevelt Avenue, Jesus' intercontinental exchange with his children was not all playful. His daughters were angry with him for becoming involved for a time, as other migrants often do, with another woman, even if he was now sitting amicably beside his wife. "Please try, Father and Mother, to stay together," pleaded Maribel, who can attend college in Cuenca because of the hundreds of dollars her father sends home every month, "If you separate, what will happen to us? We are a family; please don't break up."

Her younger sister, Nadia, clearly the more voluble one, was more sentimental. "Don't do it just for us—do it for you two," she said. "I need love, and the little boy coming up, he needs love. Try again. Forget the problems from before."

In contrast to a telephone, videoconferencing allowed Jesus to see—not just hear—Maribel's anger and Nadia's fear. "I can promise you I will try," he told his daughters, kneading his calloused workman's hands in shame. "I don't want any more problems. I want to change what I did before. It's going to be good because one more guy is coming. I want to try."

The call went on like this for forty-one minutes, lasting beyond the half hour that Jesus had booked, but the daughters kept returning to the main topic on their minds. "You remember when we were children," Nadia said. "You told us not to fight, to be peaceful with one another. Now you do it. Do it now."

Videoconferencing is favored not just by the most prosperous immigrants but more often by poorer and illegal immigrants because they cannot afford to travel back home or are afraid they will not be allowed back into the United States. Jesus, for example, left Ecuador because he could barely support his family on a shoemaker's wages, but he cannot fly back to visit his children because he has no legal documents.

While the videoconferencing systems have long been available here, they have only recently been introduced in the less technologically advanced countries that most immigrants come from, so the eureka moment of connection is a new phenomenon. Banco del Austro, the Ecuadorian parent company of Austro Financial, has provided the service for a year and a half in its offices in Azogues, Canar, and Cuenca, Ecuador's third-largest city and a place that wasn't connected by paved road to the rest of the country until the 1960s. When I saw Jesus, they were planning to open a branch in Quito, the capital, which they did a few months later. Diego Pinos, a genial, courtly man who manages the *videoconferencia* for Austro Financial Services, said that he handled thirty conferences a weekend and that business was especially brisk during the Christmas season. Another Ecuadorian company, Costamar, has a satellite-linked service at five locations, and in 2003 two American-born, non-Dominican Harvard roommates opened a videoconferencing service to the Dominican Republic, Face to Face Media, on Dyckman Street in the Inwood section of northern Manhattan.

For some, videoconferencing provides the only way to communicate in real time. Paola Palacios, who manages the Cuenca end of the conversation for Banco del Austro, told me of two Ecuadorian brothers, both deaf and mute and separated by continents, who were able to talk for the first time in sign language because they could see each other's hand movements on a television screen.

Immigrants started leaving Ecuador for New York in the 1960s, but the number has multiplied seemingly exponentially as the country, unstable and riddled with official bribery and nepotism, has failed to generate enough jobs for its 13.3 million people, many of whom idle in the squares of its cities and towns. Ecuador, a mountainous country situated along the Pacific and bisected by the equator, exports coffee, cocoa, and bananas, but its major industry is oil. When petroleum prices slackened in the 1990s, the economy sank and the banking system collapsed, requiring the acceptance of the dollar as legal tender and causing the substantial loss of countless personal savings accounts. There were seven presidents between 1996 and 2005, including two deposed by marauding mobs. Opportunities for higher education are scarce, forcing even modestly educated Ecuadorians to seek degrees overseas.

Some simply fly to New York on a visitor's visa and never leave. But the desperation of most other penniless migrants was highlighted in August 2005 when a rickety wooden ship meant for fifteen passengers but carrying ninety-four sank in the ocean. The migrants were hoping to make it to Guatemala and then by land to the United States, where some were planning to join parents they had not seen for years. Some of the dead passengers had paid smugglers, known as coyotes, up to $12,000 for this voyage. "Their dream was just to get out of poverty," said Manuel Coyago of Ecuador, who lost three sons on the doomed ship. "How can we live here earning five dollars a day?"

All that turmoil has shown up in the proliferation of mestizo faces in Jackson Heights and other parts of Queens. New York City in 2000 had 114,944 Ecuadorians, almost twice as many as it had a decade earlier, and more than half lived in Queens neighborhoods such as Corona, Jackson Heights, Elmhurst, and Woodside. A fine series on Ecuadorians by Dustin Brown of Times Ledger Newspapers, a community chain in Queens, said Ecuador had received $1.3 billion in émigré remittances to families in 2000, an amount second only to oil revenue. The money that has been sent is evident in the American-style houses blossoming on Ecuadorian hillsides, the cell phones teenagers carry, the NYPD and Yankee caps. But the price has been the heartbreak of wives separated from husbands, fathers and mothers from their children. Videoconferencing provides a small dose of relief.

One New Year's Eve, Laura A., who was fifty and left Ecuador eleven years before, was able to see her husband, four sons, a daughter, three daughters-in-law, and six grandchildren all at once as they squeezed into and around the couch in a tiny room in Cuenca. The latest grandchild, swaddled in white, was just two months old, and she had never seen him. I watched from a corner out of range of the cameras as Laura sobbed with joy mingled with what I'm certain was the persistent regret that, once again, she could not be there to hold her blood kin. "He has the same face as his father," she told her family, according to my translator, Carmen Mazza. It occurred to me later that this was a thought she could not have expressed were she speaking long-distance on a telephone.

Her daughter and daughters-in-law were quickly in tears, which she was able to see as well. "Please don't cry," Laura said. "Not today. I'm going to be happy today. I'm OK, so don't you cry." She asked her three grandsons to stand. "You are so beautiful, guys," she said, according to my translator. She could see one granddaughter's long pigtails. She could see that one son was getting fat and admonished him, "You have to lose weight." She could see that her daughter, Gabriela, eighteen, was staying in shape because Gabriela, hands on hips, showed off her figure.

Laura stood up, too, in front of the camera and exhibited her still-youthful figure. Of course, the presence of the camera made her more self-conscious, even vain, than she might have been with a telephone. "I dressed in black to look slim," she said at one point, adding, "Can you see my wrinkles?"

She had been particularly concerned about twenty-year-old Danilo, her youngest son, who has struggled with a drinking problem but seemed at that moment to be winning the battle. She asked him to step forward and, seeing his long, sad face, said, "I'm always thinking about you a lot." Her oldest son, Pablo, who is in his mid-twenties, and her husband, Jaime, began to cry. "Pablo, don't cry," she said. "You're a man. You have always been a strong person. I will be back with you, and I will raise that grandchild."

She could not resist giving some grandmotherly advice. "Maybe you should breast-feed the baby," she said to a daughter-in-law. "That's why she cries." She told them she knew how difficult the daily struggle to get by was in Cuenca. "But have courage and look forward. . . . It's too bad I have been apart from you and have not been able as a mother to raise you," she said.

The day was particularly haunting because it was on a New Year's Eve that she left Ecuador. Her jewelry business in Cuenca had failed, and she hoped to find a new source of support in New York City, as many of her friends were doing. It meant leaving behind Danilo and Gabriela, both young children, and she has never stopped kicking herself for that part of the decision, even as she understands that migration made economic sense. Danilo, the troubled son, was only nine when she left. She makes a good living setting diamonds for a jewelry company in Long Island City, Queens, but she never got the appropriate immigration documents and so has never returned, though when we spoke she was working on getting a green card.

"Get together tonight and enjoy the evening as a family," she said, her voice quivering. "Though I'm here, my heart is with you every day of my life. You are very precious to me. You should always be together and love each other. Any problem you encounter as a family can be solved if you love each other and teach your children to love each other."

For forty minutes, thanks to videoconferencing, she was together with them—virtually—as a family in the same small room.

. . .

SATELLITE TELEVISION IS another medium for helping immigrants feel connected to the countries they left. It does not bring their families into a room for them to see, but it does allow them to be stirred by the same news and entertainments as their relatives or friends, which means they continue sharing the same cultural flotsam and jetsam as if they had never left home. Imagine yourself as an American living overseas, then returning and not knowing about the television Mafia boss with a musical name who is seeing a shrink or that Martha Stewart spent some time in jail or that Sandra Day O'Connor left the Supreme Court or that the St. Louis Cardinals won the 2006 World Series. You'd be at a loss. That's how immigrants here once felt when they returned to their homelands, warped time travelers to their own land. But there's less of that feeling now that there's a closer communion with life back home.

Wherever I went along Roosevelt Avenue, television sets in the shops were on, but tuned to home countries; almost no one was watching English-speaking channels. Lucy Mangual, who owns Libreria Cuarzo, a bookshop that sells religious books and articles, was watching Mexican television and looking forward that night to watching her favorite soap opera, *Herida Del Alma* (Pain of the Soul). "For Spanish people, they have a lot of feeling for what they left," she told me.

Aashish Patel, who manages the Patel Brothers supermarket of Indian foods, was planning to gather with a half dozen compatriots that night at a local motel for a Super Bowl party of sorts, complete with beer and potato chips. Only the world-class game they planned to watch—until dawn, mind you—was not football, but cricket between India and Australia, beamed live from abroad. "We feel we are in India like that," Patel told me.

Anil Merchant, who came here nineteen years ago from Bombay, keeps the television in his five-chair beauty salon on Seventy-fourth Street in Jackson Heights tuned to an Indian TV channel that broadcasts a stream of sinuous MTV-like songs and Busby Berkeley dance numbers, many with a playfully erotic edge. He also likes to keep up with the doings of local Indian politicians. "CNN doesn't cover it," he told me. "We don't know John Kerry. We heard about him, but we're more interested in Indian politics."

Marshall McLuhan's global village is thus breaking into its global parts. Relative newcomers can relax in front of a television without being baffled by English. They can immerse their children in their native tongues, narrowing the generational distance.

All that fragmentation has some scholars worried; the availability of international channels makes it too easy for immigrants to continue to cling to their homelands. Neal Gabler, senior fellow at the Norman Lear Center for the Study of Entertainment and Society at the University of Southern California, told me that although the phenomenon of foreign channels produces many benefits, it chips away at the "common cultural references" that have allowed for whatever melting is supposed to take place in the American pot. "The things that unite us will be lost in another competing identity," Gabler said.

Satellite television also reduces the urgency to learn English. Immigrants who arrived in the 1950s and 1960s often used television to learn American idioms and mores; baseball alone was a master teacher. Brooklyn Dodger games taught my friend Simon's father, Sam Herling, not only a smattering of vernacular English, but also about an American sense of fair play, the rude democracy of the bleachers, and, for a Jew from the anti-Semitism of prewar Poland, the preciousness of a society that could finally accommodate Roy Campanella and Jackie Robinson on a formerly all-white team.

Pyong Gap Min is a Korean-born professor of sociology at Queens College who speaks English fluently and watches Korean soap operas almost every night with his wife. He worries that some of his compatriots may be using television to isolate themselves. "In a foreign environment they live comfortably, enjoying Korean food, going to Korean churches, working in Korean businesses, and now seeing Korean television," he said. "This frees them from learning American English and American customs."

Mudassar Khan, a twenty-seven-year-old Pakistani who runs an electronic appliance store in Jackson Heights, thinks that such worries—that satellite TV is encouraging cultural isolation—are overblown. "During the day you're surrounded by American culture," he told me.

"The only time you feel Pakistani culture is when you're home watching TV."

Besides, the toothpaste can't be put back into the tube. Satellite and cable TV are here to stay. UHF television stations such as Telemundo and Univision long ago proved that a mix of soap operas, game shows, and news in a native language can draw a profitable audience. By the late 1980s, recalled Barry Rosenblum, president of Time Warner Cable of New York and New Jersey, his company was hearing from Greek, Korean, and Indian businessmen who also wanted to start channels that would package programs from overseas, supplemented with news of their New York ethnic neighborhoods. By 2005, the satellite provider Dish Network was offering fifty international or foreign-language channels, including Polish and Portuguese. Across the country, Time Warner Cable offered thirty, including channels in Arabic, Russian, Greek, Persian, Filipino, and Vietnamese. In New York alone, more than 90,000 of Time Warner Cable's customers get the international channels for roughly $9.95 a month above the standard cable price.

Some channels are beamed directly from abroad to providers here, and then quickly distributed to home televisions. Others are repackaged here by local entrepreneurs from either satellite feeds or videotapes. The satellite EcuaTV, for example, mixes programming from five Ecuadorian stations—the soap operas known as *telenovelas* as well as soccer matches.

Khan, the electronics store owner, who immigrated here as a teenager and graduated from Baruch College, watches mostly American television. Most children of immigrants end up doing so. Still, Khan orders the Dish Network's South Asian package of Indian and Pakistani channels for his parents, Mohammad and Sanjeeda Khan, with whom he lives. They like to watch Pakistani news, a soap opera called *Lab-e-Derya*, and two popular Indian serials about working women, *Jassi Jaissi Koi Nahin* and *Kkusum*. (The spoken forms of Pakistan's Urdu and India's Hindi are closely related.) He often watches the soaps with them and takes note of the differences between the lives they portray and those shown on American TV. "When a guy gets married in South Asia, he usually lives in the same house with his parents," he said. "In the English soap operas, the kids move out."

JACKSON HEIGHTS

...

WHERE TO GO

Banco del Austro (TELECONFERENCE YOUR RELATIVE IN ECUADOR)
80-08 ROOSEVELT AVENUE; *(718) 899-7805*

Comandato (APPLIANCE STORE—IF YOU WANT TO BUY A
REFRIGERATOR FOR SOMEONE IN ECUADOR) ROOSEVELT AVENUE
AND 81ST STREET

Jackson Heights Historic District (STATELY CO-OP APARTMENTS,
MANY WITH INTERIOR GARDENS, INCLUDING GREYSTONE
APARTMENTS, 80TH STREET BETWEEN 35TH AND 37TH AVENUES,
AND HAMPTON COURT ON 78TH AND 79TH STREETS, BETWEEN
35TH AND 37TH AVENUES)

Roosevelt Avenue between 74th Street and Junction Boulevard
(LATIN AMERICAN BAZAAR, WITH FLAMBOYANTLY DECORATED
SHOPS CATERING TO IMMIGRANT NEEDS, INCLUDING MONEY
TRANSFERS, PHONE CARDS, AND 220-VOLT APPLIANCES)

74th Street between Roosevelt Avenue and 37th Avenue (AN
INDIAN BAZAAR, WITH SARI SHOPS, JEWELRY STORES, RESTAURANTS,
AND PATEL BROTHERS SUPERMARKET)

WHERE TO EAT

Barzola (ECUADORIAN SPECIALTIES INCLUDING SOUPS, MILKSHAKES,
AND SEVICHE) 92-12 37TH AVENUE; *(718) 205-6900*

Delhi Palace (WHITE-TABLECLOTH INDIAN) 37-33 74TH STREET;
(718) 507-0666

Jackson Diner (INDIAN BUFFET) 37-47 74TH STREET; *(718) 672-1232*

El Palacio de los Cholados (LATIN AMERICAN ICE MILK AND CREAM
CONFECTIONS) 83-18 NORTHERN BOULEVARD

Pollos a la Brasa Mario (COLOMBIAN ROTISSERIE CHICKEN)
83-02 37TH AVENUE; *(718) 457-8800*

Chapter 9

Family Ties and Knots in Flushing

. . .

BY ALL APPEARANCES, ASHRAT KHWAJAZADAH AND NAHEED MAWJZADA are thoroughly modern Millies. Long-haired, dark-eyed, and in their early twenties, they spurn the hijab, or head scarf, and other modest garb worn by Afghan women, preferring hip-hugging slacks. Both of them have also taken a route somewhat controversial among the enclave of Afghans in Flushing, Queens. They went to college. Khwajazadah, a stylish dresser with a glossy mane of black hair and onyx eyes, studied speech pathology at Queens College, and Mawjzada, more informally dressed with a ponytail, majors in political science at Adelphi University. Both also defy the Afghan ideal of a reticent woman, with Mawjzada speaking up forcefully when men talk politics at the dinner table.

But there are incongruities. Both are strikingly beautiful women, yet, by design, they have never dated. Like most young Afghan women in Flushing, they are waiting for their parents to pick their spouses. "It's been drilled into your head since you were a little girl: 'Don't talk with guys, don't ruin your reputation, everyone will gossip about you,' " Khwajazadah told me.

Her tone was sardonic, suggesting she found such social strictures suffocating. She came here as a two-year-old with parents who were fleeing the Soviet occupation of tradition-bound Afghanistan, but she has grown into a high-spirited, sophisticated, and very American woman. So she surprised me a moment later when she went on to contradict herself and defend her refusal to date. "I'm happy with my decision," she said. "I'm very close with my family and that helps me, because they want to do what's best for me."

These two women illustrate the ticklish dilemma facing young Afghans, particularly women, in testing how far to go in forsaking tradition. Growing up in a comparatively freewheeling society but with parents—often uneducated and unable to speak English—who are trying to cling tightly to conventions, they have had to strike an anxious balance.

To be sure, the Afghans' transition to America is an old immigrant story—one that could be told about the Irish, Italians, and Jews. Those newcomers too looked on with anger or resignation as their children gradually (and their grandchildren cavalierly) adopted the prevailing culture. What is occurring in the Afghan community of Flushing is occurring also among newer groups seasoning New York's stew, such as the much larger, prosperous, and well-schooled Indian community scattered around Flushing as well as more upscale suburban patches.

But the Afghan version seems particularly hearty at this early point in their settlement in this country. It is not uncommon in Flushing for parents to make sure their daughters are engaged as young as thirteen and married by sixteen, and even those who get engaged years later, having waited until they finished college or graduate school, will submit to an arranged marriage. Defiance can lead to a painful social ostracism, and few young women are strong enough to defy.

Afghanistan, one of the poorest, most tribal countries, has drawn more than its share of world attention, first in the Bush administration's response to September 11 and now as the government of Hamid Karzai struggles to establish a semblance of democracy amid a persistent insurgency. Few Americans, however, know that for almost three decades Afghans here have actually formed a discrete community in the humdrum brick apartment buildings and stand-alone houses of Flushing. There are 5,446 Afghans in New York City and more than 9,100 in the metropolitan area, according to the 2000 census, with the two densest enclaves in the southern half of Flushing in the blocks below Queens College, and in a largely Chinese and Korean area in the northern half. The 751 Afghan renters in a single census tract along Kissena Boulevard form the nation's densest Afghan concentration (the census breaks counties into tracts of varying sizes usually containing between 2,500 and 8,000 people).

Flushing, founded by English settlers in the seventeenth century, and for most of the twentieth century a bastion of Protestant and Catholic churches and middle-class whites, now has four Afghan mosques, a half dozen kebab houses, and at least one Afghan butcher. Women in hijabs and robes can be seen walking down Flushing's lively sidewalks pushing strollers or carrying plastic bags laden with fruit and vegetables. On Sunday Afghan families can be spotted in Flushing Meadows Park—the site of two World's Fairs—barbecuing kebabs. Kouchi Supermarket is a virtual Afghan bazaar, selling not only native spices, breads, apricots, sugared almonds, and newspapers but also *rabab*s (mandolins) and *karam*s (billiards-like board games). Almost next door is Afghan Kabab Palace, a gaudily ornamented eatery that serves skewers of succulent marinated lamb with long-grained basmati rice. The mosques especially would have pleased John Bowne, a seventeenth-century landholder whose Flushing Remonstrance to Stuyvesant is considered one of America's earliest thunderbolts of religious freedom. In the wake of September 11, though, that tolerance broke down. Afghans, like other Muslims, were wantonly attacked. An owner of Kouchi Supermarket, Saeed Azimi, told a colleague, "I have three children born in this country. How do I explain this to them?"

New Yorkers commonly encounter Afghan men in the 200 or so fried-chicken takeout joints they have come to own in the city's black and Latino neighborhoods and in the 800 ubiquitous sidewalk coffee carts where skyscraper workers line up for their morning fixes. They might be treated by an Afghan doctor in the hospital emergency room or ride in a taxi with an Afghan cabdriver, and there are even half a dozen Afghan police officers. The women, though, are more out of sight. A quarter of Afghan women have never been to school, and only half have completed high school, according to a study by Andrew A. Beveridge, a sociology professor at Queens College, and Kaisa Hagen, a student there. Only one-quarter work outside the home. The reason is Afghanistan's deeply patriarchal culture, which seems to have migrated here.

"Men have corrupted views of Islam and actually believe women are second-class citizens and are there to take care of them," said Manizha Naderi, the director of Women for Afghan Women, which offers counseling and instructional programs out of a threadbare office on Union Street. "They don't let them go to school or to work." Males have so much higher status in a family that it is not uncommon for men to remarry if their wives bear them only daughters. And violence toward wives, Naderi said, is more common than the community will admit. "There's a saying that the food your husband feeds you doesn't come for free," she said with a wry grin. "And men actually think they have a right under the Koran to beat their wives."

Naderi, now in her thirties, was four years old when her parents left Kabul for Kandahar and there paid a driver to smuggle the entire family—her father, an electrical engineer, her mother, and three children—on a single motorcycle across the desert into Pakistan. She described that improbable dusty adventure for me in poignant detail.

We left Kabul on a bus. My mother had sewn any money and jewelry in her undergarments under her burka. She had to carry it on her body because there were lots of thieves on the way to Kandahar. Many times along the way thieves and mujahideens stopped to search the bus and the passengers. They took my father out every time. We were afraid that they might shoot my father, but thankfully they didn't. When we reached Kandahar, we spent a night in the house of a relative of my aunt's husband. Then the next day, we had to cross the desert. We hired two motorcycles—one for my aunt's family and one for our family. I was five at that time. I remember that day very clearly. I was sitting in front of the driver, on the engine, then it was the driver, then my father and then my mother. My father was holding my three-year-old brother in his arms. My mother was holding my nine-month-old sister. I remember the way we were sitting very clearly because the engine of the motorcycle had burned my thigh and I was crying. My mother was angry at me for crying. We traveled one hour through the desert into Pakistan.

Thousands of other Afghan families fleeing the Soviet occupation that began in 1979 made similarly treacherous odysseys to seek asylum in the West. A second wave of refugees—at least 7,000—came here after the Taliban took power in 1996. Many of those who could not abide that government's unbending zealotry—thieves had their limbs amputated, women were banned from schooling themselves or working—flocked to the New York area but others to Afghan enclaves in the Washington, D.C., area or Fremont near San Francisco. Fremont is home to 10,000 Afghans, and the Bay Area beyond has another 30,000. Altogether, the United States has 200,000 Afghans. Though it is slowly prospering and stepping into American routines, Flushing's Afghan community is still quite poor, with a sizable proportion of families receiving Medicaid or on welfare. The median Afghan family income of $27,273 is about $11,000 below the city's median.

There are sharp differences among the Afghans that are not revealed in statistics. Afghans I met in Flushing told me that refugees from Kabul are less bound by tradition than those from the villages. Those who fled the secular Soviets are more conservative than those who fled the Taliban. Some bear scars from having joined the mujahideen, the fighters for Afghan independence who eventually ousted the Soviets in a CIA-financed effort. Yet more than a few Afghans here are champions of the harsh Taliban. Afghan politics plays out in Flushing. Mohammed Sherzad, a Flushing imam, was once the spiritual leader of the city's largest Afghan mosque, Masjid Hazrat-I-Abubakr Sadiq, on Thirty-third Avenue. A domed temple of turquoise and white with slim arched windows and a lanky minaret, the mosque contrasts with the surrounding workaday blocks of redbrick houses and apartment buildings. In the wake of the September 11 attacks, Sherzad ejected a group of its founders, contending they channeled money to the Taliban. The group took him to court, accusing the imam of a disingenuous power play, and regained the mosque. Sherzad, an ethnic Pashtun—the same mountain people from whom Karzai hails—is now imam of a smaller mosque with the identical name on the second floor of a low building on Union Street.

Some Afghan Muslims who have been here for decades are so acculturated they put up Christmas trees. Others, including some who speak English with a Queens accent, are returning to a new Afghanistan or at least shuttling back and forth, even though it is a land where indoor plumbing is scarce, few roads are paved, and the Taliban is resurgent.

One Afghan American opened a cement-mixing plant in Kabul and divides his time between there and Flushing; another, a cabdriver, returned to his home in Mazar-i-Sharif in September 2003 to marry an Afghan woman. Naderi also shuttles back and forth. In 2003, she and her organization opened a secular school for 1,500 boys and girls in the teeming Zar-e-Dasht refugee camp in Kandahar that after three months was absorbed into the government system. She's also organized conferences to spread the word on what rights women have under Islamic law, as opposed to what men tell them they have. In 2006, three years after we first spoke, Naderi and her family returned to Afghanistan for good.

But most Afghan families are here for the long haul and so find themselves struggling to keep up the essentials of their culture as their children are exposed to the louche ways of American teenagers in a ravenously consumerist culture. Families are particularly strict with daughters, enforcing curfews and requiring them to wear modest clothes and only meager makeup. For more than a few families, even the notion of educating their daughters beyond high school is regarded as daring, not just because education will tug them away from the attractive simplicity of traditional life but because the young women may start seeing young men on the sly. The most exigent families keep their daughters close after ninth grade, insisting that they return home promptly after school. Some will pull their daughters out of high school, even moving to another state if officials enforce the attendance law.

For the young women who do attend school, the contrast between their lives and those of Americans often rankles. They see their American counterparts roaming the neighborhood freely after school and flirting with boys. Rebellious young Afghan women will leave the house with head scarves, then strip them off on the way to school and rouge their faces and line their eyes. On the way home, they wash off the makeup and restore the scarf.

More community leaders, though, are encouraging girls to educate themselves. As we sat shoeless on the floor of his mosque, Imam Sherzad, an athletic, confident man with a trim beard who likes women in his congregation to have their heads covered, told me he looks favorably upon women who postpone having children until they finish college. "A good woman is one who is educated, both for her children and her society," he said. "In the Koran a person who is not educated is not equal to a person who has education. The not educated is compared to a blind person."

Naderi estimates that almost half of young Afghan women here do end up going to college. Indeed, Dr. Tahira Homayun, a New York gynecologist whose husband is an economic adviser to Karzai, believes young Afghan women outperform their brothers in school because struggling families press boys to give up their classes for jobs needed to pay the bills.

But economic necessities and the allure of education have had little impact on the ironclad convention that reserves for parents the authority to arrange their children's marriages. Naderi let me sit in on a basic English class taught by an Episcopal nun, Ellen Francis, who had learned Farsi in Iran (Dari, the language most Afghans speak, is a dialect of Farsi, more commonly known as Persian). All six students were dressed in robes and head scarves, and their hands were stained with henna, which women apply at the end of Ramadan to signal their return to the joys of physical life. There was a wide spectrum of experience. One woman in a purple jacket had been principal of a girls' school in Afghanistan, then fled after her husband was slain by a Taliban swordsman. Two women had never been to school. I watched the six women pronounce "bad," "fad," and "rat," identify articles of clothing such as a sweater, socks, and pants, learn to follow such street directions as "Go two blocks straight and one block to the right," and mouth some basic responses to Americans' questions such as "Fine, thank you. I am good." They seemed eager to learn the lingua franca, yet when we spoke after class, with Francis translating, it was clear that tradition still runs as deep as the henna staining their hands.

"Afghan people can't meet each other prior to getting engaged—it's an embarrassment for the family," was the peremptory statement of a sixty-five-year-old woman, a mother of six, who, like everyone else in the class, was uncomfortable with having her name in print.

Naderi and Mawjzada told me that an Afghan man's honor hinges on the pristine conduct of his wife and daughters. "If the girl has a good reputation, the family has a good reputation," said Mawjzada, a coffee vendor's daughter who sometimes works for Naderi. If a young woman chooses to find her own spouse, her father's stature will be diminished, the family name will be tainted by gossip, and her sisters may afterward find it harder to marry. Many Afghan parents despair of ever finding matches for their American children—"They say all the boys are corrupted and all the girls are corrupted," Naderi told me—and fathers will ask relatives in Afghanistan to scout for prospective spouses or will return home personally to seek them out.

Not surprisingly, parents are more willing to close their eyes to a son who is a Don Juan, and ordinary dating for young men is certainly shrugged off. Bashir Rahim, a twenty-nine-year-old computer technician who lives in Flushing with his mother, three brothers, and five sisters, said that if he meets a girl who interests him at a family gathering, he might ask her for her address, then send his parents to her home to start a conversation about marriage. "In general men are in control all the time," he said. "If they date, some parents won't agree with it, but they are more tolerant."

Young women learn by trial and error how far they can stretch tradition, but defying the code outright exacts a steep price. Those who choose to break conventions do so furtively. Naderi, smirking sardonically, told me that many young Afghan women here do have boyfriends, "but the family doesn't know about it."

Naderi, who came to this country as a nine-year-old in 1984, grew up in Jersey City, graduated Dickinson High School there, worked in a Wendy's, and was married at age sixteen to a man she chose, defying her parents. "I was a rebel," she said with a mischievous smile. As a result, her mother, who is modern enough to wear Western dress, and her grandmother did not speak to her for ten years, not until her daughter, Karima, was born. "My mother still tells me she doesn't have a face," she said. "She tells me she can't look at people because they know her daughter married in this way."

Naderi's friend Masuda Sultan had an even more wrenching story. She is an auburn-haired, brown-eyed Harvard graduate student who is urbane, poised, and gregarious. Her fair skin and unaccented English allow her to navigate easily in Western as well as Middle Eastern worlds. She has at times worn a head scarf or burka but is more comfortable in jeans. As she told me about her marriage, I found it difficult to match the young woman who endured her anachronistic experience with the person sitting before me. She was born in Kandahar in 1978, and when she was five her family escaped Soviet-occupied Afghanistan by hiring a car to spirit them across the treacherous Khojak Pass into Quetta, Pakistan. They came to Brooklyn and later moved to Queens. Her father prospered as a partner in Palace Fried Chicken in Harlem. Though she knew as early as age ten that she wanted to be a lawyer, her parents discouraged her. "Too much school," they told her. "How are you going to find someone to marry?" Still, she was a star student, though one not immune to a newcomer's foibles. Throughout high school, she confused the words "prostitute" and "Protestant" and sometimes walked by a church with the nervous curiosity of someone passing a brothel.

When she was fifteen and a student at Flushing High School, her father contrived with a friend to have her married to a doctor, a surgeon, who at thirty-one was twice her age. The friend, Sultan recalled, "suggested I would make a good match for his brother, knowing little about me except that my parents were good people. Family reputation is a big deal. I was reluctant. I wanted to go to college and thought I was too young."

She had seen the doctor only once before, and, after a betrothal ceremony called the *nikah*, which was held in a Flushing hotel and blessed by an imam, she got to see her future husband only three more times before the wedding, twice in the presence of a chaperone. "I didn't know how I was supposed to feel," she told me. "Looking back, I should have realized that this wasn't the best match for me, but at the time I had no idea what to expect from a relationship. I'd never dated before."

Although she insisted she wasn't forced to go through with the marriage, in reality she didn't have much latitude. Her parents and the community had made clear to her that if she married an outsider—someone who was not both Muslim and Pashtun—she'd be disowned. "I agreed to this marriage and actually thought it could work out. When your actions are limited and you're from a certain world and you're young and you respect your family, you go along with their wishes even if you have extreme doubts. I saw my parents and people my age, and it worked out for almost all of them."

The wedding was held in Pakistan in August 1995, and the night before, her mother asked her to follow an old custom: provide the new in-laws with a bloodstained cloth as evidence of her virginity. Once they were married and back in New York, her husband rarely spoke to her and insisted she remain subservient. He acquiesced to her going to college but did not really grasp that Sultan would need several years more of graduate school to qualify as a lawyer instead of the schoolteacher her parents wished her to become. When it became clear after the wedding that Sultan wanted to put off having children perhaps until she had finished law school, her husband turned cold.

"The core issue was really a different philosophy of what it means to be Afghan and what it means to be American," Sultan said. "The expectation was that my life and career weren't really factors in terms of the priorities of us as a couple. Ultimately I was being treated as a child and my role was set and I was told what I could and couldn't do. We weren't speaking to each other on the same plane. I was the child and he the parent."

With the strain in her marriage evidently irreconcilable, Sultan lapsed into a deep depression. She stopped going to school, dropped housework, stopped seeing people, started taking antidepressants. Her parents tried to prevail on her to work things out. But after three years she and her husband lost the will to do so. Feeling despondent, she swallowed a bottle of his Valium. Afterward, she returned to her parents' Queens home. He finally agreed to a divorce, a rare and humiliating event among Afghans.

Since living on her own was considered inappropriate, Sultan moved back into her parents' home, sharing a room with one of her two sisters, the hijab-wearing Sara. Among Afghans, blame for a divorce falls on the wife, but even her more secular friends found it difficult to believe that she could leave her husband for the reasons she did. " 'Did he beat you, or was he a womanizer?' people wanted to know," Sultan told me. "They were surprised why I left and looking for a legitimate reason why."

Sultan shuffled jobs for a time, including work for Women for Afghan Women. By the time I sat down with her for an interview, she was twenty-six years old, had scuttled plans to become a lawyer, and was doing graduate work in public administration at Harvard's Kennedy School of Government. She ultimately completed her master's and began spending time in Afghanistan training women to become political and business leaders. "Economic empowerment is the key to letting women realize they have power in the world," she told me. She was also working on a memoir she intended playfully to call *My War at Home*, which was published in 2006. She has received offers of marriage from divorced Afghan men—single men prefer virgins—but none appealing. "It's been difficult for my family, but they see I'm happy and have been able to keep my Afghan identity," she said. "I'm still Islamic. I'm still me."

She was also surprisingly optimistic about trends in the Afghan community. Since her marriage, she said, some customs have slowly withered, and more families are aware of the importance of higher education for women. "Lots of girls have arranged marriages still, but more often than not the way it is happening is the girl knows the guy. They've met in school or at a family event. They basically arrange it with their families so it looks like an arranged marriage. It's a creative solution to the whole thing."

CREATIVE SOLUTIONS TO the erosion of Old World ways are evident also in the Indian community. It is an older, more middle-class group whose initial settlers in the late 1960s were doctors, chemists, and academics admitted under special American visas offered to take advantage of the availability of well-schooled English-speaking Indians at a time of shortages in those professions. Bypassing the tenement stage of immigration, the Indians settled in the modest apartments of Jackson Heights, Elmhurst, and Flushing in Queens. Many have now done well enough to establish thriving Indian enclaves in suburbs such as Edison and Woodbridge in New Jersey. The 2000 census counted 454,686 Indians living across the New York metropolitan area. The Indians have left behind bustling shopping and dining districts including Seventy-fourth Street in Jackson Heights and Lexington Avenue near Twenty-eighth Street in Manhattan, where dozens of Indian-owned stores sell

saris, gold jewelry, and Indian spices and chutneys. Visiting Indian enclaves, I found wonderful examples of inventive approaches to blending
old and new.

Dr. Bodh Das, a courtly cardiologist at Lincoln Hospital and Medical Center in the Bronx, saw the power of age-old Indian traditions
fade with each of his three daughters. When he came here in the late
1960s, he planned to have his daughters find their husbands the old-
fashioned way—within the Hindu caste into which he was born. But he
found his success diminishing the longer the daughters were exposed to
America's freewheeling mating rituals. With his eldest daughter,
Abha—the one who had spent the least time growing up in America—
he hit the jackpot, getting her to return to India in 1975 to wed a man
she had never met but who hailed not only from the same Kayashta subcaste but also from the same obscure offshoot. With his second daughter, Bibha, he was less successful. She married a Kayashta, but from a
different branch. "So there was some transgression in this marriage," the
silver-haired Das told me with a wry stoicism worthy of another father
who struggled with three modern-minded marriageable daughters,
Tevye of *Fiddler on the Roof.*

Das' third daughter, Rekha, the most Americanized, strayed even
farther. She refused to return to India to find her mate and married a
man outside her father's caste whom she met in school. It was what Indians call "a love marriage."

As Das' experience shows, the peculiarly Indian system of stratifying
its people into hierarchical castes—with Brahmins at the top and Untouchables at the bottom—has managed to stow away on the journey to
the United States, a country that prides itself on its standard of egalitar-
ianism. The excruciatingly complex caste system dates back thousands
of years to the origins of Hinduism. As I learned talking to some experts, Hindus tell of a deity who morphed into an entire society of humans grouped by categories of work and in a sharply defined pecking
order. The deity's head turned into the Brahmin caste of priests and
scholars, his hands into the Kshatriya caste of warriors and administrators, his thighs into the merchant and landholding Vaishyas, and his feet
into Shudras, the skilled workers and peasants. An underclass rung was
reserved for the Untouchables, known as Dalit, or downtrodden, who

worked in the most "polluting" jobs, such as cleaning streets or toilets. Whatever its economic and religious foundations, the caste system—which in time sprouted more than 3,000 *jati,* or subcastes, tinged by geography, language, and employment—became ironbound. Until recent decades, village Untouchables would step out of view whenever a Brahmin walked by, and tea stalls would reserve separate dishware for the Dalit. Not surprisingly, the Dalit were breathtakingly poor.

After India gained independence from Britain in 1947, the legal forms of caste were abolished, and Untouchables and other lower castes began benefiting from favorable quotas that reserved certain percentages of jobs in government and admission to college for their members. By the mid-1960s, the social aspects of the system were also slackening among urban and educated sectors of Indian society, precisely the groups that furnished most of the doctors and engineers coming to the United States. It could have been expected that notions of caste might have withered.

Yet, even in this country, not just marital but business arrangements too are still sometimes colored by caste. Indians can easily tell one another's caste by characteristic last names or by hometowns, and if that doesn't do it, asking a few innocuous questions usually solves the riddle. Arun K. Sinha, a member of the Kurmi caste, whose roots are in land cultivation, is owner of the Foods of India store, a shop on Curry Hill at Lexington Avenue and Twenty-eighth Street in Manhattan. He complains that wholesalers from a higher Gujarati caste insist that he pay cash rather than extend the credit they give to merchants from their own clan. E. Valentine Daniel, a professor of anthropology at Columbia University, says some Indian executives will not hire Untouchables, no matter their qualifications. "It's even more than a glass ceiling; it's a tin roof," he said. Daniel, former director of Columbia's South Asian Institute, told me of the resistance he faced among upper-caste Indians on an academic committee when he wanted to name an endowed chair in Indian economics after a noted Untouchable, Dr. B. R. Ambedkar, a Columbia graduate who helped draft the Indian Constitution. Others told of Indians they know who cold-shoulder members of the lower Dalit caste and won't invite them to their homes.

But the caste system is withering here under the relentless forces of assimilation and modernity. Education seems to erode such traditions, and Indians may be America's most educated immigrant group: 66.7 percent of adults over twenty-five hold a bachelor's degree compared to a national average of 27 percent. Indeed, vestiges of the caste system often seem more a matter of sentiment than cultural imperative. Upper-caste Indians here insist they do not bother to probe someone's caste, and few Indians would admit to refusing to eat in a restaurant because its food was cooked by an Untouchable, something upper-caste Indians might have done fifty years ago.

Mostly caste survives here as a kind of tribal bonding, with Indians finding kindred spirits among people who grew up with the same foods and cultural signals. Just as descendants of the Pilgrims use the Mayflower Society as a social outlet to mingle with folks of familiar backgrounds, a few castes have formed societies such as the Brahmin Samaj of North America, where meditation and yoga are practiced and caste traditions such as vegetarianism and fasting are explained to the young.

"Right now my children are living in a mixed-up society," said Pratima Sharma, a fortyish software trainer with two daughters who heads the New Jersey chapter of Brahmin Samaj. "That's why I went into the Brahmin group, because I wanted to give my children the same values."

Ads in New York City's Indian newspapers testify to the persistence of caste, with one family advertising for a "Brahmin bride" and another seeking an "alliance for U.S.-educated, professionally accomplished" daughter from the Bengali Kayashta caste. Madhulika Khandelwal, director of the Asian American Center at Queens College, thinks that the influx of less-educated relatives of Indian immigrants of the 1960s and 1970s has tended to revive caste distinctions. "The underlying hope is that you have a woman or man from the same caste," Khandelwal said. "That way the marriage supports the family tradition. You are assuring, to the best of your ability, that the couple live through those traditions expressed in food, dress, vocabulary, and other things."

Hariharan Janakiraman of Queens is a mid-thirtyish Brahmin from the Vadama branch, which emphasizes teaching. Choosing to become a software engineer, not a teacher, was his one rebellion. But he intends to let his parents select his wife from his caste. His parents will consult his horoscope and that of the bride and make sure their planets and attendant moods are aligned. They will ask the prospective bride to prepare some food, then sing and dance, the latter activity to make sure all her limbs work.

"If I get married to a Dalit girl, the way she was brought up is different from the way I was brought up," he said. "If I marry people from other castes, my uncle and aunt won't have a good impression of my parents, so I won't do that."

Ranjana Pathak too maintains many Brahmin traditions. When she and I had lunch near her Long Island office, where she is a quality-control chemist, she was eating only fruit to mark an Indian festival. But she has found other traditions painful. She agreed to an arranged marriage, but her in-laws never quite warmed to her because she comes from a lower subcaste of Brahmins.

"Until today it has left a bitter taste in my mouth, and those are things you never forget," she said, the hurt audible in her voice. "That's why I won't do it to my children."

FLUSHING

...

WHERE TO GO

Hindu Temple Society of North America (ORNATE HINDU TEMPLE)
45-57 BOWNE STREET; *(718) 460-8484*

Kouchi Supermarket (AFGHAN MARKET AND DEPARTMENT STORE)
75-01 PARSONS BOULEVARD; *(718) 380-7670*

Masjid Hazrat-I-Abubakr Sadiq (DOMED TEMPLE OF A MOSQUE
AND THE ORIGINAL) 141-47 33RD AVENUE; *(718) 358-6905*

WHERE TO EAT

Afghan Kabab Palace (AFGHAN FOOD IN A NATIVE SETTING)
75-07 PARSONS BOULEVARD; *(718) 591-8700*

Chapter 10

A Kosher Kingdom in Midwood

. . .

IN THE LATE AUTUMN OF 2004, THE CITY'S ORTHODOX JEWS WERE IN a tizzy.

Just six months before, a rabbi in the new heart of Orthodox New York—a neighborhood in central Brooklyn known as Midwood—had spotted a tiny crustacean swimming in the city's tap water. Jews, of course, are forbidden to eat crustaceans such as shrimp and lobster by the portentous decrees of the Five Books of Moses. Yet rabbis long ago realized that only those creatures that were visible could be prohibited, since water everywhere in the world contains all manner of microscopic organisms—shrimplike creatures included—and the Torah would never have barred Jews from drinking water. The problem in Midwood was that this Sherlockian rabbi had spotted the crustacean with his naked eye.

At first, the ensuing dustup about whether the crustacean rendered the city's water unkosher seemed like an amusing but arcane case of hairsplitting in a particularly exacting Jewish enclave. Rabbis here and in Israel began handing down sometimes-contradictory rulings on whether New York's water needed to be filtered. As with the original Talmudic debates, the distinctions rendered for various situations turned out to be superfine, with clashing judgments on whether unfiltered city water can be used to cook, wash dishes, brush teeth, even shower, and whether Jews could filter water on the Sabbath since such an activity might constitute an obscure form of forbidden work.

Rabbi Yisroel Belsky, a leader of the Torah Vodaath rabbinical seminary and an important voice on kosher matters, told me there was no requirement to check for things that were impossible to see before there were microscopes. "If everybody goes around thinking that whoever doesn't filter water is actually eating things that are *treyf*," he said, using a word for unkosher, "there will probably be all kinds of disputes between individuals and marriage problems that can cause a cleavage." Nevertheless, he went along with the recommendation—as a recommendation, not a prohibition—so that communal uniformity and peace could be sustained.

The discovery changed the daily lives of tens of thousands of Orthodox Jews across the city. Jews worried that they might violate the kashruth laws—or worse, that they might cause their guests to sin—summoned plumbers to install water filters. Dozens of restaurants and food shops such as Negev Home Made Foods in Midwood did the same, and posted signs in their windows trumpeting their water as filtered. In Brooklyn, a landlord started a firm overnight that he called Eshel Filters, and the company adopted as its slogan "The bug stops here." One September, just before the Sukkot holidays, when many Jews invite neighbors over for a light meal, the company installed thirty filters a day ranging in cost from $99 to $1,150. Many homeowners held off, but in time the communal pressure became insurmountable. Even if you thought the water issue was a tempest in a teapot, what if your friends, relatives, or guests took it seriously and might not eat at your table? As a result, an entirely new standard was now being set for what constitutes a kosher kitchen. "I don't want people in the community to be uncomfortable in my home," Laurie Tobias Cohen, an Orthodox Jewish woman who is executive director of the Lower East Side Conservancy, told me, explaining why she put a filter on the faucet of her apartment in Manhattan's Washington Heights.

The dispute charmed me in its particular details but did not surprise me. As a yeshiva student I grew up in the Orthodox world, and as a journalist for almost forty years I have periodically covered controversies within its colorful if sometimes esoteric culture. In writing about immigrants in New York, I was drawn to Orthodox Jews because they are an expression of a group that over the generations here has steadfastly rejected many—though far from all—of the trappings of assimilation while maintaining an identity with many similarities to that of their ancestors who came over from Russia and Eastern Europe starting in the 1880s. While other Jews who shared the same immigrant ancestors embraced secular American life with full-throated enthusiasm, they kept the faith, and one contemporary expression was the filtering of water. "In a society where people feel via the Internet and television their very values are under attack, there's a need for people to reassert their level of religiosity," William Helmreich, the professor of sociology and Judaic studies at the City University of New York, told me. "And one way this is done is by discovering new restrictions which give people the opportunity to demonstrate their adherence to faith."

Just a year before the crustacean brouhaha, I had written about another startling and seemingly anachronistic tempest—a book banning, in this case the rabbinical banning of an obscure tome called *Making of a Godol: A Study in the Lives of Great Torah Personalities,* which had become the *Lady Chatterley's Lover* of the Orthodox world. It was not an erotic potboiler but rather a respected Talmudic scholar's affectionate biography of an esteemed Lithuanian rabbi who had the good fortune to meet up with some of the most revered Torah scholars of his time. What made the book so controversial was that its portraits of rabbis were not typical saintly idealizations. The Lithuanian sages—a *godol* is a great sage—are shown wrestling with the lures of secular life and with their own sometimes crusty personalities. Even as they display remarkable analytic powers in tackling Talmud, they read Tolstoy, have relatives tempted by communism, write love letters to their fiancées, are mercurial and moody. The response by other sages was Deuteronomy-like. The head of a yeshiva in Brooklyn said that it would be better to buy a crucifix than to read the book, and twenty-three leading American and Israeli rabbis issued an edict condemning it. The author eventually softened the portraits.

As with the controversy on filtering water, it dawned on me that something bigger was going on in the Orthodox world, something that seemed to testify to the increasing self-confidence of more zealously observant Jews. They had a right to be assertive because they are becoming a larger proportion of the city's remaining Jews. The number of Jews has been declining since 1957, when 2 million New Yorkers, or one out of every four, was Jewish. In a 2002 survey by UJA-Federation of New

York, the number had dipped below 1 million. New York still had the world's largest Jewish population—more than Jerusalem or Tel Aviv—but it was half of what it had been fifty years earlier. Prospering Jews, like prospering Americans of all kinds, were moving to the suburbs, and the New York metropolitan area—as a whole—has roughly the same number of Jews it did decades ago. But far fewer live within the city's boundaries. The Bronx, once practically a shtetl, with large colonies along the Grand Concourse and Pelham Parkway, now has only about 45,000 Jews, mostly in an enclave in the northwestern Riverdale section and in aging numbers in Co-op City. That figure is scarcely more than the number of Jews in Staten Island.

The study's figures suggested tectonic shifts in an ethnic and religious group that had shaped the culture, music, language, politics, and very accent of the city itself. The proportion of Jews who call themselves Orthodox continued to grow over the previous decade, and by 2002 there were 331,200 Orthodox Jews, a third of the city's Jewish population. Although the earlier, 1991, survey did not specifically count the number of Orthodox Jews within the city's boundaries, the proportion of Orthodox in a region encompassing the city's five boroughs and three suburban counties was measured in both surveys, and that increased from 19 percent to 27 percent. One impressive yardstick of the ascendance is the increase in the number of yeshivas in just a decade, from 172 in the city in 1991–92, with 58,959 students, to 221 schools with 68,604 students in 2001.

With growing self-assurance, the Orthodox have become far more conspicuous and forceful about their beliefs. When I was growing up in the 1950s and 1960s in Manhattan and the Bronx, a time when the brutal consequences of anti-Semitism were fresh in Jewish minds, a Jew in a yarmulke was a rare sight in all but a handful of neighborhoods. Today, Orthodox Jews not only wear yarmulkes on the subways, in theaters, and at work in white-shoe law firms, but on the Sabbath they can be seen walking along sidewalks with prayer shawls draped over their shoulders, an open—and detractors might say brazen—declaration of arrival. On Simchat Torah, the holiday celebrating the start of another year's cycle of Torah readings, observant Jews all over the city take their Torahs out into the streets to dance and revel in frenzied abandon.

In the bustle and clamor of a Manhattan workday, at the most prestigious law firms, brokerages, and banks, thousands of Jewish New
Yorkers now take time out from their jobs to say the required afternoon
and evening prayers with one another. At the global law firm of Weil,
Gotshal & Manges in the General Motors Building, Jewish men from
around the neighborhood gather just before sunset in the twenty-eighth-
floor office of one of the firm's partners. There, beside tall windows overlooking the groves of Central Park and the swirl of its ice rink, prayer
books are passed out, skullcaps are put on, and the men murmur their
obligatory prayers. There are two daily services in General Motors and
two in the Empire State Building—one in a garment manufacturer's
conference room on the fiftieth floor, in Sephardic style, and the other
on the sixth floor, in Ashkenazic style. Such profusion seems to illustrate
the old joke about the Jew stranded on a desert island who builds two
synagogues because the second is "the one I won't go to." Indeed, a website known as GoDaven.com lists 195 places in Manhattan where Jews
can find an afternoon minyan, the quorum of ten preferred for prayer.

Not all these worshipers in such unlikely places are Orthodox—
many are Conservative, Reform, and even so-called cultural Jews trying
to say Kaddish, the mourner's prayer, for a father or mother who died
within the previous eleven months, at a spot convenient to work. But
Orthodox Jews organize and command these services. J. Philip Rosen, a
partner at Weil, Gotshal, appreciates the perspective this prayer break
offers on what matters in life. "It's private time; it's not billable time," he
said. "It's a recognition of the importance of religion in your life. No
matter what else is going on, you find the time to pray."

As a moderately observant Jew, I appreciated the availability of these
minyanim after the death of my father in December 2003. I felt a need
to say Kaddish as often as I could, first to honor him and the tradition
of the Galician town from which he sprang, but later to heal my own
soul. There was something about standing in the presence of other
mourners—all communing with the mystery of death, with the finality
of loss—that was strangely comforting. No one in the minyanim I attended at Weil, Gotschal or the Empire State or the cozy Garment
Center Congregation actually wept for their relatives. But there was a
thick common grief contained in the prayer of men, and sometimes

women, who stood up, shut their eyes, bowed their heads, and chanted or murmured the same timeless seventy-five Aramaic words that Jews have been saying for thousands of years: *Yisgadal vyiskadash shemey raba* . . . Whether we were corporate executives or baggy-pantsed working stiffs, we all connected with that chain. I too was part of it, and almost every time I headed back to *The Times*, I felt better.

It is the most rigorous brands of Orthodoxy that are becoming the most muscular. In my childhood in the 1950s, Orthodox synagogues drew worshipers who wanted a service the old-fashioned European way—one that was exclusively in Hebrew, where men and women sat in separate sections, and where men took care of all the synagogue rituals—but in their private lives, those worshipers might be less than observant. My immigrant father worked on Saturdays because that was his boss's requirement and my father did not feel he had the stature to argue. Many of my synagogue friends were happy going to public schools. More than a few of the grown-up worshipers indulged in the characteristically Jewish misdemeanor of eating Chinese food—shrimp included.

Today, as the most stringent continue to gain clout in such neighborhoods as Midwood, Orthodoxy is not just surface style. It has become embedded in the habits and outlooks of a new generation raised in fervent yeshivas that insist upon submission to halacha, or Jewish law, and that eye the secular world—particularly the Jewish secular world—with a caution born of bitter experience with its seductions. Younger Orthodox Jews are proud to be *frum*, or observant, and call each other *frummies* in slang. The most all-encompassing sects of Orthodoxy such as the Hasidim are stronger and more exacting than ever.

The growth of the right-wing Orthodox—and such controversies as the *Godol* book—have raised questions about the state of intellectual freedom in the fervently Orthodox world and about its relations with the wider Jewish world, a culture that is generally known for valuing freewheeling intellectual exploration. On the liberal flank, Orthodox Jews observe all the dietary laws and Sabbath rituals, but they attend colleges, watch television, and engage in secular pursuits. To the right are the more rigorously observant known as *haredim:* Hasidic groups such as Satmar, headquartered in Williamsburg, Brooklyn, or Bobov and Belz, centered in Borough Park, Brooklyn, that revere particular

European-bred sages and demonstrate a zestful engagement with Torah, and the groups known as "black hats," which are equally strict in observance but whose culture centers on the great yeshivas in Baltimore; Lakewood, New Jersey; and Flatbush, Brooklyn. Samuel Heilman, a professor of sociology and Jewish studies at the City University of New York and an author of a 1992 book about the *haredim* called *Defenders of the Faith: Inside Ultra-Orthodox Jewry,* said that as Jews of all stripes have been able to navigate freely in all sectors of American society, the walls in the *haredi* world have grown taller and closed in.

"When the ghettos were locked from the outside, these kinds of issues never happened," he said. "But when they're locked from the inside, a great deal of energy has to be expended to keep the walls of virtue up so that people on one side have no contact with people on the other. Books and media are one way the walls become permeable."

Many children who grew up in so-called modern Orthodox families now make observance a far more encompassing part of their lives than their parents did. "The biggest news is the dawning of the black hat," Heilman says. "The father is wearing an Izod jersey and the son looks like he came from Lithuania."

The remarkable shift in the city's Jewish landscape is also having an impact on its politics. The Orthodox tend to be more conservative than other Jews on such issues as abortion and gay rights, and they can vote in near-bloc strength for candidates who deliver such services as housing and subsistence payments, important matters for groups with a high birth rate and many low-income families. That explains why politicians court Orthodox votes more aggressively than those of more fragmented Jewish constituencies.

Another result of all this ferment is that the historic pattern of New York Jewish geography has been turned upside down. Only two decades ago, there were a few black-hat and Hasidic neighborhoods in Brooklyn—Williamsburg and Borough Park, for instance—surrounded by a vibrant mix of Jewish styles everywhere else. Now secular Judaism seems to flourish mainly in Manhattan, surrounded by vigorous Orthodoxy everywhere. Orthodox Jews' numbers are expanding in neighborhoods that once held an eclectic mix of Jewish beliefs, neighborhoods such as Midwood and Flatbush in Brooklyn, Riverdale in the Bronx, and Far Rockaway, Hillcrest, Fresh Meadows, and Kew Gardens Hills in Queens. Playing on the Hebrew word *haredi,* for the stringently observant, Professor Helmreich of the City University told me: "We are witnessing the gradual *haredization* of the outer boroughs."

Take Midwood. It is a genteel neighborhood of eighty-year-old houses with deep front porches and overhanging eaves broken up by weathered apartment buildings. There was a substantial community of Orthodox Jews back when the neighborhood was developed—a major synagogue, Talmud Torah of Flatbush, was built then—but the Orthodox were sprinkled among the largely proletarian and lower-middle-class plain vanilla Jews, among them the parents of Woody Allen, who graduated from Midwood High School.

Today, unsung as it is, Midwood, when combined with its neighboring zip codes of Flatbush and Kensington, has grown into the largest concentration of Jews in the entire New York area—32,500 Jewish households with 107,800 people—even larger than the far more celebrated neighborhoods of Borough Park or Williamsburg. According to the UJA report, more than half of Midwood's Jews identified themselves as Orthodox. Others suggested they are part of the Orthodox orbit, with 62 percent telling the survey they keep kosher and an astonishing 92 percent saying they send children to so-called Jewish day schools—most of which are Orthodox yeshivas.

Many neighborhood institutions have been appropriated by the Orthodox for their needs. Vitagraph Studios, which was built in 1907 to make silent movies and became a division of Warner Bros., is now Shulamith School for Girls. Other schools include Yeshiva Chaim Berlin, Yeshiva of Flatbush, Yeshiva of Brooklyn, and, on the periphery, the nationally known Yeshiva Torah Vodaath and its rabbinical seminary, Mesivta Torah Vodaath. At most of the male yeshivas, teenage boys and young men sit at long tables unraveling the meaning of Talmud passages in an ancient singsong, their passion evident in their swaying and the uplifted thumbs that punctuate their arguments. The neighborhood also has Touro College, which was founded in 1971 as a nonsectarian institution emphasizing Jewish studies and has several campuses around New York. In Midwood, though, it holds classes on separate days for men and women so the sexes can't mingle.

The main commercial streets, Avenue J, Avenue M, and Coney Island Avenue, might as well be the main streets of a shtetl. They are a jazzy kaleidoscope of shops that cater to an Orthodox clientele, kosher restaurants including Garden of Eat-In and Essex on Coney, whose pastrami is fabled across Brooklyn; groceries such as Glatt Zone and Negev Take Out; and bakeries such as Isaac's Bake Shop and Ostrowsky, said to have the neighborhood's best challah. Even the Dunkin' Donuts is kosher. The clothing stores are under rabbinical supervision to make sure the prohibition against mixing linen and wool is not violated, and hat stores such as Hat-Dashery sell the large-brimmed black fedoras popular with Orthodox men. There are several wig stores, including Ita's Wig Salon and Vizions in Wigs, since rigorously Orthodox women are prohibited from showing strangers their own hair. And for people of the book, there are several bookstores—even secular bookstores are an uncommon sight in the outer boroughs—such as Eichler's, that sell tall volumes of Talmud and commentaries.

On Friday mornings, the streets are bustling with black-hatted men, and women pushing baby carriages and buying challahs, fish to make gefilte fish, beets for borscht, and potatoes and beans for a stew known as a *cholent,* to be prepared for the crowning point of the week, the Sabbath. With sunset approaching, shopkeepers lock stores and draw down protective grills and the street becomes a ghost town. The rhythm of the year is set by the holidays. Before Sukkot, for example, a half dozen shopkeepers wall off corners of their stores to sell sets of *lulav* and *etrog*—a palm frond joined with myrtle, willow, and a lemonlike fruit—which are waved in six directions during prayers.

The reasons for the exodus of so many more secular Jews from the outer boroughs include a desire to gravitate toward the excitement of Manhattan or the spacious homes and safe, solid public schools of the suburbs. While in some neighborhoods departing Jews have been replaced by Asian, Hispanic, and black newcomers, in others they have been replaced by Orthodox families, who cluster in compact communities so they do not need a car to get to the synagogue on the Sabbath, when driving is forbidden. Queens and Brooklyn each have only six Reform synagogues left, and the Bronx has three. In the 1960s, Brooklyn alone had eleven Reform synagogues. In Queens, the majority of Conservative synagogues have lost members, with the largest, the Forest Hills Jewish Center, seeing its rolls drop to 800 families from 1,800.

I found a vivid example of the Orthodox insurgency in Kew Gardens, one of the city's suburbanized treasures with Tudor, colonial, and Victorian homes surrounded by prewar apartment buildings set in a hilly, tree-shaded enclave in central Queens. Thirty-three years ago, the middle-class members of the Anshe Sholom Jewish Center, a Conservative house of worship, were so flush with success that they built a modernistic new temple. But almost immediately, the congregation began losing younger families to the suburbs and older ones to Florida. The trickle became a flood. By 2003, there were just two bar mitzvahs all year and the Hebrew school had one student left. The congregation could afford only part-time salaries for the rabbi and cantor. And the High Holidays cruelly reminded the aging remnant how much their temple had been humbled. "I remember when they ran a second service in the basement, it was so crowded," Jay Graber, an earthy seventy-six-year-old printing salesman, told me. "Now we have one service and we put up less and less seats, and we can't even fill them."

Two years later, Anshe Sholom could no longer afford its rabbi and was searching for a tenant for its basement catering hall. The news was, nevertheless, good for the Jews. For in that same Kew Gardens neighborhood, there has been a heady upswing of the Orthodox. Indeed, it was to an Orthodox school that Anshe Sholom was trying to rent its catering hall. In tracing the neighborhood's metamorphosis, I was told that the first signs were evident in the late 1970s after the opening of a school for the advanced study of Talmud by adult men, Yeshiva Shaar Hatorah. Orthodox families began snatching up homes close to their teachers—often the homes of Conservative or Reform Jews who had retired to Florida or died—and by 2003 Rabbi Yoel Yankelewitz, executive director of the yeshiva, estimated that there were 700 Orthodox families in Kew Gardens. If the trend continues, Kew Gardens' future can be glimpsed next door in Kew Gardens Hills. The neighborhood that was once a mix of Jewish beliefs now counts all but one of its thirty synagogues as Orthodox, and its shops are so uniformly kosher that its leading ice cream parlor, Max and Mina's, sells flavors like lox, garlic, and hummus.

Orthodox Jews are now blazing trails into the most unlikely places. In 2003, I learned that an old classmate of mine at Manhattan Day School, the yeshiva I attended through eighth grade, had arranged to hire Madison Square Garden for a performance of the Ringling Bros. circus during Passover in front of an exclusively Orthodox audience. I could not resist going along. The Torah commands Jews to be joyful on three holidays: Passover, Sukkot, and Shavuoth. How much more joyful could anyone be than at a circus? Here's how organizers made the Ringling Bros. circus kosher not just for Passover, when leavened bread is forbidden, but for the arcane predilections of its Orthodox audience of 19,000. They sold hot dogs without rolls and bought two brand-new cotton candy machines to make sure they were uncontaminated by leavened products. They reserved areas of the garden for those extrascrupulous souls who believed that for an event like this men and women should not sit together. And they insisted there be no female performers, including the Lycra-clad star aerialist and horse trainer Sylvia Zerbini, aka the Circus Siren.

"It's not because we don't like ladies," Rabbi Raphael Wallerstein, my former classmate and now a yeshiva principal in Brooklyn, told me. "I'm married with thirteen children and over thirty grandchildren. We love ladies. It's out of respect for them."

For several years, Rabbi Wallerstein, the unofficial impresario of the Orthodox world, had booked Passover or Sukkot events at a sports complex and amusement park in Elizabeth, New Jersey. But he wanted this year to be different from all other years. "So we said, 'Why not give Ringling Bros. a call,'" he remembered. "They're the biggest and the best. You never know." Not only did he get the owners to rent him the Garden, but they obeyed all his requests. And why not? He was providing a full house in midweek.

The band started the afternoon by playing "Dayenu," a rousing song at the Passover seder that children love. And David Larible, the master clown they call the Prince of Laughter, wore a yarmulke to perform a miracle that more than one youngster must have thought was right up there with the parting of the Red Sea: He turned another performer into a goat for several heart-stopping seconds. Through the performance, the children shrieked, gasped, guffawed, and gazed in wonder like all children who drink in a circus, maybe more so because most of these children don't have televisions and have never seen a circus. "I was scared he was going to rip him up and eat him," said Lazer Schlesinger, a twelve-year-old with side curls, after seeing the lion tamer put his head in a lion's mouth.

Not only Ringling Bros. but much of corporate America has found it profitable to accommodate the Orthodox. Hundreds of mainstream companies agreed to have their food production supervised by rabbis, and the Union of Orthodox Jewish Congregations, or Orthodox Union, claims that 230,000 discrete products made by 2,500 companies in sixty-eight countries carry its seal of approval. The power of this market was evident when Jews in Midwood and other Orthodox colonies complained to then-owner Kraft Foods about its plan to use a milk-infused chocolate in its Stella D'oro cookies. At the time, Stella D'oro was one of the few widely available brands that were made without milk or butter, and Orthodox Jews loved to munch them right after the Sabbath afternoon meal, where meat is traditionally the main course. (Usually up to six hours must pass before a milk product can be eaten after meat.) The cookies are pareve, meaning they have no trace of meat or dairy, and so can be consumed with either food. Stella D'oro's Swiss Fudge cookies are so treasured for their meat-congenial chocolate centers that they have been nicknamed *shtreimels,* the term for round fur Sabbath hats. Yet, in the few hours that I was exploring the facts of the story for *The New York Times* and calling Kraft for comment, Kraft did an about-face, announcing that it would continue using the same pareve chocolate. It was another demonstration of black-hat power.

MIDWOOD

...

WHERE TO GO

Eichler's Book and Religious Articles (TALMUDS AND TORAH
COMMENTARIES) 1429 CONEY ISLAND AVENUE; *(718) 258-7643*;
WWW.EICHLERS.COM

Hat-Dashery Shop (WIDE-BRIMMED FEDORAS OR HOMBURGS)
1419 CONEY ISLAND AVENUE; *(718) 252-1336*

Yeshiva Torah Vodaath (FERVENTLY ORTHODOX BOYS' SCHOOL)
425 EAST NINTH STREET; *(718) 941-8000*; THE RABBINICAL
SEMINARY IS AT 452 EAST NINTH STREET.

WHERE TO EAT

Essex on Coney (HUMBLE DELI WITH FABLED PASTRAMI) 1359 CONEY
ISLAND AVENUE; *(718) 253-1002*

Garden of Eat-In (KOSHER DAIRY RESTAURANT) 1416 AVENUE J;
(718) 252-5289

Ostrowsky Bakery (CHALLAHS AND CAKES) 1201 AVENUE J;
(718) 377-9443

Chapter 11

Domestic Disturbances in Rego Park

. . .

WITH THE BREAKUP OF THE SOVIET UNION IN THE EARLY 1990S, a rather obscure group of Jews started streaming out of the Central Asian lands of Uzbekistan, Tajikistan, Turkmenistan, Kazakhstan, and Kyrgyzstan, and they soon formed a thriving colony in the central Queens lands of Rego Park, Forest Hills, and Kew Gardens. Dark-eyed, dark-haired, with lush eyebrows and a slightly olive tint to their pallid faces, they were known as Bukharans, after an Uzbek city that once formed the center of their anomalous culture. They came here steeped in a tribal pride in traditions seen nowhere else in Judaism—among them their penchant for holding frequent memorial dinners where poets commissioned for the occasion recite eulogies while mourners feast on ample servings of stuffed grape leaves. In less than a generation in Queens, they have grown to 40,000 strong, establishing a string of synagogues, a yeshiva, and colorful restaurants packed nightly with celebrants or mourners. But this remarkably tight-knit community has also been grappling with a demon that seems to have slipped in with the baggage they brought from Central Asia.

Back in the Old Country, Bukharan Jews lived among patriarchal societies where the husband ruled the household and sometimes enforced his will with a raised hand. After all, the Old Country qualified as what the writer V. S. Naipaul has called a "wife-beating society," a description that fits most of the world's nations. But here Bukharan men, like those of many other immigrant groups, are confronting the values and laws of a new land and have discovered—sometimes after spending time in jail—that violence against wives is not acceptable.

That is why a delegation of three synagogue nobles set off some time ago to the home of a jewelry worker in Rego Park, the center of the Bukharan diaspora. The man, an immigrant in his late thirties, had experienced setbacks at work, his income diminishing in a seasonal job for which he was paid by the piece. His malaise was not helped by the fact that his wife was doing just fine at her bookkeeper's job and was evolving into the breadwinner. He ended up taking his frustration out on his wife and struck her several times in the course of an argument, leaving her black and blue. She called 911 and the police locked him up in Rikers Island until his wife dropped the charges. The Bukharan community—still forging its reputation among New Yorkers—was disgraced, as much by the jailing as by the hitting. Now, Rabbi Shlomo Nisanov, the bearded leader of Kehilat Sephardim of Ahavat Achim in Kew Gardens Hills, and two other emissaries, Gabi Aronov, who sells kosher meat, and Abraham Itzhakov, an elderly émigré who had been an apparatchik in Uzbekistan, needed to teach him about the rules of the American game—not to mention the right way for people to treat one another.

It was a delicate mission that tested the wile and sensitivity of the rabbi, a genial man who was raised in a suburb of Samarkand in Uzbekistan and came here in 1979 as an eight-year-old boy. Like many immigrants, he is enchanted with certain American expressions and uses them more often than he should—but to charming effect. He will describe a lavish wedding as "the whole nine yards," and then use the same expression to describe the meager furnishings his family brought from Uzbekistan. Nisanov wanted to change the man's behavior without giving him a lecture that could make the man despise himself. He also did not want to unravel a family with three children. "You can't just make the guy feel bad" is the way Rabbi Nisanov put his dilemma to me. "When you clap, it takes two hands."

At the meeting, the jeweler claimed that his wife deserved the punishment, that she did not "know how to respect her husband." So the rabbi reminded him that he came from "a respectable family," not one known for its loutish behavior. "Individuals are allowed to disagree, but that doesn't give me the right to beat you up," the rabbi told him. "To raise a hand on another person, let alone your spouse, you are considered an evil person." Finally, the rabbi was firm: "You can talk with words.

You don't have to hit. No matter how many pressures you have, you don't pick up a hand against the wife and kids."

The man seemed chastened, but the rabbi confided later that the man was most upset not by his own behavior but at his wife's offense against household protocol. "That he hit his wife didn't bother him—it bothered him that she called the police," Nisanov said.

In listening to Nisanov, I realized how the Bukharans of central Queens have become a prime exhibit in the scarcely remarked-upon underside of the vaunted immigrant dream. Newcomers from most countries learn that immigration is brutal on families. As legal refugees from the former Soviet Union, the Bukharans can come over as families, unlike some of the migrants who spirit on their own across borders. But the strains are just as subversive. Bukharan wives typically land jobs before husbands. The men may have been engineers or government officials in the Old Country and reject jobs they feel are unworthy of them. The women are less finicky and will work at such messy, low-skill jobs as home health aide and cashier. Suddenly breadwinner roles are reversed. Even if the husbands reluctantly take jobs they feel are beneath them, the wives often end up earning more money. At work, the wives come to know accomplished and outspoken American women. Steadily, subtly, their relationships with their husbands shift. Some men chafe at their diminished status. A few—not many, but enough to worry the Bukharan community—take their anger out on their wives. "When you don't bring money home, you get angry and you don't know who to get angry at so you get angry at your family," Rabbi Nisanov says. "If you get angry at your neighbor, he'll call the police. In your own family you're protected."

What's more, Bukharans still have to cope with the same unhinging frustrations as other immigrants—their clumsiness with a strange language, their bewilderment at New York's convoluted grid of streets and subway tunnels, the isolation from families forsaken in the Old Country, the loss of cultural touchstones. Merely getting oneself understood is a daunting moment-to-moment challenge. With no other kin around, the pressures on a spouse to provide affection, companionship, wisdom, are more urgent. Minor disappointments can seem catastrophic; early stumblings foreshadow failure of the whole immigration enterprise. Children looking on at such inelegant bungling cannot help but sense the chasm between their parents and more rooted Americans, and sometimes lose respect.

I saw these tensions in my own parents' marriage, which barely survived the transplantation from Europe. My father's skills as a farmer were useless in New York, and he took the first job he could find—as a roustabout in that ironing-board-cover factory in Newark. My mother too snatched the first job she could find—sewing hats. As a woman in the 1950s, she would rather have stayed home and raised children. But now she was earning as much as he was—and, with overtime in Easter bonnet season, sometimes a good deal more. She lost whatever deference women of that era owed their husbands and was not timid about letting him know of her disappointment, sometimes in front of her children. That took a toll on my father's confidence. But though he sometimes brandished his arm in anger, he never struck her. He was not that kind of man. With only a fifth-grade education—typical of Polish peasants—he never found a better-paying, cerebrally taxing job and so never felt sure enough to parry her carping. He shrugged it off, which only made his children lose regard. Once, when I was a teenager, I was walking to synagogue with my mother and I could sense she was agitated. She recounted an argument with my father the night before and startled me by talking of divorce. She never took even a tentative step toward a breakup, and in time their marriage settled into what would prove a durable—and loving—bond. But to their son those first years after they immigrated were often filled with foreboding.

The problem of wife beating among the Bukharans is probably no greater than it is for any other immigrant communities and may even be less. I called people who work with other ethnicities such as Emira Habiby Browne, executive director of the Arab-American Family Support Center in Brooklyn, who told me Arab men are also frightened of losing power in the family. "The immigration experience lends itself to domestic violence," she said straightforwardly.

Indeed, many of today's immigrants come from cultures where wife beating is so routine, women have come to rationalize it. A concise statement of the problem appears in the novel *A House for Mr. Biswas,* Naipaul's masterpiece about life among the ethnic Indians of Trinidad.

Pondering what approach he should take toward his new wife, Biswas observes that most women were disappointed if the man did not dominate them with the threat of beatings. Biswas' sister-in-law "talked with pride of the beatings she had received from her short-lived husband. She regarded them as a necessary part of her training and often attributed the decay of Hindu society in Trinidad to the rise of the timorous, weak, non-beating class of husband."

However widespread the problem, the Bukharans, tribal and intensely private, have not been happy having the problem aired in Jewish community newspapers. I had a long chat with Boris Kandov, president of the Congress of Bukharan Jews of the United States and Canada, and Lana Chanimova Levitin, often referred to as his minister for culture, over a formidable lunch at Uzbekistan Tandoori Bread in Kew Gardens. They filled me with tandoor-baked bread stuffed with meat; a vegetable soup known as *lagman;* and *palav,* a rice dish laced with carrots and meat. Through much of the conversation, Kandov tried to divert me from the story I was working on, insisting that "this problem is in any community, especially immigrant community": "There is a saying, you don't take the garbage out of your home," he told me. "You clean your home, you sweep your home. You don't bring your problems outside."

Understandably, the community's leaders would rather the media focus on the thousands of solid families and of children who have gone on to college and become doctors and engineers. Kandov himself is a shining model. In sixteen years here, he has built a fleet of 500 cars—Prime Time Limousine. Levitin, who came in 1972 from Samarkand, is a thriving real estate broker on Long Island. One daughter graduated from Columbia University and a second was studying at Fordham. Bukharans in general are proud of their thirty kosher restaurants, where families gather nightly for weddings, birthdays, and memorial services, dining on kebab while listening to musicians in brocaded silk caftans play the lute-like *tar* and hand drums. They would rather attention be paid to a six-story, $7 million building that has risen in Forest Hills and combines a synagogue, cultural center, and museum. It is the seat of their chief rabbi, Yitzhak Yehoshua, and houses twenty Torah scrolls donated by Bukharans. They would prefer a focus on a new $7.3 million yeshiva in Rego Park, the Jewish Gymnasium, where children of Bukharan families—observant, as most are, or not—study for free. Both institutions were financed by Bukharans around the world such as Lev Leviev, who, according to Forbes, controls the world's largest source of rough diamonds and is worth $2.6 billion.

Until they came here in large numbers, Bukharans were obscure even to most American Jews, whose roots are in Eastern and Central Europe. The Bukharans trace their lineage to the Jews who stayed in Central Asia after the Hebrew exile in Babylonia ended in 538 B.C. They lived in scattered settlements along the Silk Road, the ancient trade route linking China and the Mediterranean, serving as merchants, silk dyers, and court musicians. In virtual isolation from world Jewry, even the Sephardim, whom they most resemble, they cultivated idiosyncratic traditions, sometimes absorbed from the surrounding Near Eastern cultures. They preserved these traditions under Muslim potentates for a millennium, and under the czars, and kept them alive even when the Communist commissars forbade public worship. They also sustained their peculiar dialect, Bukhari, a variation of Persian flavored with Uzbek, Tajik, and Hebrew, though they spoke Russian as well. Even pogroms did not destroy the community. Levitin, the cultural minister, recalled how Muslims brazenly burned Jewish houses and raped women during the Six Days' War of 1967. Communist officials stood by.

Bukharans trickled to the United States in the 1970s along with other Soviet dissidents. Then, after the collapse of Soviet rule and the instability that allowed a hostile Muslim fundamentalism to flourish, thousands more Bukharans immigrated here or to Israel. Americans greeted them warily, sometimes disparaging them as bumpkins with a clannishness that allowed three families to live in a single apartment, not grasping that that was the Bukharan way. "We like to live next to each other," Rabbi Nisanov said. "I live next door to my sister, three blocks from my mother. Six blocks over is my grandparents. My wife's cousin is three houses down. We congregate together, and everybody knows everything."

There are, according to Kandov, 50,000 Bukharans in America, in Los Angeles, Atlanta, Cleveland, and Colorado, though 40,000 live in New York. In Rego Park and Forest Hills, Bukharans have set up clusters of characteristic shops on Sixty-third Road and 108th Street, selling velvet caftans, brocaded caps, crusty tandoor-baked breads, and *samosi* pastries filled with nuts. One bakery, Beautiful Bukhara, is owned by a Bukharan, Misha Kandov, and his son Ruben, but their chief baker is a Muslim, Ramazan Samarov, they knew back home.

Much of communal life revolves around mourning ceremonies. Bukharans not only sit shiva—the seven Jewish days of mourning in which the closest blood relatives confine themselves to home—but friends and more distant relatives gather in restaurants for those seven days to raise money to pay for the funeral and aid the grieving family—and help the restaurant's business as well. Additional memorial services are held thirty days after the death, then monthly for the first year, then annually, again in restaurants or sometimes in halls that hold a thousand people. These are not somber affairs, but celebrations of a life zestfully lived that can last for hours, with poems to recall the deceased and absurd amounts of food. All this makes for an unusually insular community, not to mention a proliferation of restaurants.

During weekday prayer services, Bukharan men repeatedly drop coins for charity into a container. On Friday nights, instead of gefilte fish, Bukharans eat fried fish in garlic sauce, a delicacy said to date to the First Temple. Bukharans keep one foot in their homeland, where 25,000 of their brethren still live, sending packages of matzo for Passover and paying stipends to make sure graves are preserved.

To the wider New York community, Bukharans are notable for the role they played in stabilizing Rego Park. When other whites were unwilling, they settled into the modern apartments in Lefrak City, a complex of twenty eighteen-story buildings and 25,000 tenants. As a result, they restored racial balance after a 1970s federal housing discrimination judgment brought in hundreds of poor black families and sent virtually all the complex's middle-class Jewish residents fleeing. By 1995 Lefrak could count 500 Jewish families who occupied roughly 10 percent of the apartments.

Whatever their triumphs here, the problem of spousal abuse has been a sore point and has galvanized the community's attention. Lali Janash, a case manager at the Esther Grunblatt Service Center for Russian Immigrants, blamed the problems on a failure to grasp American mores. "The problem is whatever was okay in Russia is not okay here," she said. "The same as child abuse. To spank a child in Russia is okay." Levitin recalled how different family life was in Central Asia, when kinfolk lived around a courtyard and the husband's mother was often the dominant woman. "The men would get anger and frustration out at their wives and the next day they would kiss her and bring her flowers," she said. "The man wasn't ostracized. The mother-in-law would say to the wife, 'Aren't you happy when he buys you something? So he hits you once or twice; it's not a big deal. If you take his love, you can take his abuse.' "

That mind-set persisted here—inflamed by the upheaval of transplantation. Although many barbers, jewelers, and professors resumed their occupations, many went to work as taxi drivers or factory workers; others could not find work. Rabbi Nisanov told me about a characteristic complaint he received from a twenty-five-year-old jeweler whose wife was a physical therapist. "How can I live with my wife when she's making fifteen thousand dollars more than me?" he told the rabbi. "She's going to start commanding me."

In Rabbi Nisanov's shul I met many of these diminished men, Bukharans like his uncle, Abraham Itzhakov, who was, as Rabbi Nisanov described, the chief bookkeeper of Uzbekistan in a land where clout was crucial to a person's self-worth. He was in his early sixties when he came, still sturdy and fluent in eight languages—but not English. "Who's going to employ him?" Nisanov said. "But his knowledge is vast."

Sometimes, Bukharan women told me, wives can provoke their husbands. At a communal celebration, I had a long conversation with Zoya Fuzailova Nisanov, the rabbi's mother. She described herself as an independent woman, someone who twenty years after she left Samarkand made a success of herself as a jewelry contractor. Nonetheless, she offered a good deal of sympathy for the men. Some men, she said, are indeed violent, unfaithful, or engaged in drug dealing. But sometimes, wives enticed by American freedoms and affluence goad their husbands on, Mrs. Nisanov claimed. "She says to him, 'She has a car. Why don't I have? She has a fur coat. Why don't I have?'

"Women in this country find themselves faster than men," she said.

"But people don't realize that the family is more important than money. Sometimes you have money, you cannot build the family again."

Then too, once in America, the women are more likely to fall back on the authorities for help. "In Bukhara, they never call the police," she said. "Here they call the police."

By the time I spoke to them, the Bukharans had arranged for several communal conferences on domestic violence with the help of the office of the Queens district attorney, Richard A. Brown. "We always have this problem, but now the women are speaking out, the rabbis are speaking out, and we're not just shoving it under the rug like we did before," Rabbi Nisanov said. Levitin runs workshops on women's legal rights through her organization World of Women Immigrants. Another organization known as Beit Shalom—a peaceful home—holds twelve weeks of summertime workshops training women to counsel compatriots. Lessons for prospective brides and grooms start out with an Orthodox religious emphasis, teaching couples, for example, to abstain from sex during prescribed periods before and after menstruation. They then move on to pointers that might raise feminist eyebrows. They tell new grooms to be understanding of working wives who don't have supper ready when the husbands come home and urge them to salve their hunger by stopping at a coffee shop. They tell wives to be sensitive to husbands' moods and urge them to look their best, to realize, as instructor Leah Davidov told me, that when the husband is in the outside world "he sees women dressed nicely."

"Many men don't want to come home, because she wants to tell him all the problems and he wants to get free," said Davidov, a fiftyish immigrant from Tashkent.

Chief Rabbi Yitzhak Yehoshua, a tall man with a straight back and a long beard, reinforces such lessons by reminding his community that the Torah and Talmud prohibit physical and verbal abuse, and that marriage requires consensus, not imposition of one spouse's will.

A new generation raised here regards routine assaults on women as an anachronism unfit for an egalitarian country. Olga Nisanov, the rabbi's wife, urges women not to tolerate violence and to contact professionals or rabbis if husbands degrade them. Svetlana Kariyev, Rabbi

Nisanov's mother-in-law, has seen palpable changes. She came here from Tashkent, studied at the University of Cincinnati, and is a microbiologist at New York University Medical Center. She raised two children, and her husband, Amnun, working in a factory and owning a shoe store, always helped with the children. "People are depressed while they're looking for a job," she said. "Once things fall into place, they look at life differently and are more aware of civilized life. For the past ten years I've seen men more willing to take care of children, take them to school, and be aware of their discipline and how they're doing. Before, the man had his business and the woman took care of the children. Now the father gives a lot of attention to education and they are good to their wives."

Janash thinks the intimate, gossipy nature of Bukharan culture is serving to reduce the abuse problem, with people letting one another know that hitting a wife is unacceptable. "Women are more courageous and they take a step," she said. "They don't suffer in silence anymore." Still, Bukharan women often do not report assaults, fearing they will lose their husband to divorce or deportation, that he will take the children back to Central Asia, or that a scandal will make it difficult for the couple's children to marry. And many men still don't get it. Gloria Blumenthal, director of acculturation at the New York Association for New Americans, which helps immigrants find jobs and housing, recounted the time several Bukharan men sought her help in blocking the deportation of a friend accused of a crime against his wife. What was the crime? she asked. Rape, they said. When she refused to help, Blumenthal said, "they looked at me like I was crazy."

IN MANY WAYS, the Bukharans have it easy when compared with the multitudes of illegal Latino and East Asian immigrants who trek their way individually to New York for the kind of money they can't make back in their dysfunctional homelands. Many of these immigrants leave spouses and children behind, harboring the illusion that they will soon bring their families over to settle forever in America. But despite such technologies as videoconferencing, many illegal Latino migrants end up divorcing the wives or husbands they left behind, and they do so with such frequency that a cottage industry of divorce lawyers has cropped up. I glimpsed a sense of this in walking along Roosevelt Avenue—the spine of the nearby Jackson Heights neighborhood and a pulsing street shadowed by the elevated subway line that seems to exist merely to cater to the needs of immigrants. In the swarming montage of commercial signs, I noticed how often I would see signs for *abogados*—lawyers—followed by two words, *inmigración* and *divorcios*, that seemed to go hand in hand.

Every year, tens of thousands of Latino immigrants tearfully kiss their spouses and children farewell and make their way to the American border, sneaking across or flying in on tourist visas they will probably let lapse. A study by the Department of Homeland Security estimated that in 2004 there were 10 million illegal immigrants in the United States, and that 3.6 million had simply overstayed their visas; only 4,164 of those overstay cases were ever investigated. The married Latino immigrants come here to secure gritty jobs because the wages, while small by American standards, go far when sent back home to support their children. The lowest-wage Mexican workers, for example, earn $4 a day; here they can earn two and three times that much per hour. The money is addictive. Although many immigrants come planning to remain a year or two, they often find themselves staying five and ten years as they come to realize that risking a journey home might mean never returning to the United States. Phone cards and videoconferencing keep some immigrants connected to their spouses, but others sense their husbands or wives back home becoming strangers. Some succumb to loneliness and meet lovers. Some seek out American citizens for sham marriages that they hope will lead to the brass ring of legal residency. Together all of these types provide more than enough business for the dozen or more divorce lawyers along Roosevelt Avenue.

One of the busiest is Jesus J. Peña, a compact Cuban immigrant with dark, plush eyebrows and silver sideburns. He works out of the second floor of a squat two-story taxpayer building, and the blue awning trumpeting his services—"Abogados"—fairly touches the sides of the elevated subway. His office handles ten divorces a week, charging $900 for most.

"The human race is a very optimistic race," he told me, radiating the weary wisdom of a too-well-experienced man. "Everyone thinks they come to the United States and will make enough money to build a house and educate their kids and then they will go back. The first year they don't make enough money. The second year they don't make enough money. After fifteen years, they're still not making enough money and they're still here. You may find a girlfriend, and that's when you need a divorce."

Peña has seen so many quirky divorces that he has come to adopt a stoic shrug toward the parade of human schemes and illusions. He sighs at how often men with wives and children come here clandestinely at the risk of splintering families. When I stopped by, one of his clients was Rodolfo Rodriguez, a thirty-seven-year-old illegal Mexican immigrant. In Mexico, Rodriguez was earning $129 a week at a Nestlé yogurt plant in the Tlaxcala area east of Mexico City. He hugged his wife and six children good-bye, and with the help of a smuggler to whom he paid $1,500, he walked across the border and made his way to the Bronx. He found work as a packer at a Manhattan meat market, a job that paid $400 a week, and sent half his earnings like clockwork to his family in Tlaxcala. He came in to see Peña in the summer of 2005 because, despite his conscientiousness, his wife had divorced him the year before in Tlaxcala on grounds of abandonment. Rodriguez, round-faced with a black mustache and doleful brown eyes, was sent into a tailspin. "I was depressed, because when I came to this country, I thought I was doing the right thing by helping my family financially," he told me through a translator.

Nevertheless, he confided that he had found a Puerto Rican girlfriend that he was thinking of marrying. In fact, he was here to see Peña because he wanted to know what precisely was the status of his previous marriage. Although it may not be the case with Rodriguez, Puerto Ricans are prime prospects for immigrant remarriages because they speak Spanish and are citizens from birth. Peña told him the divorce was legal, and that he could remarry here. Although marrying an American citizen does not mean access to a green card for someone who entered illegally, as a practical matter immigration investigators seldom bother immigrants who have American spouses. Whatever he chooses to do, Rodriguez let me know that immigration has left a bitter taste in his mouth and he would so warn his countrymen. "If you have something valuable such as a family, I would tell them not to come."

Even when long-distance separation is not an issue, the pressures of immigration—the vulnerability of a spouse who is not a citizen, the isolation from family—can destroy a relationship, and in some cases, the breakups are accompanied by the kind of violent abuse that echoes the Bukharan problem. Dorchen A. Leidholdt, director of the legal center at Sanctuary for Families, a citywide organization that provides shelter and counseling for female abuse victims, said 85 percent of her clients were immigrants who endure beatings and humiliation because of their uncertain status. She introduced me to Du-juan Zhang, a winsome twenty-four-year-old who came in May 2005 from Guangdong Province on a fiancée visa to marry a Queens dentist, a naturalized American citizen who had met her on a trip to China. Zhang told me how her husband first hit her on their wedding night and how he thwarted her from familiarizing herself with American culture, never teaching her how to ride the subway or giving her money for shopping. When she asked to take English classes, he accused her of trying to meet other men. When she suggested that she work in his clinic, he hurled a heavy backpack at her.

The following July he punched her in the stomach with a closed fist and swatted her with a shoe. In pain, she furtively phoned a friend and had her call the police, who took her to a hospital and arrested her husband. When I spoke to Zhang, her husband was facing prosecution in Queens and she was living in a shelter. But Zhang is still worried because she is here alone and now is illegal to boot. Her visa has expired and her husband has refused to file the paperwork that would give her a conditional green card as his spouse. Leidholdt was petitioning to get Zhang residency as a battered woman who made a good-faith marriage. Still, Zhang was nervous about her future. "My husband is rich, and he's a citizen of America," she told me. "I'm an immigrant from China. I don't have any money. I don't have any relatives here."

In her anguished isolation, she embodied the deep loneliness of so many immigrants, a loneliness that explains why changing countries is so traumatic and why it must be noted that expatriation is almost never Hollywood's romanticized idyll. If more Americans understood this, they would not be so quick to support harsh roundups and deportations for people who come here, however illegitimately, just to earn a living.

REGO PARK (AND FOREST HILLS)

...

WHERE TO GO

Bukharian Jewish Center (SYNAGOGUE AND CULTURAL CENTER AND SEAT OF CHIEF RABBI ITZHAK YEHOSHUA) 106-16 70TH AVENUE, OFF QUEENS BOULEVARD, FOREST HILLS; *(718) 520-1111*

Bukharian Jewish Museum (COLLECTION OF 2,000 PIECES ON HOME AND RELIGIOUS LIFE) 65-05 WOODHAVEN BOULEVARD, REGO PARK; BY APPOINTMENT ONLY; CONTACT ARON ARONOV AT *(212) 898-4135*

WHERE TO EAT

Beautiful Bukhara (A BAKERY THAT ALSO SELLS EMBROIDERED CAFTANS) 64-47 108TH STREET, FOREST HILLS; *(718) 275-2220*

Da Mikelle II (BUKHARAN RESTAURANT AND BANQUET HALL) 102-39 QUEENS BOULEVARD, FOREST HILLS; *(718) 997-6166*

International T. K. Gourmet (BUKHARAN MARKET) 97-28 63RD ROAD, REGO PARK; *(718) 896-0617*

King David (WHITE-TABLECLOTH BUKHARAN RESTAURANT) 1010-10 QUEENS BOULEVARD, FOREST HILLS; *(718) 896-7686*

Tandoori (BUKHARAN RESTAURANT THAT SELLS ITS OWN BREAD) 99-04 63RD ROAD, REGO PARK; *(718) 897-1071*

Shifting Sands on the Grand Concourse

. . .

FOR THE STRIVERS WHO MOVED THERE IN THE 1940S AND '50S, the Grand Concourse was their Champs-Élysées, a broad boulevard of Art Deco and other stylishly sedate apartment buildings that filled their craving for modest touches of class such as sunken living rooms, marble-tiled lobbies, even uniformed doormen. It was the height of petit bourgeois living in the Bronx and often derided as such by their children—this writer included. But for people weary of two wars and a Depression, living on the Concourse was a chance at modest graciousness and respectability, a statement of having arrived at a comfortable perch, with other, higher perches still in the distance.

Those sunken living rooms were occupied by postal workers, locksmiths, bureaucrats, teachers, shopkeepers, even local doctors and lawyers. To a teenager, the residents seemed to flaunt a smug delight in having arrived on the Concourse, and nothing seemed to capture their complacency more than the ritual of hauling out folding chairs on a mild afternoon or evening, setting up on the sidewalk, and reviewing the passing parade. Distinctions of status were calibrated by what synagogue one belonged to, the Conservative temple or the Orthodox *shtiebel,* whether you went for the summer to a hotel, a bungalow colony, or just the Bronx's own Orchard Beach, whether you ate in the deli or ventured to a Manhattan restaurant. But whatever one-upmanship there was, all was apparent harmony on the High Holidays, when every Jewish family would cram as if by command into four-block-long Joyce Kilmer Park near Yankee Stadium and show off their Sunday-best finery and their children.

Except for a handful of flinty survivors, those residents are long gone. While Robert Caro in his landmark biography of Robert Moses blamed the demise of the middle-class Concourse on the gash in the neighborhood produced by the Cross Bronx Expressway's construction in the late 1950s and 1960s, I would argue that what happened had a more complicated dynamic. Residents of the streets radiating off the Concourse had already begun leaving slowly in the 1950s, and left more quickly in the 1960s, snatching at the next step up the ladder of success—a house in the newly tamed wilderness of northern Queens or even Westchester or Long Island. Meanwhile the humbler streets far to the east and the west of the Concourse in neighborhoods including East Tremont, Highbridge, and Morrisania were turning over, as Jews, Irish, and Italians were giving up tenements and ramshackle wood-frame houses for fancier apartments, and black and Puerto Rican strivers were taking their place.

With each passing year, those waves of racial change lapped closer and closer to the Concourse. Then apartments started going begging on the Concourse itself, sometimes because tenants moved to Florida but sometimes because the children of those bred on the Concourse wanted to move away—to the electricity of Manhattan or to the comforts of the burgeoning suburbs. Landlords found it easy to fill buildings with referrals from the city's welfare department, most of them black and Latino families for whom landing on the boulevard seemed a stroke of good fortune. The blending of newly bourgeois whites and poorer blacks and Spanish speakers did not take—it happens easily almost nowhere—particularly because too many of the newcomers had the kinds of problems the Jews and Irish had come to the Concourse to escape. Their new neighbors made them uncomfortable, and they never gave them a chance to defy expectations, lumping the good families together with the bad. Then too the schools that had turned out college-bound Americans as if on an assembly line were losing their best students and declining, unable to solve the riddles of working with children from fractured homes. The moment that I knew life was changing in my bland neighborhood was when my mother found a tall man standing just inside the door of our unlocked fifth-floor apartment claiming he was looking for a Mrs. Goldberg. This intruder was black, and his bewildering presence in a building that was almost entirely Jewish raised my mother's suspicions. We rustled the man out and my mother urged me to call the police.

"He was looking for Mrs. Goldberg's apartment," I said, siding with the intruder.

But sure enough, that night, while I was at the movies with my mother in our local movie theater, the Kent, my father suddenly appeared in the aisle with a look of alarm that seemed to glow in the dark. We had a boarder living with us in a small room right near the door—like more than a few families, we took in boarders to satisfy the rent—and my father told us that the boarder had come home and discovered that watches and jewelry had been taken from his night table. My Concourse innocence was shattered.

There were enough incidents of muggings, burglaries, and plain thuggish behavior to accelerate the exodus. Jews, who always keep a metaphorical suitcase packed, fled en masse. Year by year during the late 1960s and '70s, I noticed that the High Holiday crowds in the park were growing thinner. When Co-op City opened in the swamps in the northern Bronx, with its lure of bargain-basement home ownership, the crowds in Joyce Kilmer Park vanished. One by one the European bakeries, pastrami-slicing delis, and kosher butchers closed. The Concourse Plaza, outside whose door my brother and I would sometimes wait to spy a resident Yankee baseball player, became a welfare hotel. With membership plummeting, rabbis handed the keys to their synagogues over to Baptist and Pentecostal churchmen, who retained the Mogen Davids and arched tablets carved into the stonework, letting them remain like pentimenti of a lost time. A deep slump settled over the boulevard, with one or two buildings succumbing to the abandonment sweeping across the southern Bronx.

But the avenue has come back. Mayor Edward I. Koch put his mind to getting the city to fix up empty buildings it had been warehousing and to putting up new buildings on the lots of brush and trash. By 2005, the city owned fewer than fifty abandoned buildings in the Bronx, where it had once owned more than a thousand. The Concourse is now bustling with new breeds of immigrants who also see the Grand Concourse as their boulevard of dreams and appreciate those same lingering, if tattered, touches of Art Deco elegance, even if they have wholly different outlooks on how they should be preserved. Dominicans have moved up from Washington Heights, Albanians and Cambodians fleeing wars and persecution have found refuge in the Concourse's northern end, and there has even come a more exotic strain than the Bronx is accustomed to—West Africans from Ghana and Nigeria. All probably are feeling the same heady sense of ascendancy, of having climbed from steerage to at least cabin level, that the Jews, Irish, and Italians felt when they first came to this airy boulevard and its decorous houses.

It is the Ghanaians who have planted an entire novel culture into this spine of the Bronx, with their lilting accents, spicy foods, chromatic kente cloth clothing, tribal facial cuts, and uncommon mores, none more odd than their twist on the timeless yearning of new Americans for owning a house. When Ghanaians immigrate here, they too save up to buy a house, but the house they yearn to own is in Ghana. These Ghanaians, some of them living pinched lives as taxi drivers and nursing home aides, may never actually return to Ghana to live. But that is where they want to locate the concrete trophy that declares they have arrived. Beyond the standard rationales that people use to buy so remote a house—a good investment or haven for retirement—there is one explanation that speaks volumes about the city's growing Ghanaian population: "You can own a home here, but no one's going to know about it, so you have to own a home in Ghana," said Kwasi Amoafo, vice president of Ghana Homes. "Then everyone who matters to you can see you've made it in America."

I discovered the Ghanaians and their odd fixation in the most pleasing way possible, serendipitously, by driving along the Concourse and noticing African shops sprinkled among the more Latino-flavored stores. One of these bore the sign "Ghana Homes Inc." I stopped in to inquire what this business was all about and discovered I had stumbled across an enchanting folkway. Amoafo and a partner, Kwasi Kissi, started this business in 1999; it helps Ghanaian immigrants buy houses in Ghana. A three-bedroom cement house there can be bought for as little as $30,000, so $6,000 in savings may be all it takes to put a deposit down for a piece of the planet in a lush and stable land.

Amoafo and Kissi are catering to peculiarities of West African tribal tradition. Ghanaians, as well as Nigerians and Ivorians, come from lands where ties to clan and family are primal and primary. For every Ghanaian, the extended family—parents, siblings, uncles, cousins, aunts, and grandparents—grounds one in the universe. In times of difficulty, the entire family pitches in to share the burden of repair, and at times of joy, the entire family shares the elation. Sons and daughters typically live with their parents until they have started their own families, and when they do, they choose to live with or next to their parents. Still, it is the building of a house that marks an individual's "cultural coming of age," Chudi Uwazurike, a senior fellow at the Institute for Research on the African Diaspora in the Americas and the Caribbean, told me.

Ghanaians started leaving Ghana in the 1970s when a succession of military governments sent the economy into a tailspin. Those who came here were often professionals, bureaucrats, and merchants. Many were well educated, since Ghana, the first African colony to gain independence from Britain, made schooling the focus of early development. The new immigrants sent money back to Ghana and persuaded relatives to join them here, swelling the migration. Now those who have settled into their lives here can finally concentrate on saving up for that house—in Ghana.

Frank Samad came here twenty-five years ago after finishing high school in Ghana and started work as a security guard. He dropped his Ghanaian given name and chose Frank because there were two Franks who worked at his firm and he saw that it was a name people rarely mispronounced. He found better jobs, eventually managing a supermarket. After ten years, he opened Kantamanto African Market on Tremont Avenue just west of the Concourse. Kantamanto, which means "one who honors his word," stocks smoked mudfish, ground yams, pumpkinseeds, the tuberous root known as cassava, and smoked grasscutter—a very large rodent related to the guinea pig that runs wild in the bush and comes right after chicken and fish as a Ghanaian's preferred source of protein. It also carries kente cloth, African magazines, and phone cards that make possible a six-minute call to Ghana for $10. In New York he has always lived with his wife and three children in a rental apartment, but in 1993 he and his brother—a contractor—began building a four-bedroom house. It was located in a suburb of Accra, Ghana's capital of 2 million people. Now he stays there on his yearly visits home.

"When you look at it, it doesn't make sense," he admitted as we spoke in the rear of his store. "I'm not living there, and with the money I put in there, if I used it here I could have tripled the size of my store. But when I go to Ghana I have a place to live. I wouldn't like to bother my relatives or live in a hotel. That would be a letdown. After all those years here, I would go back to Ghana and it would be like being homeless. So with that kind of pride, anybody who makes a little money will buy a house in Ghana."

In a broader sense, the story of the Ghanaian houses illustrates once more the big difference between the immigrants of today and those of the past. Today's immigrants keep one foot in the Old Country largely because they can do so easily with jets (flights back home to Ghana can be had for $700) and cheap phone cards. "Always in the back of their minds is the idea of returning one day," Amoafo said of Ghanaians. But it is largely a pipe dream. "I can tell you that ninety percent will never go back. But it defines their thinking."

The fact that Ghana Homes can exist as a profitable business testifies to the remarkable growth of the city's Ghanaian population, particularly in the census tracts along the Concourse, as the pioneers send word home that life here is good. Ghana, a country the size of Oregon with 20 million people, has an economy that can't keep up with the growth of its population. The 2000 U.S. Census revealed that the number of immigrants born in Ghana tripled in a decade, to 14,915, of whom 9,275 live in the Bronx. If children born here were included, the ranks of Ghanaians would expand by several thousand.

Ghanaians bring with them a courtly culture that is at odds with the rough-hewn Bronx stereotype. Ghanaians encourage a smile for strangers, patience in daily dealings, and respect for elders and for women. A visitor to a Ghanaian home will be given a seat and water to drink before he is asked the purpose of his visit. Ghanaians appreciate a well-crafted phrase that deftly captures some wisdom about living. Ghanaians also tend to socialize within their own tribes, and there are dozens, including Ashanti, Ewe, Ga, Akwamu, and Akuapim, each with its own dialect. Akuapim, Amoafo told me, speak a very dignified dialect, while the Ashantis' conversation is more robust and forceful. Ghanaians of all tribes come together under the banner of the National

Council of Ghanaian Associations, which sponsors an annual picnic in a state park, at which Ghanaian politics is dissected and thousands of dollars are raised for Ghanaian hospitals.

Ghanaian life here is felt daily by New Yorkers in the cabs they drive and in nursing homes, where many Ghanaians take care of the frail elderly. (A tall, engaging, and graceful Ghanaian mother of five—her name was actually Grace—took care of my father at the Hebrew Home for the Aged in Riverdale before he died in 2003.) Since many Ghanaians arrive here with advanced degrees, Ghanaians are sprinkled throughout the top ranks of the city's banks, hospitals, and colleges. Kofi Annan, the seventh secretary-general of the United Nations, is a Ghanaian, the grandson of Ashanti and Fante tribal chiefs who studied at Macalester College in St. Paul, Minnesota, and received a master of science degree in management from MIT. As with other Ghanaians in his larger tribe, his name took a standard pattern, with Kofi indicating a boy born on a Friday, and Annan indicating that he was the fourth child of his family.

More than 400 Ghanaians live in Tracey Towers, the two circular forty-one-story buildings at the Concourse's northern end that are the Bronx's tallest and were completed in 1972 as part of a government-subsidized program aimed at keeping moderate- to middle-income families in the area. They socialize in several Ghanaian-inflected Pentecostal and Seventh-day Adventist churches along the Concourse. They're also visible in African groceries and variety shops that dot Highbridge and Morris Heights west of the Concourse and a half dozen sometimes-ragtag restaurants, such as the African and American Restaurant on University Avenue near Burnside Avenue.

The restaurant's owner, Mohammed Abdullah, a burly man of forty-seven when I spoke to him, started working here as a gas station attendant in the Bronx after he came over from Accra in 1980. He brought his own home-cooked lunch to work, and his co-workers were so enamored of what they tasted, they paid him to make them lunch. Soon he was operating a restaurant incognito out of his fifth-floor apartment at 184th Street, three blocks off the Concourse, his landlord none the wiser. Finally he decided to become legitimate, opening his enterprise in a former donut shop in 1987, closing it, then, for $15,000, opening African and American Restaurant in what had been a Dominican fried-chicken shack. Abdullah, who has two tribal cuts on his cheeks, catered a Kwanzaa celebration for Mayor David Dinkins. He has done well enough to buy a house at West 179th Street for himself and the twelve children he has had with three wives, two of whom he was married to at the same time and one who died in Africa. (As a Muslim, he told me, he is allowed to have two wives, though I sensed he hadn't checked with New York authorities.) Six of his children were living with his mother-in-law in Ghana so they could go to a school where drug addiction and punkish behavior are not as unavoidable as they are in Bronx schools.

We sat at one of his oilcloth-covered tables, and he fed me spicy baked steak and spinach laced with crushed sunflower seeds. "This neighborhood is not really a good place to raise children," he told me. "I send them home so they get better schooling and to be respectful and not mingle with the kids that, you know, will give them bad ideas."

It's not just mischief but the values children pick up that clash with Ghanaian attitudes toward family and clan, as Abdullah made charmingly clear. "The way my children are brought up, they have a sense of mother and father," he said. "In the past, we find they grow up and all they care about is their wife. His mother and father are a headache for him. They lose that sense of family."

To help cement that sense of family, he bought a second house—in Ghana—which he visits yearly. But he is also reaching out to his black American neighbors, since they are so much larger a pool of potential customers. He serves them soul food, while at the same time enticing them to try his baked steak and sunflower spinach. "Now most of them don't eat soul food anymore," he said.

As with Abdullah, many Ghanaians have been in New York long enough that there are struggles between the habits of the immigrant generation and those of Ghanaians born here. Amoafo told me that many Ghanaian mothers are exasperated by teenage girls who want to wear tops and slacks that expose their midriffs, just as their American friends do. At the same time, those mothers are being introduced to liberated American women and becoming less docile with their husbands. "A woman becomes more vocal and a man is totally at a loss of how to deal with her," Amoafo told me. Wanting a woman unspoiled by American impertinence, some Ghanaian men have their families back home find them a bride. Too often these marriages don't work out, sometimes because the cultural chasm is too great but sometimes, according to *African Abroad*, which has news in English of Ghana and Nigeria, because some of the native women come to the United States planning "to jump the marriage" as soon as they can, to tap American opportunities on their own.

Given the values they bring with them, Ghanaians also struggle with Bronx streets. They sometimes look down on their poorer black American neighbors, who they feel are not as industrious as they are and whom they see as too willing to live on government handouts. "African Ghanaians have very little in common with black Americans," Amoafo said. "They have different worldviews, different values. There's nothing in common in terms of aspiration." If Ghanaians form relationships with American blacks, it is with those in the middle class, he said.

Amoafo, a handsome, sinewy man of medium height who holds a legal resident's green card, came to the United States in 1973 as an exchange student with American Field Service. He attended high school in Tacoma, Washington, started out at a college in Baltimore, and got two years under his belt at New York University. He drove a taxicab and worked as a Wall Street administrative assistant and ten years ago started Ghana Homes with Kissi, who like him belongs to the Kwahu tribe, a division of the Akan group. Amoafo, his Kenyan wife, and their two boys and two girls live on the Concourse near 167th Street, less than a block south of where my family started our Bronx sojourn.

Amoafo and Kissi's Ghana Homes stands out as a curiosity even among the Ghanaian businesses. Situated in the ground floor of a Concourse apartment house near Tremont Avenue, it pays its overhead by handling money transfers and travel arrangements. But Amoafo and Kissi make their real profits selling the houses, representing developers in Ghana as well as the country's main mortgage company. Amoafo and Kissi reassure potential customers that they can avoid the disheartenment of murky property titles or the fraud typical of some transactions.

The houses are ranches or two-story affairs, usually part of a development. They cost anywhere from $30,000 to $300,000. Owners who live in the United States often arrange to rent the houses out or let family members use them. Still, they envision returning to their Ghanaian clans as soon as they put together a nest egg. One of Ghana Homes' customers, Austin Batse, a computer consultant in Durham, North Carolina, had wanted to return to Ghana to help build up the country practically since the day he immigrated here as a ten-year-old. In 2001, he bought one of Ghana Homes' houses for $63,000. Batse has never been to his house, but he asked his sister in Ghana to visit the house with a wedding photographer, and they shot a video that gives him deep joy to look at.

"For a lot of people it's a status symbol of getting out of the position you were in," Batse told me by telephone. "Someone who's not highly educated and works at a low-income job comes up with the down payment on thirty thousand dollars and achieves that type of house in a very nice area. You can be someone coming from a village, but you return in a totally different class because of the power of what you've been able to earn here."

THE GHANAIANS HAVE taken part in the revival of the Grand Concourse and the gathering renaissance of a borough that two decades earlier was known for its landscape of eviscerated buildings and Fort Apache air of menace. Buildings all along the boulevard have been sandblasted or had their graffiti scrubbed off. In some cases the interiors have undergone wholesale renovation. These buildings have increasingly been filled with working families. Two notable bookends to the revival of the main stretch of the Concourse were unveiled in 2005. First, the Yankees announced plans to build a new stadium in the Bronx just north of the House That Ruth Built. The replacement will have echoes of the original stadium circa 1923 and seat up to 54,000, some of those inhabiting the fifty to sixty luxury boxes. But the new stadium is not without its touch of tristesse. To erect it, contractors will destroy two neighborhood parks, Macombs Dam Park, currently a track for runners who have at times included Olympians, and Mullaly Park, which I played in as a teenager. I still remember standing at home plate and hitting a ball that soared out of the park and struck the horizontal girders of the Jerome Avenue el, a truly towering home run in my subconscious field of dreams. Yankee owner George Steinbrenner, though, has a way of getting his way. He stopped wanting to flee the Bronx about the time the

Yankees started winning World Series again and their attendance sky-rocketed, doubling in a decade to a sport record of 4,200,518 in 2006. Surely the increasing appeal of an enhanced Concourse neighborhood helped draw fans.

The second crowning Concourse milestone was the reopening of the Loews Paradise in October 2005. The theater, the Bronx version of Radio City Music Hall, originally opened a few weeks before the stock market crashed in 1929 with a showing of the "all-talking" film *The Mysterious Dr. Fu-Manchu.* The Paradise gave generations of working-class and lower-middle-class strivers a taste of Old World opulence and gave generations of teenagers a haunting setting for their first kiss. "It was meant to take people out of their humdrum existence and bring them into a world of unimagined wealth and luxury," Lloyd Ultan, the Bronx historian, told me.

The Paradise was designed by legendary theater architect John Eberson, and its atmospheric show included twinkling stars, rolling clouds, and flying pigeons. The stage was embraced on three sides by a Venetian garden, with walls dripping with sculptured vines, cypress trees, and classical statues. The vaulted lobby was surrounded by fluted and gilded mahogany pillars and an arched balustrade of royal proportions. Every nook seemed to be filled with cherubs, nymphs, and recumbent lions. In three domes set into the lobby's filigreed ceiling, Eberson had painters execute dreamy murals of ersatz half-nude deities: Sound, Story, and Film. On the lobby's north wall Eberson placed a Carrara marble fountain of a child on a dolphin and filled the fountain with goldfish. For the cream-toned terra-cotta-and-marble façade, Eberson designed a mechanical clock topped by St. George astride a charger slaying a fire-breathing dragon on the hour.

I remember riding by bus along the Concourse one weekend in 1957, when I was twelve, and glimpsing a long line of teenagers against the Paradise marquee, which displayed Elvis Presley's name and "Jailhouse Rock" in oscillating lights. For the teenagers, this opening was the biggest public event in their short history in the Bronx, and I recall thinking I would never be cool enough to be included. A few years later my graduation from the Bronx High School of Science was held in the Paradise, and I remember walking by the fountain with its capering goldfish and looking up at the twinkling midnight blue sky. I wondered what memories my classmates at Bronx Science had, so I called a few of them. Diane Levine Edelstein remembered the Paradise balcony as something of a lovers' lane—though for nothing much more daring than a long kiss.

"You walked in and you felt you were in another world, you weren't in a movie theater," said Edelstein, now a senior research assistant at the Albert Einstein College of Medicine. "We always sat in the balcony because you felt closer to heaven. I remember watching the stars and not looking at the movie." And Phyllis Gross Greenbaum, now a publisher of community newspapers in the Washington-Baltimore area, touched a sympathetic chord when she told me why the Paradise stunned her and her friends. "I don't think many of us grew up with that kind of elegance," she said.

For thirty years, after the middle class left the Concourse, the Paradise was either boarded up or sliced into multiple screens. The new owner, Gerald Lieblich, acquired the theater for $4.5 million and restored much of its Italian baroque grandeur, getting workers to clean the statuary, install 4,000 burgundy seats, and repaint the blue ceiling. The stars, however, won't twinkle, because making them do so proved too costly. The goldfish pool will not be replaced because it would interfere with a concessions stand.

And the Paradise did not reopen as a movie house. Its opening-night bill in October 2005 was a salsa and merengue concert, clearly a bid to cater to another generation of strivers who did not grow up with that kind of elegance—Latinos, who now make up half the borough's populace. The entrepreneurs leasing the space also plan to hold gospel and rap concerts, live boxing matches, nostalgia acts that might appeal to onetime Bronx residents, and once again, high school graduations.

Despite such ornaments as the Paradise, the revival of the Concourse has exacted a price, one that is heartbreaking to old-time exiles. The Concourse was designed as a residential street, conceived as such by engineer Louis Aloys Risse in 1870. It was finally built between 1902 and 1909, then extended farther south in 1927 so that the completed boulevard was almost 200 feet wide and stretched for four and a half miles between 138th Street and Mosholu Parkway (roughly 207th Street). The boulevard really began to flourish in the 1930s and '40s, after the completion of the IND subway line, which ran underneath and produced stations every few blocks that became the impetus for commercial development on the station cross streets. Enterprising developers took advantage of the enchantment with Art Deco to create alluring buildings with stylish touches including polychrome brick, set-back steel-casement windows, and terrazzo lobby floors. The Concourse became the borough's parade route, the site of its government, and its most prestigious address. Those who grew up there or lived there as celebrities included Milton Berle, Babe Ruth, E. L. Doctorow, the singers Roberta Peters and Eydie Gormé, and the journalist David Halberstam, who lived in the stately thirteen-story Lewis Morris Apartments near 175th Street, where a white-gloved doorman opened doors of arriving cars. The Concourse's other iconic gem was a smaller cream-brick Art Deco structure at 1150 that was known popularly as "the fish building" for the tropical mosaic flanking its doorway.

The residential character of the boulevard survived the racial turnover, but paradoxically that character is being chipped away by the thoroughfare's revival. On the ground floor of the fish building there are now a barbershop and a tax preparer's office, each with a prominent sign. In the Lewis Morris, where three-quarters of current tenants receive federal rent vouchers, the ground floor houses three clinics, each with a two-foot-high banner that advertises its acceptance of Medicaid and insurance plans. Indeed, scores of stores and clinics have been carved out of what were once ground-floor apartments. The wave seems to have accelerated in recent years so that almost every block between 161st Street and 196th Street now has a grocery, a barbershop, a beauty parlor, a travel agency, or a pharmacy, and some stretches are chockablock with stores and outsize signs. When I was growing up, only the blocks flanking the borough's shopping district of Fordham Road had stores; the only signs elsewhere were discreet doctors' shingles.

"Why do you have to have a sign up there saying 'Family Dentist'?" Michael Saccio, a forty-eight-year-old prop man living in the fish building said to me. "On Park Avenue you see a little gold plaque. This guy is advertising like he's giving away something free."

Preservationists, historians of the Bronx, wistful former residents, and some government officials say they are heartsick at what they regard as an aesthetic blight on a once-genteel street. They are trying to stop the commercialization by creating a Concourse historic district or by enforcing more strictly a 1989 zoning law that bans stores in all but a few places and limits signs in most of those locations to twelve square feet. In 2003, the borough president, Adolfo Carrión, Jr., asked the city's Department of Buildings to step in, and an inspector soon issued 170 violations at seventy to eighty buildings. The owners were given forty-five days to correct the transgressions. But Sid Dinsay, a department spokesman, admitted that "to my knowledge" none of the stores had been closed, though legal proceedings against some had begun. Meanwhile, enforcement of the signage laws has been suspended since early summer 2003, when the city council imposed a moratorium after receiving heated complaints from shopkeepers about the costs of changing signs. Carrión, an urban planner by training, told me he would like to find a way to steer merchants toward the busy commercial cross streets and away from the boulevard. Otherwise, the Concourse's sense of place would be damaged. "When you drive down Fifth Avenue or Central Park West, you know where you are," he said. "The place has a personality. The Concourse should be one of those places in our city where we make a statement about how we care about our city."

But even as the Concourse nears its one hundredth anniversary in 2009, official talk about a crackdown seems to be so much lip service. The fact is, preservationists say, that few residents are clamoring for enforcement. They have different needs and tastes—a desire for a nearby grocery to buy a container of milk for their children, more chances for jobs in those neighborhood stores, outposts of vitality to discourage muggers on desolate nights. They are not as concerned about keeping the almost pristine residential character of most of the boulevard and have welcomed the stores springing up on nearly every block and the signs that sometimes accompany them. For the old-time exiles, it may be heartbreaking to see the changes in their cherished Grand Concourse, but not to the newcomers. For them, the avenue's history is, well, history. "I think the people around here are more interested in having the stores," Thomas Hernandez, a construction worker, told me as we chatted on the 169th Street corner. "You don't have to go to a supermar-

ket three blocks away. As long as people have demands—buying cigarettes, baby milk, stuff like that—this is not going to faze anybody."

Carlos Fernandez, the manager of Claris Record Shop, across from
the fish building, told the story of how the store's owner was hauled into
court six months before, and residents turned out in force to support him.
"Otherwise, they have to go six blocks to buy a CD," Fernandez said. Dr.
Jagdish N. Markale, an immigrant from Bombay who owns the dental
clinic across from the fish building, said he put up his sign a year ago out
of fear that other dentists with signs might lure patients away. The
street's history, he said, is not as important to residents as a grocery store,
and added bluntly, "The government has to consider their priorities
rather than that of the people who used to be here fifty years ago."

GRAND CONCOURSE

...

WHERE TO GO

The Fish Building (ART DECO GEM, WITH A MOSAIC AT THE
ENTRANCE WITH AN AQUARIUM THEME) 1150 GRAND CONCOURSE
NEAR 167TH STREET; OTHER NOTABLE ART DECO BUILDINGS ARE AT
750, 888, 1947, 2155, AND 2830 GRAND CONCOURSE, AND A STROLL
REVEALS DOZENS OF OTHERS.

Kantamanto African Market (AFRICAN GROCERIES AND PRODUCTS)
61 EAST TREMONT AVENUE; *(718) 583-5250*

Lewis Morris (ONCE THE GRANDE DAME OF GRAND CONCOURSE
APARTMENT HOUSES) 1749 GRAND CONCOURSE AT 175TH STREET

Loews Paradise Theater (MOVIE PALACE) 2403 GRAND CONCOURSE;
(718) 220-6144

WHERE TO EAT

African American Restaurant (GHANAIAN DELICACIES)
1987 UNIVERSITY AVENUE; *(718) 731-8595*

Chapter 13

Nursing Americans in Norwood

. . .

THE NEW YORK ECONOMY IS HONEYCOMBED WITH ETHNIC NICHES. Greeks own the diners and coffee shops, Koreans the fruit stores, South Asians the newsstands, and Afghans the sidewalk coffee carts and barbecued-chicken shacks. Brazilians shine shoes, Mexicans peddle flowers, and West Africans hawk umbrellas. For decades many of the firms that wash the windows of office buildings were owned not just by Ukrainian Jews but by Jews from a single town in Ukraine. And of course all of these joined the more storied occupational niches, some of which survive now only in legend, such as the Jewish garment workers, Italian stonemasons, and Irish cops (Irish and other whites no longer make up the bulk of police recruits; more than half are black, Hispanic, or Asian).

I stumbled across another niche when my father was hospitalized with a stroke in 2003 at Montefiore Medical Center in the Bronx. I could not help but notice how many of the nurses tending him were Filipino. I could explain why so many were immigrants—Americans don't want to do the dirty, often unnerving work of ministering to the old and very sick. But why were so many from a single foreign country? I asked the Filipino nurses and not only learned why but discovered that there was a surgical case at the very same hospital that epitomized the Filipino role. As I walked around the streets outside the hospital, I also discovered that Filipino nurses had gently recast the character of that Bronx neighborhood, a place that calls itself Norwood.

Arlene Aguirre, a woman from a squalid Filipino village where she lived in a small hut with no running water, arrived in New York in September 2003 for some extraordinary surgery—the separation of her conjoined eighteen-month-old twins. Carl and Clarence had been born with the tops of their skulls fused together, preventing them from moving about independently. They spent their days in bed lying on their backs in a single line. The Montefiore surgeons mapping out their separation were going to do it in a way no one had ever dared before—in stages, with four operations over a year's time and many months of rehabilitation at Blythedale Children's Hospital in Valhalla, New York. They were fortunate in finding that the boys' brains were not fused, a factor that could allow for separating them without producing significant brain damage, if any. Still, the unprecedented operation in a city where Aguirre hardly knew a soul was complex and perilous and she was profoundly fearful for her children.

But by coming to a big-city hospital she found herself caressed by compatriots in a way she might not have been had she come for, say, a job on Wall Street. At Montefiore, she was swarmed by Filipino women. "People called to each other, 'Did you hear there are conjoined twins and they're Filipino?' " recalled one of the women, Clemencia Wong. The Filipino women brought Aguirre *pancit*, a noodle dish as standard in the Philippines as French fries are here, and adobo, a garlicky chicken dish, and took her shopping at a nearby grocery that carries Filipino products. They gave her a phone card to call relatives back home and took her underwear home to launder. A half dozen women prayed with her at the twins' bedside in the tenth floor Pediatric ICU, and a special mass was held in the chapel. This was not just a spontaneous outpouring of love but the result of a plan devised by twenty Filipino nurses meeting with Dianne Aroh, the hospital's head nurse, to make sure Aguirre's ordeal was as cushioned as possible.

One-quarter of Montefiore's nursing staff is Filipino, a figure not too dissimilar from those in many other hospitals in the city, where women from a constellation of Caribbean islands are their only rivals for dominance. Filipinos in the New York area are practically defined by this single occupation. Thirty percent of the 173,000 Filipinos work as nurses or other health practitioners—four times the rate for the entire population. Many of the rest are their spouses, children, or aging parents. I talked about the phenomenon with several nurses in a conference room at Montefiore.

"If you meet a Filipino girl and say, 'You're a nurse,' you're probably right," Clemencia Wong, a pediatric nursing instructor at Montefiore, told me.

"And if you meet a Filipino man, he'll probably say, 'My wife is a nurse,' " chimed in Pio Paunon, a Filipino man who is the nurse manager at Montefiore and the president-elect of the Philippine Nurses Association of New York.

I learned that for more than three decades, American hospitals have aggressively recruited nurses from the Philippines, sometimes enticing them with bonuses of thousands of dollars. One male nurse at Montefiore told me the going rate at one time was $7,000. Hospitals prize Filipino nurses because they speak English with ease and bring with them professional schooling not too dissimilar from that of American nurses. The Philippines, after all, was an American colony or commonwealth from 1898 to 1946, except for four years of Japanese occupation. Its government, schools, and professional training programs were modeled on those of the United States, and the American government in the early twentieth century regularly sent Filipinos to such American colleges as the University of Illinois to instruct them in engineering, agriculture, and medicine.

There are other winning qualities that speak particularly well of Filipino culture. Hospital administrators value the nurses for their strong work ethic—not always true of other nurses—and their loyalty to employers. "They're extremely respectful of patients and their family members," Aroh, the nursing chief at Montefiore, said of her Filipino staff. "And they're very flexible, willing to take new assignments on the spur of the moment, willing to work extra-long hours." They are not as ready as some other nurses to switch hospitals for a pay raise or a shorter commute. Filipinos also bring a tenderness to their work that seems to stem from a culture where people insist on caring for their own aging or sick relatives. Nursing homes are uncommon in the Philippines. That tenderness stands in sharp contrast to the brusqueness that seems to be an accepted part of the experience of having a beloved relative confined to a hospital bed. "The family is the center of your life and it's your upbringing," Lolita B. Compas, a Filipina who is president of the New York State Nurses Association, told me.

The Filipino connection is crucial because American hospitals are drastically short of nurses, with fewer students entering the profession and more nurses leaving to retire or because they are frustrated by unpleasant working conditions. Hospitals and nursing homes have been appealing to immigration authorities for help, and these officials have made it easier for nurses to obtain visas and the green cards that give them permanent status. Nurses in the Philippines seem to have benefited the most from these preferences. A 2001 national survey by the Commission on Graduates of Foreign Nursing Schools found that 41 percent of the 789 nurses who responded had received their education in the Philippines, with Canada second at 26 percent. There were more nurses from the Philippines than from all of Europe and South America combined. Compas estimated that there are 10,000 Filipino nurses in the three states that make up the New York City area.

It should be noted, however, that what has been helpful to the United States is hurting the Philippines. So large is the exodus of nurses that in November 2005 the Philippine Medical Association called a conference to discuss the crisis, which some described as an approaching collapse of the country's health system. A former health secretary, Dr. Jaime Galvez Tan, estimated that 100,000 nurses had left the Philippines to work abroad since 1994, with more leaving than can be replaced by nursing schools. Britain and the United States were the most popular destinations.

As I looked into the matter, it became easy to understand why the lure of America is irresistible. With enough overtime and experience, nurses can earn $80,000 a year, more than twenty times what they would make in the Philippines. The average pay at Montefiore is $75,000. That money allows them to buy homes in suburbs such as Bergenfield, New Jersey, where 3,133 Filipinos live in a community of 26,247. For a not particularly large suburban town, it manages to have a store that sells nurses' uniforms. And its mayor for a time, Robert C. Rivas, claimed to be the only Filipino mayor in the Northeast.

Nursing in America also allows Filipinos to send money back home to pay for finer schools for their brothers and sisters. Maria Dolores Egasan, an intensive-care nurse who was at the Aguirre twins' bedside after their second operation, came here in 1989 and married a Filipino security guard at the Metropolitan Museum of Art. She got her job at Montefiore through her mother-in-law, a nurse, who has five sons, four of whom are married to nurses. Her life is not exactly regal, but she has been able to put her brother, Ferdinand Colon, through Concordia College in Manila, and he is now a computer engineer in Saudi Arabia. She also put her sister, Fernandita, through secretarial school. For someone from her modest background, passing the test of the Council of Graduates of Foreign Nursing Schools seemed like a ticket to prosperity. "We came from a third world country, and I think this is our passport to earn a good living," said Egasan. "It's like winning the lotto if you pass the CGFNS. You will earn dollars and send them back home and send your brothers and sisters to school."

The prevalence of nurses has also helped give Filipinos here an uncommon and upscale profile for a group of immigrants: 57.8 percent of the city's 60,602 Filipinos are female; 49.7 percent have college degrees; and the median income of full-time workers is $41,000, far higher than the city median. Filipinos are now rising to senior levels in the health industry. When I spoke to her, Dr. Consuelo Dungca was a senior assistant vice president for clinical affairs at the city's Health and Hospitals Corporation. And of course, Compas, an instructor at Cabrini Medical Center, where 75 percent of the nursing staff is Filipino, was president of the New York State Nurses Association.

FILIPINOS OFTEN THINK of themselves as ethnic chameleons, people whose history of living under a variety of colonizers—Spanish, American, Japanese—allows them to adapt to any culture. The State Department estimates that there are 2 million Americans of Filipino ancestry, with concentrations in California, Hawaii, and Illinois larger than that in New York. But most Americans would be hard put to list Filipinos among the country's major immigrant groups, so scattered within the mainstream have they become. Indeed, Filipinos in the New York area have never formed a single Little Manila, no sharply defined enclave.

Jersey City, with 15,860 Filipinos, has the closest thing to one along aptly named Manila Avenue near the Holland Tunnel. Indeed, what brings Filipinos together in one place are the hospitals, and there are significant concentrations in neighborhoods with large hospitals, such as Elmhurst in Queens and Manhattan's Stuyvesant Town.

Since the north Bronx has such hospitals as Montefiore, North Central, Albert Einstein, Jacobi, and St. Barnabas in its midst, such neighborhoods as Norwood, Bedford Park, Belmont, Bronxdale, Fordham, Jerome Park, Morris Park, Pelham Parkway, Wakefield, and Williamsbridge together boast more than 2,500 Filipinos. Down Gun Hill Road from Montefiore is a grocery store, the Philippine Food Center, that sells imports including Lily's Peanut Butter, coconut gel, lychee nuts, as well as SkyFlakes crackers and *pancit* noodles. It also has a sizable stock of both amorous and violent Filipino videotapes. Simon Robles, the elderly man behind the counter when I sampled some of the foods, told me the store is actually owned by his daughter, Felicitas Carino, a nurse at Montefiore. Norwood has no Filipino restaurants, but Filipinos might take the subway to treat themselves to a paella at upscale Cendrillon in SoHo, or, if they want to be surrounded by compadres, drive across the George Washington Bridge to Bergenfield, New Jersey, which has a cluster of Filipino shops and a very good homespun restaurant, the Bamboo Grill. Filipinos flock to the Bamboo Grill on weekends to indulge another of their national passions—ballroom dancing.

Filipinos socialize heavily through church. Unlike other Asians, Filipinos hail from a country that is 85 percent Roman Catholic, the religion of their Spanish colonizers. In Norwood, St. Ann's on Bainbridge Avenue holds a service with Filipino liturgical flourishes on the first Sunday of the month. The choir is made up mostly of Filipino nurses. In heavily Filipino churches across the city, Filipinos take part in novenas—nine-day cycles of prayer devoted to Mary or other saints in the days preceding holidays—and they stage processions between churches. "Religion is still one unifying component," Bert Pelayo, publisher of the *Filipino Reporter*, told me.

Yet for these Filipinos beguiled by the American siren song, the price can be excruciating. When she came here in 1967 as one of the first Filipino nurses at Columbia Presbyterian Hospital in Washington

Heights, Clemencia Wong left behind her parents, four brothers, and a sister in Quezon City. Egasan found herself so busy working nights that in 2003 she decided to send her daughters, Jewel, twelve, and Jamila, six, back to the Philippines to be cared for by her mother. She keeps in touch with them with phone cards and finds her longing for them only partly relieved by the news of how well they are doing at the schools she can now afford. "That's your consolation," Egasan told me.

A good part of their earnings, the nurses say, pays for regular trips back to their homeland and for gifts for kinfolk. "Every time we go home, it's Christmas for them," Wong said. Still, the distance from family is a permanent ache and explains why Filipinos depend on compatriots, whom they call *kababayans* (fellow Filipinos). "There's a Filipino custom that everyone becomes your uncle and aunt," said Leonora A. G. Dubouzet, a Montefiore nursing administrator. "For those of us who don't have relatives, the friends become our next of kin. The kids will call a friend of their parents Tita—aunt—or Tito—uncle—as if they were blood relatives." And Wong added that "those who managed to have parents come here, those parents become the grandparents of all."

Wong and other nurses like her have remained close to the nurses they first got to know as greenhorns. "We were all single together, and we've had christenings, and now we're up to the weddings of our children," Wong said. Indeed, the network of nurses is so tight-knit that many find their spouses among the relatives of other nurses. Egasan, known as Dottie, came here in 1989 and met her husband through his sister, a nurse at St. Barnabas.

Sometimes the nurses' world seems a little too insular. Their spouses, the nurses say, complain that whenever Filipinos get together the conversation turns to shop talk: disagreeable patients, excessive paperwork, stressful workloads. One way they avoid the topic is by an evening of karaoke. Every Filipino home seems to have a microphone that allows friends to impersonate Sinatra and Elvis. It is another Filipino passion.

The nurses pride themselves on not spending their time exclusively with other Filipinos. "If you come to a Filipino gathering, they are so diverse," Dubouzet said. "I'm married to a Puerto Rican. Clemencia is married to a Chinese man." Blending easily into other cultures, said Dubouzet, means sometimes "we don't know who we are."

Some erosion of cultural tics is intentional, an adjustment to American medicine. Compas has had to train Filipino nurses not to politely nod yes when they mean no or can't understand a request. Like people from many cultures in Asia and Africa, Filipinos are embarrassed to refuse. She has also had to caution Filipinos not to get insulted when American nurses summon them with a come-hither finger gesture. "Back home, using your finger to [say] come here is like calling a dog, so a person will resent that," Compas said.

But nurses do worry that assimilation and homogenization are reshaping their lives. They are particularly concerned about who their American-bred children will become. Filipino youngsters, easily making friends in polyglot communities, are shedding Tagalog, the leading Filipino language, and picking up distinctly urban slants on life such as dressing in hip-hop clothing. *The Filipino Express* community newspaper reported in December 2005 on a conference of seventy mostly elderly Filipinas who met to talk about the displacement they feel in a country where kinship is not as valued as it is in their homeland. One retired nurse, Virginia B. Bersamin, who is on the teaching staff of the City University of New York, said that elderly parents find their American-raised offspring preoccupied with their own careers and with shopping for gadgets and luxuries. These grown children relate to their parents mostly as babysitters for the grandchildren.

Paunon, who has a daughter, fourteen, and a son, thirteen, worries that Filipino culture is so malleable that its values will dissolve in its peculiar encounter with so colossal and ravenous a culture as America's. "We're very vulnerable," he said. "Our kids have nothing to hold on to. We blend in so well with other groups, we forget we're Filipino."

NORWOOD

...

WHERE TO GO

Montefiore Medical Center (MAJOR NEW YORK INSTITUTION
AFFILIATED WITH ALBERT EINSTEIN MEDICAL SCHOOL) 111 EAST
210TH STREET; *(718) 920-4321*; WWW.MONTEFIORE.ORG

Philippine Food Center (SMALL MARKET THAT SELLS IMPORTS SUCH
AS COCONUT GEL, LYCHEE NUTS, AND SKYFLAKES CRACKERS)
234 EAST GUN HILL ROAD; *(718) 515-8405*

St. Ann's Church (CATHOLIC CHURCH THAT HOLDS FILIPINO-
THEMED SERVICES ON FIRST SUNDAY OF THE MONTH) 3519
BAINBRIDGE AVENUE; *(718) 547-9350*

WHERE TO EAT

NORWOOD BOASTS ONLY WORKADAY RESTAURANTS, SO FOR GOOD
FOOD HEAD SOUTH ACROSS BRONX PARK TO THE ARTHUR AVENUE/
BELMONT NEIGHBORHOOD AND TRY ROBERTO'S OR DOMINICK'S. FOR
FILIPINO FOOD,

Bamboo Grill (ACROSS THE GEORGE WASHINGTON BRIDGE) 54 SOUTH
WASHINGTON AVENUE, BERGENFIELD, N.J.; *(201) 384-5951*

Chapter 14

Bewildering Flavors in Richmond Hill

. . .

WALK DOWN THE MAIN STREET OF RICHMOND HILL IN QUEENS—Liberty Avenue—and you might think you are in Bombay or Calcutta.

Many faces on the sidewalk are the purplish bronze of the Indian subcontinent. The accents have a South Asian singsong. Saris drape the shop windows and the smell of curry is everywhere. But almost all the residents in this neighborhood are neither Indian, nor Pakistani, nor Bangladeshi—they are not even from the subcontinent—and more discriminating New Yorkers have come to know the difference. The Indians of Richmond Hill are actually from the South American country of Guyana or from the Caribbean islands of Trinidad and Tobago. They are the descendants of Indians who almost 200 years ago crossed the Indian and Atlantic oceans to plant roots in the Western Hemisphere, but in that time they have evolved a distinct culture. When that still-raw culture encounters the ancient Indian civilization on the alien soil of New York, the result seems to be a chafing uneasiness or at least a cool distance.

This may surprise some New Yorkers. After all, immigrants have usually found their first foothold in the neighborhoods of their more established ethnic kin—even if the welcome mat was not always wholeheartedly rolled out. Irish-brogue newcomers moved into cloverleaf enclaves of the northwest Bronx, off-the-boat Italians went into a Bensonhurst adorned with front-yard Madonnas, and Soviet Jewish refugees found shelter among the knish parlors of Brighton Beach. But such an easy osmosis does not always happen. The Guyanese and Trinidadians of Indian descent have ended up living quite apart from their forerunners. Though they share a religion, language, and heritage, these Indo-Caribbeans have not felt particularly embraced by the more flourishing Indian communities of Flushing, Elmhurst, and Jackson Heights in Queens, nor have they made overtures to embrace the Indians. Instead they have cobbled together their own fragrant neighborhood of roti, sari, and gold shops among the row houses of Richmond Hill. "From my experience, we're not Indian," Latchman Budhai, my cicerone to this flavorful neighborhood, told me. "We look like Indians, but we're not Indian."

He is a graying man in his late fifties with a broad salt-and-pepper mustache and the sturdy build of a policeman, which he was for many years in Guyana. His grandfather was born in India and made the journey to the northern coast of South America in 1880. In Georgetown, the Guyanese capital, Budhai wanted to become a teacher and found his ambition frustrated. In a Christian-dominated government, such jobs were reserved for Christians. He came here in 1976 on vacation and decided to seize America's opportunities, working for many years as a security officer at the Mayflower Hotel on Central Park. He helped found the Maha Lakshmi Mandir, a Hindu temple whose members are Guyanese Americans, in 1983 and was for years its president. As such he got to know Queens politicians and became a go-between with bigwigs such as Helen Marshall, the borough president (whose mother is Guyanese), and the Reverend Floyd Flake, the former congressman. In greenhorn groups there is often one canny wheeler-dealer like him, someone who despite a foreign stamp manages to penetrate the Byzantine ways of power brokers. Yiddish-speaking immigrants might have called him a *macher*.

Yet he talked candidly about the belittlement he has often felt at being thought not quite up to the standards of New York's Indians. He tried to form a civic association with Sikhs and other Indians and failed. He has not been accepted by Sikh credit unions. "I was totally excluded, [or] should I use the word 'ostracized,' " he said. "The Indians from India stick together." His best illustration concerned his wife, Serojini. In 1983, she won a beauty pageant for Indians sponsored by the United Nations, but she was never awarded the top prize, a trip to India. The organizers, Budhai said, had learned she was Guyanese.

I heard other stories like that not only in Richmond Hill, but just about the same time I gave a talk on ethnic New York to a journalism class at Baruch College in Manhattan, and one student, Priya Mahabir, a twenty-nine-year-old senior, happened to be Guyanese. She was born in Georgetown, and her family has a copy of their ancestral pioneer's Indian birth certificate. In her case it is that of her great-grandmother, issued in the northern state of Uttar Pradesh, India's most populous. She told me that Indian friends of hers sometimes distinguish between East Indians and West Indians, and have told her she's "not really Indian."

"I would be really offended by that," she said. "Indian people have to be better than you are. People from India think of us as being coolies, and that's something we find very offensive. Indian people are very much into status, so they sort of look down upon people that they feel [are] beneath their status."

To appreciate the chasm between these kindred communities requires an understanding that actually long-settled immigrants and their raw cousins have not always gotten along. Historians have noted how, during the late nineteenth century, German Jews, a comfortable generation removed from Europe, kept less-polished Jewish arrivals from Eastern Europe at a condescending arm's length, although many created the institutions that helped the newcomers assimilate. Cubans who fled the island after Castro's revolution were sometimes less than welcoming to the refugees of the 1980 Mariel boatlift.

"Certainly the major impulse is to help the less fortunate parts of the community," John Mollenkopf, director of the Center for Urban Research, told me. "But, at the same time, people giving help are the more assimilated, whereas people who need help are at the bottom and don't have the prestige and status. There's more of a tendency of the more established people wanting to distinguish themselves from the newcomers."

My family too felt that some of the lower-middle-class Jews, while almost always warm and friendly, needed to maintain a relationship of mentor and protégé, of expert and novice, with us. They were children of Eastern European immigrants and we were actual immigrants. Any signs that we were exceeding our ranking—by buying too pricey bar mitzvah suits, by gaining admission to the Bronx High School of

Science—might have prompted compliments, but ones laced with a touch of resentment.

Most Guyanese, and the smaller number of Trinidadians in Richmond Hill, are descendants of Indians who were contracted to work on Caribbean sugar plantations in the decades after slavery was outlawed in the British colonies in 1838. They were poor, lower-caste people mainly from the states of Uttar Pradesh and Bihar. While they planned to return, they often found that their families had disowned them as tribal defectors and did not want them back. Spurred on by rumors of fortunes made, the influx of penniless indentured laborers persisted into the first decades of the twentieth century.

There were so many Indians, they eventually formed a majority in Guyana, the former British Guiana, and 40 percent of Trinidad and Tobago. They also became prominent leaders. Cheddi Jagan was elected Guyana's president in 1992 in what were regarded as the first free elections since independence in 1966. Rohan Kanhai became a legendary cricketeer. V. S. Naipaul won the Nobel Prize for his novels, including *A House for Mr. Biswas,* which portrayed in darkly comic fashion the sometimes hapless culture of ethnic Indians in Trinidad trying to break free of ironbound Indian traditions.

Indo-Caribbeans began immigrating to New York not only because of the liberalized immigrations law of 1965 but also because of political and economic upheavals in Guyana and Trinidad. Indians from Asia had settled in New York slightly earlier and in larger numbers, but the economic and educational divide between these groups—the Indians tended to be doctors, engineers, and chemists, the Guyanese babysitters and blue-collar workers—made bridging their diverging civilizations all the more formidable. "While these two groups share a common ancestry, their historical experiences and the timing and nature of their immigration set them apart," Khandelwal, the Indian immigrant who directs the Asian American Center at Queens College, told me.

For most Guyanese, even those who remember their India-born grandparents, the passage of time has chiseled away much of their Indian character. It has diminished their fluency with Hindi and given their English patois a more rhythmic lilt and sense of humor. A Guyanese might say "Yuh can't suck cane and blow whistle" as a way of avoiding two tasks at the same time, or "When you want fuh swim river yuh gat fuh plunge inside furss" to encourage taking a risk. Guyanese curries are less spicy. A shop that serves the flat roti bread filled with meat is a distinctly Caribbean conception; Indians eat curries with a tortilla-like bread to accompany their main course or to sop up the gravy, not as a filling. Guyanese and Trinidadian music, while Indian influenced, is marked by a faster West Indian style that has come to be known as chutney soca.

Tofayel Chowdhury, owner of Fabric Depot and one of a handful of shopkeepers on Liberty Avenue who actually come from India, observed that virtually no Guyanese wear saris every day as many Indian women do. Guyanese wear them on ceremonial occasions and their palette is more pastel than vivid. Even Guyanese names are distinguishing, with last names often derived from Indian first names, an artifact of the demeaning way British planters addressed their Guyanese workers.

While Guyanese parents limit their children's dating choices to serious suitors, they do not insist on choosing spouses, something many Indian parents still do. This is particularly true for young women. Mahabir, the Baruch student, told me that "your parents wouldn't want you to have five or six guys before getting married—one or two at the most. With women, parents want to know the intention of the person dating. We've gotten away from arranged marriage, but it's not quite there."

The 2000 census identified 24,662 people in Richmond Hill who were born in Guyana and 7,384 who were born in Trinidad—numbers widely regarded as gross undercounts. These figures also do not include the Guyanese and Trinidadians born here. In Richmond Hill, almost all the Guyanese and Trinidadians are of Indian descent. But in wider New York many Guyanese and Trinidadians are black, and they have chosen to live in West Indian neighborhoods of Brooklyn such as Crown Heights, East Flatbush, and Canarsie, showing that a racial divide is alive in the West Indies as well. In all, the census counted 130,496 Guyanese-born residents in all of New York City, 43 percent of whom were black, and 88,794 from Trinidad and Tobago, 78 percent of whom were black. Racial data for Indo-Caribbeans is quite misleading, however, a numerical reflection of their ambiguous position. The main census form gives Guyanese only a few racial categories to choose from, and Indian (as opposed to Native American) is not one. Guyanese, though, would find it strange to identify themselves as Asian, white, black, or Hispanic.

This confusion about ethnic identity is apparent in Richmond Hill. It is a 150-year-old neighborhood on Jamaica's southwestern edge that is filled with flamboyant Victorians and the high-stooped wood-frame and brick row homes known as Archie Bunkers. It is those houses that draw Guyanese to this Queens pocket, for in Guyana, everyone owns a home, however humble. Until thirty years ago, most occupants of those houses were descendants of Irish, Italian, and German immigrants. The latter's presence was evident in the Triangle Hofbrau, a 150-year-old hotel and tavern on a triangular piece of land that was patronized by Babe Ruth and Mae West and the last time I looked was still there, but as a medical building.

There is much that to an outsider appears Indian. The main temple, Budhai's Maha Lakshmi Mandir, which opened in 1994 in a warehouse on 101st Avenue, is indistinguishable from a typical Hindu temple in its assortment of divine statues and paintings of the elephant-headed god, Ganesh, and the four-armed goddess of wealth and beauty, Lakshmi. Every Sunday Guyanese and Trinidadian Hindus make offerings there of fruits and flowers placed on elaborate altars. The temple offers evening classes in the sacred language of Sanskrit and in Hindi dance and music. Budhai even thinks Guyanese are more devout than Indians. "We keep the religion more than they do—this is a fact," he told me.

Liberty Avenue's video stores are stocked with romantic musicals from India's Bollywood industry, which are particularly popular with Guyanese girls. Natasha Warikoo, a Harvard doctoral student in sociology who studied Guyanese teenagers, pointed out that these girls look "to an Indian culture based in India rather than the Caribbean for 'authentic' Indianness." Gold stores have the same appeal as they do in Indian neighborhoods, though the jewelry on Liberty Avenue is less deftly fashioned.

Richmond Hill's restaurants, though, are distinctly unlike those in an Indian enclave and are a reflection of a people with roots in poverty who haven't yet grown accustomed to white tablecloths and Muzak. The most characteristic are the shops that sell roti—curry-filled wraps—and there are one or two on practically every block: Richie's Roti Shop, Singh's Roti Shop, Bobby's Roti Shop, and St. John's Restaurant, which by some estimates has the best goat curry roti. Most are about as elegant as a Blimpie's, with a deli-style glass counter of hot trays from which servers scoop up various stews and fill round flat breads. There are fancier places, such as Kaieteur on Lefferts Boulevard, named after a 741-foot-high Guyanese waterfall, that do offer white tablecloths and savory dishes including rice and duck. There are also Guyanese bakeries—Brown Betty and Little Guyana—that sell such peculiarly Guyanese treats as blackeye cakes, currant roll, and pineapple tarts, and the longtime J & B West Indian Grocery, which stocks Caribbean products including bitter-melon, taro root, and sugar cane.

Every spring, Guyanese and Trinidadians have their own celebration of Phagwah, a Hindu holiday that Indians call Holi but which Indo-Caribbeans have infused with the spirit and high jinks of Latin American Carnaval or Mardi Gras. The streets of Richmond Hill are ablaze with floats teeming with people in Indian costumes. Musicians play Indian drums and cymbals, even if the rhythms are Caribbean. Children dressed in white clothing spray one another with red, yellow, and blue dyes from old Formula 409 spray bottles.

While the coolness between Indians and Guyanese was palpable to me, some Indians I spoke to thought too much is made of the chill. Uma Sengupta, a native Indian who is a Democratic assembly district leader, said the distance between Indians and Indo-Caribbeans simply represents an abrasive encounter of two different cultures. There need not be any haughtiness involved. "Even if they don't mix, that doesn't mean they look down," she said. Some Guyanese leaders also prefer to see the glass half full. Dr. Dhanpaul Narine, who was an unsuccessful candidate for city council in 2005, contended in a letter to me that Indo-Caribbeans "have always held India close to their heart" and show a keen interest in news of India. Whenever there is an earthquake there, Guyanese and Trinidadians raise tens of thousands of dollars in Richmond Hill for relief.

Warikoo, the sociology doctoral student, feels too much is made of there being a separate Guyanese enclave in Richmond Hill, pointing out that the Indian subcontinent is so fragmented linguistically, religiously, and geographically that many of its subcultures here have carved out their own neighborhoods. Indians from Gujarat, for example, have clustered in Forest Hills, Bangladeshis in Ozone Park. Almost 5,000 Sikhs—native Indians with a distinctive religion that blends Hinduism and Islam—have settled in Richmond Hill to be near their main temple. They are recognizable by the turbans the men wear.

But many Indians and Guyanese acknowledge the arm's-length reserve between the two communities. Outar Pooran, sixty-eight, who is retired from a porter's job at the Giorgio Armani store in Manhattan and is active in Budhai's temple, said some Indians speak to him with the expression "you Guyanese people." "When I speak, I say, 'We Indians,' " said Pooran, whose grandfather left India in the 1880s. "They believe our grandparents quit India, so we are like strangers to them."

In telling me this story, Pooran intimated something that Guyanese do not speak much about explicitly because it is humiliating but that Budhai and others candidly articulated. Guyanese detect a lingering snobbish elitism among the Indians they encounter here, a throwback to the caste system. In Guyana the hierarchy has withered to virtual insignificance, while it survives in India—and among some Indians here. The Indians who immigrated in the 1960s were largely from higher castes, not the lowborn castes of the original Guyanese contract laborers. Sengupta, the Democratic leader, points out that Indians came here to fill gaps in skilled occupations, and in time they obtained green cards and citizenship. By contrast, more Guyanese either came here as visitors and overstayed visas or spirited across borders.

Kris Oditt, the Guyanese owner of Brown Betty Restaurant, says Guyanese have much warmer relations with other diaspora Indians here—Indians from formerly British African colonies such as Uganda, South Africa, and Kenya. Marriages between Guyanese and Trinidadians are common; Budhai's son, for example, is engaged to a young woman from Trinidad. Marriages with Indian immigrants, though not unheard of, are far less common.

Many Richmond Hill residents say that attitudes are already changing among generations born here, that the great American ethnic blender is working its magic. Bobbie Ramnath, a travel agent, notices that Guyanese are arranging trips to India to search for their roots. When a Sikh spiritual leader was pummeled into unconsciousness in 2004 by a group of hooligans who ridiculed his turban, Guyanese joined in the protests. Guyanese in Queens are also running for local elective office and forming alliances with all sorts of ethnic organizations, even occasionally those representing Indians. "Politics will bring all of us closer," said Pooran, mentioning such Guyanese candidates as Narine and Taj Rajkumar, a City University professor who has run for office. "We'll communicate more, get to understand one another more."

Mahabir, the Baruch College senior, said that more Guyanese and Indian students at her school are crossing ethnic boundaries. She has already formed close friendships with Indians who are children of immigrants. When she walks into a classroom, she told me, the first people she notices are those of Indian descent. "We exchange a smile," she said. It doesn't matter to her whether they are from India or Guyana—and she feels her Guyanese identity may not matter much to the Indians either.

ANOTHER GROUP OF OFFSHOOTS from the Indian subcontinent is reshaping—some would say saving—a neighborhood not so far from Richmond Hill that until recent years was notorious for the city's worst murder rate. The neighborhood is Brooklyn's East New York, and it is a low-rise, largely black and Latino neighborhood on the Queens border that since the 1960s has been marred by run-down buildings, failing schools, drug bazaars, and soaring crime.

For the first half of the twentieth century, East New York was a thriving community of blue-collar Irish, Italians, and Jews who were glad to afford the plainspoken brick and wood-frame row houses or pay rents in the tenement-like walk-ups. Half of working-class Brooklyn seemed to shop on Pitkin Avenue, and the high-priced Fortunoff chain got its start in the 1920s as a series of shops along Livonia Avenue. In the mid-1950s, my off-the-boat father searched futilely for an uncle who had come here years earlier and ended up close friends with the uncle's in-laws on Alabama Avenue. Sam Lessen, a worker for the state Workers' Compensation Board, and his wife, Fanny, owned one of those flimsy wood-frame houses.

But East New York was cursed by a lethal brew of inept local leaders and foolish big-government decisions. Black families from nearby Brownsville, many of them displaced by urban renewal, were steered to empty homes and apartments, accelerating the departure of middle-class whites, some of whom simply abandoned their houses as unsellable. Meanwhile, the federal government foreclosed on too many mortgages, leaving a rash of hollow-eyed buildings ripe for arson. There were outbursts of rioting. One enclave that seemed to escape the ruination was Highland Park, a leafy plateau whose grand houses with views of midtown Manhattan are popular with black politicians and pastors. Still, by the late 1970s more than half the residential core of East New York had been leveled into rubble-strewn lots, and that blight lingered for two decades. Even five years ago developers were skittish about investing. Today, though, nearly every vacant lot, even in the most run-down areas, is spoken for. Builders are putting up two- and three-family row houses, and African American and Latino police officers, nurses, and civil servants are sprucing up older houses.

All this activity has been augmented by a group of newcomers to these parts—immigrants from Bangladesh. The country was once a Muslim-dominated part of British-ruled India, then became the eastern flank of a decolonialized Pakistan, and since 1971 has been independent. With 141 million people, Bangladesh is one of the world's poorest countries, plagued by calamitous floods and political volatility. That's why Bangladeshis emigrate. Until recent years they settled in more decorous communities such as Ozone Park. But they are now spilling over into the badlands of East New York.

Women in burkas are now a common sight along Pitkin Avenue, once Brooklyn's Herald Square. Several mosques have opened, and groceries sell halal meats. In 2004, one company, Millennium Homes, was building twenty-two two- and three-family homes on Shepherd Avenue and Essex Street off Pitkin, most of which were snapped up by Bangladeshis. Millennium's sales agent was Shariar Uddin, who had worked as a waiter at the World Trade Center and on September 11, 2001, was supposed to show up for the 4 p.m. shift. Now he was pitching houses to his countrymen, people such as Mohammed Hamid, a fifty-two-year-old engineer. Although the sidewalk was warped and flecked with weeds and there was no decent grocery or dry cleaner nearby, Uddin was emphasizing the neighborhood's future and pointing out that the houses were right next to the Shepherd Avenue subway station. He also noted that a short ride away on Liberty Avenue in Ozone Park, there was Al Amin Grocery, which stocks Bangladeshi okra and dates, frozen paratha bread, and newspapers flown in from the capital of Dhaka. As Hamid listened, even the neighborhood's racial mix, something he once might have been wary of, seemed a plus. "You need to mix up with American culture, and this is a neighborhood with mixed people," said Hamid as he put a down payment on a three-family home.

Rashida Khanam chose to buy a three-family house in East New York rather than in a more flourishing area such as Astoria, Queens, where she had been renting. She is a widow in her late forties who has been in this country twelve years and supports herself and two college-going daughters by selling bread in a Manhattan bakery. East New York prices, unlike those in Astoria, were affordable, as she found out on periodic visits to a niece who was already living in East New York. She looked for evidence of any unpleasantness such as crime but "I didn't see anything bad." "I think the neighborhood will be OK," she told me.

Some of the forces upgrading East New York are the same as those that have been gentrifying once-crime-ridden neighborhoods such as Harlem. Crime across the city has plummeted since 1990, when a record 2,245 murders were recorded—almost four times current levels. The breathtaking improvements in the reliability and ambience of the subways—even the ability to transfer from buses to trains without paying another fare—have helped revive neighborhoods far from midtown. Municipal government, starting with the Koch administration in the late 1970s, can claim credit for rebuilding properties seized by the city for tax delinquency or getting nonprofit organizations such as Nehemiah Houses—active in East New York—to rebuild. Tax abatements and city-financed construction primed the pump for private investment, encouraged banks to lend, and spurred insurers to insure.

And the city's population has rebounded after falling close to 7 million in 1980. The Department of City Planning estimates that 8.15 million now live in the five boroughs and that more than 9 million could be living here within twenty years. Much of that spurt is the result of immigration, and all those additional guests from overseas need shelter. Since comparatively little new housing is affordable in established neighborhoods, buyers and renters with shallow pockets have had to look at the city's ragged margins, gambling on once-moribund blocks such as those in East New York.

Many immigrants also look to real estate as a way to make their American fortune, often using the income stream from renting half of a two-family home as their springboard. It's not a coincidence that many of the neighborhoods gentrifying now are full of two- and three-family homes. These newcomers from overseas have been open to living among other races and willing to risk their life savings on shabby blocks.

"We're one of the last frontiers," William S. Wilkins, an official of the Local Development Corporation of East New York, told me. "It's the cheapest game in town. Where else are you going to find houses for two hundred to three hundred thousand dollars in Brooklyn?"

The sprucing up of homes has rippled across East New York. The area's surviving factories and warehouses, where products including pasta and light fixtures are made or stored, are humming with workers, with a vacancy rate estimated at less than 10 percent compared to 25 percent a decade ago. The new Gateway Mall by Jamaica Bay, with its Home Depot and Target, attracts New Yorkers from miles around. The neighborhood's most notorious school, Thomas Jefferson High School, where in 1992 two teenagers were shot to death an hour before a visit by Mayor Dinkins, has been divided into five more manageable mini-schools, with such themes as civil rights and fire safety.

"It's not Shangri-la," Wilkins said. "But if you've been renting your whole life, this is the American dream."

But the American dream can sometimes get twisted into a nightmare. Just a half year after I wrote about East New York's revival for *The New York Times,* I had to return because the Bangladeshi buyers of Millennium Homes were calling to say they had lost the homes they were promised. In six months, they said, prices had soared $50,000 to $75,000 higher, and the builder realized he could fetch far more money by selling the dwellings to newer buyers, even if that meant breaking contracts. When I arrived, working-class Bangladeshis were standing in a driving rain outside their unfinished houses. Under a canopy of umbrellas, they were huddled mournfully with children, baby carriages, and hand-lettered signs that read "We Want House" and "We Want Justice." Because of the rain, the ink was running like tears on those signs. It was a small demonstration by New York standards, no more than twenty people in the soggy dirt of a construction zone on a bleak Monday afternoon. But it signified how much the protestors craved owning homes like other Americans and how furious they were that their hopes had been dashed.

The protestors included Salimul Hoque, a thirty-nine-year-old housepainter who came from Bangladesh three years before, and people like him. He lived with his wife, Khaleda, and their two young boys and a girl in a rented house plagued by a balky refrigerator, mice, and rats. "One day a rat bit me on my toe," Khaleda told me angrily. Hoque had put down $10,000 on a house valued at $515,000, hoping he could bid farewell to that rental. Another protestor was Nazmul Chowdhury, a gray-bearded man of fifty-six with gold-rimmed glasses who worked providing information to patients at Maimonides Medical Center. Standing in the rain with his wife, Baiby, trying to explain his predicament, he seemed overcome. He claimed he was supposed to close on his $485,000 house on March 31, 2004, but that the house was unfinished and his $10,000 deposit had been returned. "I've been in this country twenty-five years, and this is my dream," he said. "I've never owned a house. I want my house back; I don't want the money."

There too was Rashida Khanam, the bakery worker who had been so exuberantly expectant six months before. Now her mood was very different, though respectful of American ways, she bottled up her grievances. But her daughter Tanzia Lokman, a twenty-one-year-old student at St. John's University, voiced them for her. She was particularly angry with Millennium's sales director, Shariar Uddin. "He promised us the house would be ready by January 2004," she said, pointing out that the rent for their Astoria apartment could have gone toward a mortgage.

The paradox was that Uddin was there with them, and had been the person who alerted me to the demonstration. He had quit Millennium because he was upset about what he called the company's deception, could not participate in an "injustice to my clients." Yet some of his customers were furious with him. "He's the biggest culprit," Tanzia Lokman said. "He trapped us. He sold all of us on that company."

I called Danny Vaswani, the president of Millennium, who contended that the families had failed to satisfy income and other requirements needed for mortgages, and had exhausted several extensions. He denied that he was exploiting a surging market. But the protesting families brought letters from banks along with a mortgage broker, Shah S. Haque, to prove that they qualified handily for mortgages. Mohammed F. Hussein, a sales manager, and Hamid, the engineer, produced binding commitment letters from banks that their mortgages had been approved. "I think he's playing a trick so people leave him alone and he can sell it off at a bigger price," Hamid said of Vaswani.

A lawyer for some of the buyers, Dennis R. Sawh, said that the only outstanding issue they faced was the need for an appraisal, which usually requires the builder to complete the house. Since seventeen of the twenty-two houses had not been completed at that point and therefore had not received certificates of occupancy, his clients' mortgage commitments had expired, creating what Sawh said was a Catch-22.

Uddin tried to mollify those disappointed with him; nevertheless, he was a powerful ally. "He's thinking these people don't have enough courage, enough support, and enough money to go to court," Uddin said of his former boss. "These people are working hard, and their only dream is buying a house."

The issues were still bubbling at the start of 2007, and Uddin told me he too felt exploited. "They used me," he said. "They used my contacts and my expertise to sell these houses."

RICHMOND HILL

...

WHERE TO GO

Liberty Avenue (A GUYANESE BAZAAR, WITH ROTI, JEWELRY AND CLOTHING SHOPS)

Maha Lakshmi Mandir (COLORFUL GUYANESE HINDU TEMPLE) 121-15 101ST AVENUE; *(718) 805-4988*

WHERE TO EAT

Brown Betty (BAKERY) 129-06 LIBERTY AVENUE; *(718) 323-6438*

Kaieteur Restaurant & Sports Bar (FORMAL DINING) 87-12 LEFFERTS BOULEVARD; *(718) 850-0787*

Richie's Roti Shop 118-06 LIBERTY AVENUE; *(718) 835-7255*

St. John's Restaurant (ROTI SHOP) 118-14 LIBERTY AVENUE; *(718) 322-5200*

Chapter 15

Arrivederci, Bensonhurst

. . .

WHAT SAL CALABRESE HAS ALWAYS LOVED ABOUT BENSONHURST, the city's largest Italian neighborhood, is that it provides the intimacies of a village. "If I walk out," he said, "I will say hello to fifteen or twenty people and they to me. 'Hi, Sal. How are you? How's your father?' Like the old days. We're from different places in Italy, but we live in the same town."

But these days Calabrese worries that Brooklyn's Bensonhurst is losing the congenial feeling that comes from a place of common habits and pleasures. Bensonhurst is losing its Italians. There are fewer men sipping espresso in cafés, fewer teenagers hanging out Italian-style on corners, fewer bakeries, pork stores, and restaurants on the main street, Eighteenth Avenue. The faces in the neighborhood are increasingly Chinese, Russian, or Middle Eastern. The 2000 census indicated that the number of residents of Italian descent in Bensonhurst had fallen to 59,112, little more than half that of two decades before, when Italians made up 80 percent of the neighborhood. More recent estimates by the census indicate that the decline is persisting unabated. Calabrese volunteers that he is part of that movement. His parents still live in the neighborhood, and he runs a thriving real estate agency there, but in 2000 he moved to Bedminster, New Jersey, to a thirty-four-acre farm where he breeds Arabian horses.

What makes the decline in Bensonhurst more remarkable—and rueful—than that in Claudio Caponigro's East Harlem is that East Harlem is an old story; it began its decline in the 1950s. But in those years Bensonhurst was just coming into full flower. Bensonhurst was "the country," a giant step up for the descendants of dirt-poor Sicilian and Neapolitan immigrants, the place they settled after enduring the tenements of Little Italy and East Harlem. By shoveling rocks to build the subways and stitching garments in sweatshops, they had accumulated the nest eggs that allowed them to flee those first squalid footholds. Now as I walked through the streets of brick row houses with flapping American flags that gave Bensonhurst its characteristic look, I could see that this second-stage Italian village was also splintering and, like Astoria, this classic is fading.

Bensonhurst's apex may have been reached around the time John Travolta made *Saturday Night Fever*, the 1977 film that captured the flashy lifestyles of young Italians in Brooklyn's Bay Ridge and Bensonhurst. These were not off-the-boat immigrants, but Italians who could finally afford cars, dance lessons, and razzle-dazzle clothes, who could dream about a triumph on the dance floor instead of a job in construction. But Italians have advanced to a third stage of the immigrant ascent. The children who grew up in those working-class and middle-class rows of brick homes are, like Calabrese, now professionals, academics, managers, and businesspeople who want suburban homes with backyards of grass, not concrete. They may come to Bensonhurst on Saturday or Sunday to shop for mozzarella or cannoli, but they no longer want to live there.

Indeed, Italian Americans are declining sharply in numbers in all the boroughs except relatively suburban Staten Island. Many New Yorkers worry not only that they will lose the Italian neighborhoods but also that the Italian spice in the city's personality will fade away. After all, it has been Italians who have given New York City much of its charm in emblems as telltale as Fiorello La Guardia and "fuhgeddaboutit," who gave us pizza and *The Godfather*, who gave us Sinatra belting out "New York, New York," DiMaggio cantering across center field, and Pavarotti at the Met (adopted New Yorkers all, but why quibble). The census shows that the number of New Yorkers of Italian descent has fallen below 700,000, compared with more than 1 million in 1980—a number that had held steady in all the years after World War II. In 1980 the proportion of Italian New Yorkers stood at 14.22 percent. It is down to 8.65 percent. (The decline parallels that of most whites; the number of New

Yorkers of Irish descent has declined from 647,733 in 1980 to 420,810 in 2000, or just 5 percent.) In the 1980s, Bensonhurst was a favorite stamping ground of John Gotti and his mob family. His son, Junior Gotti, favors Long Island. It is fitting that *The Sopranos* was filmed in Jersey suburbs such as Belleville.

This is all surprising to those who savor the anthropological and sociological rhythms of New York. More than any other ethnic group, Italians are famed for their diehard allegiance to their neighborhoods. When the Jews and Irish seeped out of the south and central Bronx, fleeing the influx of black and Hispanic newcomers, Italians stayed put. They clustered fortresslike in a pocket around Arthur and Belmont avenues, completely surrounded by black and Hispanic families but sustaining their village of tidy houses and pork shops as immaculately—and safely—as ever. Sociologist Jerome Krase says that long after East New York became a black and Latino neighborhood feared by many whites, he would find four or five Italian families on a dead-end street clinging cockily to what remained of their turf. But even a reputation for no-holds-barred toughness could not stand up to the power of a more subversive force— upward mobility.

Inevitable as population change is, a hemorrhage of Italians would be a blow to the city's character. Take just one area—politics. Italian enclaves have been a seedbed for some of the city's and state's most prominent leaders, with such names as Giuliani, Cuomo, and Ferraro. Writer Gay Talese thinks of Giuliani, who in 2007 was running for the Republican presidential nomination, as the first Italian politician to win widespread approval across the nation, a person who managed, by his performance as a crime fighter and on September 11, to shuck off the provincial "of the neighborhood" aura that burdened Cuomo. But Richard Alba, a distinguished professor of sociology at the State University of New York at Albany, predicts that, Giuliani notwithstanding, Italian politicians will become less common in the five boroughs because Italians are increasingly assimilated and dispersed and voting more often on issues rather than on ethnicity. "Giuliani is probably not the last hurrah, but one can imagine that the influence of white ethnics on the city will decline as newer groups striving for power—immigrants and non-whites—succeed in achieving it," he said.

There is, however, a wide difference of opinion on whether a shrinking Italian population will change the city's characteristic New Yorkness. Italians, after all, have left such a durable imprint on New Yorkers' dialect and physical gestures, on the city's food and music, on such stereotypical attitudes as a wariness of authority. Yet, in a long conversation I had with Gay Talese, who chronicled Italian life in America through his memoir, *Unto the Sons*, he was not lamenting some of that passing. Many of the signature images, he told me, hark back to a time when Italians, in the public eye, represented the urban underclass. He recalled how the Italians who came over at the turn of the century and before World War I were basically landless farmers—*contadini*—from Sicily, Naples, and elsewhere in the south who were fleeing the bitter poverty spawned by the upheaval of forging a unified Italy. Illiterate and unskilled, they took the first jobs they could—the women sewing garments, the men picking up garbage or paving streets—and found grubby railroad-flat apartments near work, with a tub in the kitchen and a toilet in the common hallway.

Those early Italian immigrants brought with them what Talese called a "village mentality" that has lasted more than four generations—an insularity that demanded tight family ties and the kind of loyalty from friends evident a generation later in political dynasties such as the Cuomos and the clannish structure of the Five Families that make up the Mafia. Those pioneers spoke Italian, cooked Italian, married Italian, and made their families the core around which their lives revolved. The father ruled, and more often than not he wanted his son to follow in his footsteps, even if that meant forgoing college for a job in construction. The stellar Hollywood director Francis Ford Coppola, Talese pointed out, still uses family and friends to make his movies.

But that insularity has been dissipating as Italians get university degrees, clamber up the ladder in the professions, business, and government, and marry out of their clans. Italians such as Yale president Bart Giamatti, novelist Don DeLillo, and, of course, Supreme Court Justices Antonin Scalia and Samuel Alito, Jr., are increasingly those who represent America's Italians.

But the old ways haven't vanished. Talese, who is in his mid-seventies, volunteers that he himself still retains much of the "village mentality." Although at the time we talked he lived in a Manhattan town house, was married to Nan A. Talese, a prominent book editor of Irish descent, and was a regular at Elaine's, he visited his ninety-five-year-old Calabrian mother twice a week in his hometown, Ocean City, New Jersey, and took her to a restaurant and then a casino so she could play the slot machines that give her pleasure. "I'm still a hometown, small-town guy," he told me.

Obviously, as one of the nation's premier nonfiction writers, he is not as small-town a guy as his father was. And Italians no longer have to be attached to colonies like Bensonhurst. As life moves on there is an aching sadness in the passing of a time and a culture, a painful acknowledgment that the era can never be re-created, except in books and in Hollywood. In a memory piece for *The New York Times* and in a novel he self-published called *Johnny Once*, Robert Gangi, a second-generation Sicilian American who is a leading expert on prison reform, remembered the "loud, gaudy" Bensonhurst where he lived for several years as a child and where he visited every weekend on trips to see his grandmother.

It was "a town of big skies and low buildings," he wrote, where men were called Tiny, Husky, and Johnny Once (for a person who came around once in a while). The street-corner arguments were over the relative merits of a Lincoln Continental and a Cadillac Eldorado, and one word, spoken with a slight peremptory menace, "Definitely!" could end any discussion.

I want to stand again on barely sunlit corners and flirt with the girls with showy hairdos, tight pants and heels, popping Chiclets like tiny firecrackers—sadly a lost art. I want to wisecrack with the boys with their short sleeves rolled up, shiny hair and loud voices, moving and chattering with nervous energy, more Travolta than John. I want to drive down the busy, narrow streets, squeezing past small delivery trucks parked in front of markets and restaurants, while I watch middle-aged women lugging shopping bags, and expressionless old men sitting on little porches listening to the ballgame on the radio. I want to walk to church on Sunday morning, the unlikely quiet on the streets, the absence of humans and honking cars, the only sign of life the aroma of pasta sauces—gravy, we called it—drifting out of kitchen windows of small brick houses.

A short time after he wrote the piece, I spoke to Gangi, a tall, stylish man with an open smile and a rangy Italian strut. This time he remembered the "strong physical presence," sense of style, and "grand, generous gestures" of the neighborhood's handsome men. He showed me a 1930s photograph of his father and three uncles, all nattily decked out in fedoras and double-breasted suits, proud of who they were and how they looked. "Bensonhurst was a village," he said. "There was something very secure about belonging to something that was self-contained and well defined and was foreign to people outside of it. Often I go to a suburban area and I feel like I could be Anywhere, USA. But Bensonhurst was well defined in its houses, its people, its mannerisms. There was a warmth and strength of feeling about the people who lived there that was engaging. They had definite ways of eating, of expressing themselves. It was all very good-humored and reflected the desire to stay connected, to eat, sing, and have fun together."

But there was a flip side to the village's virtues. "The other side of the coin was that it was parochial and very limiting," he said. He spoke of commonplace expressions of prejudice he often heard, even against other Catholic groups such as the Irish. "Grown-ups were very judgmental and expressed their opinion and could be hard on people who disagreed with them," he said.

But something subversive was occurring in Bensonhurst, as it was among the rest of America's Italians. Children were leaving the neighborhood for college, to local schools such as St. John's, Hofstra, and Adelphi, but also every once in a while with breathtaking delight to schools such as Columbia (Gangi, class of 1965) and Princeton (Sam Alito of Trenton, New Jersey, class of 1972).

Columbia was Gangi's ticket out of the provinciality of Bensonhurst. Except for his uncle Sonny, who went to Catholic Seton Hall, he was the first in his family to go to college. But it wasn't an easy step. His parents worried that he would lose his feelings for family and his Catholic faith. His Jewish friend Bruce Kaplan had to come "to the apartment and explain that they wouldn't lose their son to this godless, communist institution. That helped reconcile my mother." Besides, his mother, who came from Abruzzi, had been conflicted anyway. She was American enough to know that she didn't want him to be what Gangi called "a greaseball."

"They wanted me to go out into the world and be more American," he said.

His brother Alfred didn't go to college—he became a beautician. But his uncle Sonny's five children all went, and none of them live in Bensonhurst any longer.

The halting Italian progression to college stood in sharp contrast to the educational attainment of another group of immigrants, the Jews. "Italians started at a lower place in the American system," explains Alba. "They were basically peasants moving into cities, and they lacked industrial skills. They also didn't have the reverential attitude toward education that the Jews did. The pull of family tended to keep people in place and helped to make these neighborhoods more stable."

Indeed, in Bensonhurst going to college usually meant forsaking the friends in the neighborhood hangouts with whom you had less in common, and often that was a permanent break. Gangi lives on the Upper West Side, not in an Italian neighborhood. He married a Jewish woman, and his Catholic faith, he suggested, has lapsed. His Italian mores and macho mannerisms have thinned out, just like his hair. He told me of a time his mother came to dinner and called him afterward in a state. "They were terribly upset that I was doing the dishes," he said. His son, Theo, is a writer, not a common Italian occupation two generations ago (though he has taken an apartment in still heavily Italian Bay Ridge to get a whiff of his father's roots).

Yet the pull of the old neighborhood is powerful. Gangi went back to Bensonhurst on a recent Father's Day and saw a few young men "with their sleeves rolled up being very loud, and very Italian, and I immediately slipped into a comfortable pair of shoes. I was totally aware I was not home but I was in a place where I belonged."

There were other ways to leave the neighborhood besides college. With powerful talent, comedian Dom DeLuise and actor Danny De-Vito built careers by tapping the rich vein of Italian shtick they absorbed in Bensonhurst. But whichever way people abandoned the neighborhood, they left those remaining in a state of edginess. Alba thinks the most notorious incident associated with Bensonhurst—the murder of a black teenager, Yusuf K. Hawkins, by a group of local young men in 1991—was rooted in the angry defensiveness Italians began to feel as they saw the population of Italians shrink and newcomers move into their streets and schools. By some neighborhood accounts, the attack was triggered by an Italian girl, Gina Feliciano, who lived in an apartment over a Bensonhurst candy store and violated the neighborhood's mores by dating Latino men. When her Italian friends reproached her, she threatened to bring in a group of her black and Hispanic friends to beat them up. The Italian friends mistook Hawkins, who was in the neighborhood trying to buy a used car, for a member of this supposed dark-skinned posse, or so the neighborhood's defenders say. One can predict that such blowups will probably be less common because Italian styles and habits—like their insularity and suspiciousness of authority and outsiders that sometimes rises to belligerence—are also dissipating with assimilation.

To be sure, Bensonhurst is still very Italian. It is a place of quiet numbered streets lined with tightly grouped two-family brick row houses adorned with Madonnas in the small front yards and American flags snapping over the doorways. Its commercial spine, Eighteenth Avenue, is dappled with the Italian colors of green, white, and red. Il Colosseo Restaurant has penne and rigatoni that rival any of those near the Coliseum in Rome, and Tomasso's on Eighty-sixth Street is the place to snatch a whiff of the lingering culture of wiseguys along with tagliatelle Bolognese. Villabate Pasticceria's window displays wheels of orange-scented cheesecake and pastries stuffed with ricotta, drawing long lines of weekend shoppers—yes, it gives out numbers—driving in from Long Island. There are still a couple of surviving salumerias—pork product stores—such as Trunzo Brothers. SAS Italian Records has CDs of the great tenors as well as stainless steel espresso brewers and machines to grind tomatoes into sauce. Aldo Studio, the neighborhood's wedding photographer, is still famed for its collection of backdrops, including a waterfall, a grand piano, and a white Rolls-Royce, to complete the over-the-top garish Italian wedding. There are at least a dozen still-functioning hometown social clubs, including Societa Santa Fortunata and Militello Val Catania Society, though old-timers remember two and three times that number.

So Bensonhurst has a long way to go before it becomes what Professor Krase calls an "ethnic theme park" like Little Italy and Arthur Avenue in the Belmont section of the Bronx, neighborhoods where few Italians actually reside but where tourists and "Saturday Italians" flock to get their Italian blast. But its fate seems unavoidable. The Italian American residents, who once passed houses on to their own relatives or those of their neighbors, are selling them to the highest bidders: Chinese moving up from nearby Sunset Park, Russians expanding from crowded Brighton Beach, Arabs and Pakistanis moving east from Bay Ridge.

Yes, the remaining Italians are adapting. The real estate agencies on Eighteenth Avenue may bear Italian names, but Calabrese employs five Chinese-speaking and six Russian-speaking brokers among his staff of forty. Salvatore Alba, whose bakery had seen long lines for its cannoli and cheesecake ever since his Sicilian parents opened it in 1932, hired a Chinese American woman to sell Italian ices. "I figure if they can't speak English, we'll get someone to speak to them in Chinese," Alba told me when we spoke in 2002. Aldo Studio now displays a large photograph of a Chinese bride and groom standing in front of a maroon Harley-Davidson. Churches that were once heavily Italian are now offering masses in Chinese.

But the heartbreaking evidence of loss is everywhere. I revisited Bensonhurst in 2006 after a three-year absence and noticed that on Eighteenth Avenue, two of the espresso cafés had been turned into a Starbucks and a Dunkin' Donuts and that there were fewer Italian groceries. Older people told me they had to walk farther for the Italian products they need. The Feast of Santa Rosalia is still held every summer and is as teeming as ever, but only half the revelers and visitors are Italian, the merchants knowing that their sausages have become an American, not just an Italian treat. I was particularly saddened to see that the Alba Pastry storefront was covered in plywood, with construction proceeding on a replacement enterprise. It is history.

The Starbucks was a melting pot, with a slender young man in a yarmulke sitting near a young Chinese man with an iPod in his ears clicking away at his laptop, and he was sitting next to two Russian women animatedly chatting. There was now a Chinese bakery, novelty store, beauty parlor, and pharmacy on Eighteenth Avenue I hadn't noticed before, and Healing Treasure, a shop that sold ginseng, angelica, and other Chinese medicinal herbs and offered acupuncture on site. In a local example of globalization, it was run by a short, wiry Russian man with a glinting earring. "Sometimes good ginseng is the difference between living and dying," he told my wife.

Bensonhurst's Italians are fanning out to New Jersey or Long Island or across the Verrazano-Narrows Bridge to Staten Island—which lets the grown-up children remain a short drive from their aging parents. Almost no Italians are moving in. Philip V. Cannistraro, acting executive director of the John D. Calandra Italian American Institute at Queens College, studied migration in the last years of the 1990s and found that in all that time, fewer than 300 Italians had settled in Bensonhurst.

It should be remembered that Bensonhurst, famously the setting for bus driver Ralph Kramden's apartment in TV's *The Honeymooners,* was always multiethnic, though from World War II to the 1980s, the other large group was Jewish (Buddy Hackett, Jerry Stiller, Elliott Gould, Harvey Fierstein, and Abe Burrows all hailed from Bensonhurst). But the ethnicity today is new. The Jews now are mostly Russian, as the groceries, fruit stores, and pharmacies with Russian lettering attest. Along the side streets, Chinese are on the ascent, buying up two-family houses made of relatively fire-resistant brick rather than wood for $400,000 and more. They relish the neighborhood's orderliness, its schools with seasoned teachers, and the subway lines that go straight to Chinatown. Under the el at Eighty-sixth Street, there is now a cavernous Chinese store, T & H Supermarket, that sells Chinese vegetables, dishware, live carp, and more exotic fish for people who like to see their fish wriggling just before it is cooked. Indeed, it is relatively safe to predict that a Chinatown, complete with dim-sum parlors, will prosper along Eighty-sixth Street, once a thoroughly Italian street.

There have been tensions—in the public schools—where Italian children are a diminishing presence. Some Chinese parents feel Italian families have maneuvered to deny their children academic awards. In

2001, Schools Chancellor Harold Levy ordered an investigation into complaints that five Chinese students beginning their senior year were forced to leave Lafayette High School on the specious grounds that they had completed their graduation requirements. Chinese families felt some of the students might have had a shot at becoming the valedictorian, denying the honor to one of the seniors of Italian descent. Italians now compose less than 10 percent of Lafayette's student body, when in the 1960s they along with Jews composed the bulk of the school. Asian students have also been targets of bullies and of racial taunting—not necessarily by Italians but by black and Latino teenagers, who now make up a majority of Lafayette's student body. Asian leaders explain that Asian teenagers are smaller in stature, may not speak English breezily, and are taught to concentrate on getting good grades and not to confront bullies, get into trouble in school, or embarrass their families. The tensions have been so persistent and the school so ineffective that in 2006 Schools Chancellor Joel I. Klein decided to close Lafayette along with four other troubled high schools. Each high school will be broken up into four or so small schools built around a theme such as science or the environment, with roughly 400 to 500 students in each small school.

THERE HAVE ALSO BEEN cultural misunderstandings in Bensonhurst. As newcomers, Chinese work long hours and don't have time to attend to chores until late at night. Jerry Chiappetta, executive director of the Italian-American Coalition of Organizations, which runs centers for the elderly, told me about a squabble he had with a Chinese neighbor, someone he had first tried to befriend with a basket of homegrown tomatoes from his backyard. "He did admirable things with his home, but when he got into late-night hours using a jackhammer, I got a little irate," Chiappetta said. "He stopped it, but it took me blowing my gasket one night."

But aside from such incidents and those centered on the young, Chinese in the neighborhood told me they liked Italians and have enjoyed relatively amicable relationships. "Italian people are friendly, easy to talk to," said Lisa Pan, a Chinese woman who works at her family-owned business, Wei's Gift Shop, which draws Italian youngsters who prize its

Yu-Gi-Oh! Japanese trading cards. Jeiying Franco, a Chinese woman who has taught physics at Lafayette since 1984, claimed that even the incidents at Lafayette were not representative of Italian feelings. "I don't think Italian people have any resentment toward the Chinese," she said. "The Chinese are hardworking. They never bother their neighbors." The Chinese also have traditions that endear them to the Italians, said Betty Lee, an administrator at the Brooklyn Chinese American Association. Just like Italians, they buy houses so different generations of Chinese families can live together.

Bensonhurst has not yet acquired a Chinese character or even a Russian one—so dominant is the Italian—but it is only a matter of time. In this ferment, many Italians have lost their "comfort zone," said Chiappetta. He continues to see houses on his block being sold to Asian families as the Italians retire or their children marry and leave home. Each year brings fewer neighbors of the kind who make wine in their garage or grow basil in their backyard gardens and then give him sprigs to plant in his yard so he can make pesto or flavor his tomatoes. "When you have an influx of people who don't share similar traditions, it's not a question of disliking them; it's just there is less in common," he said. "And if you're on the border of should-I-move-or-not, it's one more reason to move."

Chiappetta, who has lived in Bensonhurst for forty years and graduated from the neighborhood's New Utrecht High School, recalled a time when he and his brothers lived with their parents, with their uncles and aunts nearby. But his twenty-five-year-old daughter, Kristin, lives on Long Island with his four grandchildren. When we spoke, he confided that he remained in the neighborhood principally to be near his elderly mother. "She should live to a hundred and twenty, but if she should go I would be less inclined to stay if Mom weren't around," he said. His brother, a chiropractor, has already moved to a fancier Brooklyn neighborhood, though it is still close by, only a mile away, because he too wants to be near their aging mother.

Italian families, who had perhaps the most close-knit ties of all the immigrants who came here a century ago, are dispersing. "There is a degree of sadness as people mourn the passing of an old life, an old world," Cannistraro, the Queens College professor, told me. "One of the characteristics of older neighborhoods is that the people there tend to stay put. So what you're left with is a neighborhood of old people. There cannot be anything but sadness in watching that."

Calabrese takes all the changes in stride as another turn of the American immigration wheel. "You go back to the early 1900s; Italians were moving near the Bowery and you'd have two or three families sharing a two-bedroom apartment in order to buy a house," he said. "Chinese are doing the same." Fifteen years ago, when the Chinese began to move in, there were complaints from Italians. But as they realized that the Chinese were creating few problems, all that was left was rueful resignation.

"The Feast of Santa Rosalia is still going on, but how much longer?" Calabrese said. "If you asked me fifteen years ago, I would have said it was going on forever. Now I don't know, and that makes me sad because I am Italian."

BENSONHURST

...

WHERE TO GO

Aldo Studio ("BIG FAT ITALIAN WEDDING" PHOTOGRAPHER)
6108 18TH AVENUE; *(718) 236-6300*; WWW.ALDOSTUDIO.COM

18th Avenue, between 65th Street and 86th Street (YEAR-ROUND ITALIAN FEAST)

SAS Italian Records (ITALIAN MUSIC, COFFEEMAKERS, AND PRODUCTS) 7113 18TH AVENUE; *(718) 331-0539*

T & H Supermarket (CHINESE MARKET AND EMPORIUM) 86TH STREET AND AVENUE U

WHERE TO EAT

Il Colosseo (HOMESPUN ITALIAN) 7704 18TH AVENUE; *(718) 234-3663*

Tomasso's (UPSCALE ITALIAN) 1464 86TH STREET; *(718) 236-9883*

Villabate Pasticceria and Bakery (ORNATE CONFECTIONS)
7117 18TH AVENUE; *(718) 331-8430*; WWW.VILLABATE.NET

Chapter 16

Steadfast in Gerritsen Beach and Broad Channel

. . .

NEW YORK IS AN EDGY CITY AND IT ALSO HAS AN EDGE—MILES of shoreline lapped by sea and river that surround a metropolis that after all is made up of two islands (Manhattan and Staten), the western end of another island (Brooklyn and Queens), and a large peninsula (the Bronx). Those shores on the city's edge happen to provide cunning hideaways for people who want to stay out of the New York limelight, the kind of New Yorkers who call Manhattan "the city" and rarely visit except to work. They like the end-of-the-world feeling of a place where they can go no farther, are smack up against the Atlantic Ocean or one of its lagoons, and know that out there lie the deep and the void. So, caught between razzle-dazzle and nothingness, they turn inward, stick to themselves, cultivate a crusty insularity that eyes outsiders with more than a smidgeon of suspicion, and would like nothing better than if strangers stayed strange. And yet they are as much New Yorkers as the city's 8.25 million other denizens.

There are more than a dozen of these spots in New York, but two that I visited seemed the most undiscovered, unsung, and Brigadoon-like: Gerritsen Beach in Brooklyn and Broad Channel in Queens. They are alike in their inbred qualities, in the clannish way people relate to one another, and in their gently frayed appearance, as if people this far out don't really have to dress up for visitors. But each has a distinctive face and personality and idiosyncratic story line that trumpets its singularity.

What struck me about Gerritsen Beach was how timeless it was.

While the one unchanging truth about New York's neighborhoods is that they constantly change, Gerritsen Beach defies that rule. Tucked between the better-known fishing colony of Sheepshead Bay and suburban-like Marine Park, Gerritsen Beach is a portlike cluster of 2,300 closely packed bungalows and brick homes, a village where seagulls wheel across somber skies and a lone cormorant may perch for hours on a rotted piling. Its inhabitants include the families of firefighters, police officers, garbage collectors, subway conductors, "people who make everything work," as one resident, Michael Taylor, Jr., likes to say. More recent settlers include bankers and traders, but they are often the children and grandchildren of Gerritsen Beach residents. Ethnically, most residents are of Irish, German, or Scandinavian stock. That profile was true twenty years ago, forty years ago, and even eighty years ago, when the neighborhood was first settled.

Most New Yorkers have never heard of Gerritsen Beach, and that is just fine with its residents, who are insular to the bone. Lorraine DeVoy, the unofficial historian, a demure but steely woman who works as a dispatcher for the fire volunteers, estimates that one-third of the residents can claim a relative living in the neighborhood. She accounts for a big share of kin. Her grandparents moved to "the Beach" in the 1920s, her parents stayed on, and so did she. Now, DeVoy's son Michael, a captain in the fire department, lives on Abbey Court, her son Charles, who works for the Department of Environmental Protection, lives on Hymen Court, and a third son, Jimmy, lives with her and owns the local liquor store. Those sons have given her four grandchildren that constitute a fifth generation of Gerritsen Beach DeVoys.

As a result of such ties, people look out for one another, dispelling the urban anonymity that some New Yorkers may find liberating but that most in Gerritsen Beach find chilling. "What I hated growing up here, I love about it today: Everybody knows everybody," Joe Benecke, a third-generation "Beacher," told me.

Benecke is a former marine in his late forties who earns his living as a subway conductor. His grandfather, who delivered eggs and milk by horse and cart, moved to Gerritsen Beach from Coney Island and with his wife raised eleven children. Benecke's parents stayed on and raised him there. Benecke has a brother, an aunt, an uncle, two nieces, a nephew, and a dozen cousins with homes in Gerritsen. Clannishness like that makes for a certain busybody nosiness, and growing up, Benecke bridled at having neighbors who snitched to his parents when he cut school. But after living in Sheepshead Bay and Astoria, he missed the embrace of the Gerritsen weave and moved back. Now, as a father of three boys and two girls, he sees his neighbors' watchfulness in a new light. "If my son is doing something wrong, I know about it before he has a chance to come home and give me his side of the story," he said. "Of course there are times when you want to keep something in the closet and you can't. But it's the price you pay for living here. And I'll pay that price. My laundry is not that dirty that I have to fear."

In sociological parlance, Gerritsen Beach is an enclave, and in twenty-first-century New York, tossed about by four decades of robust immigration, the number of stable enclaves is shrinking. In Queens, pockets such as Howard Beach, St. Albans, Broad Channel, Breezy Point, and Middle Village (virtually surrounded by cemeteries) still qualify. So do City Island, Woodlawn, and Harding Park (another colony of bungalows inhabited largely by Puerto Ricans) in the Bronx, and Mill Basin and Bergen Beach in Brooklyn. Enclaves tend to be either hard to reach or isolated, and Gerritsen Beach is both. There is practically only one way in—on Gerritsen Avenue. Residents need a car to get to Manhattan, or the willingness to take first the B31 bus to Kings Highway station, then a long ride on the Q line. "I had to leave the house at 7:20 to get to work at nine o'clock," Anne Dietrich, the president of the Gerritsen Beach Property Owners Association, told me, recounting her daily odyssey when she worked as a secretary to a judge.

Sharon Zukin, a professor of sociology at Brooklyn College, says that Gerritsen Beach and similar enclaves also display strong bonds among the generations; after they attend college or marry, children raised on the Beach crave returning to their parents' neighborhood, an outlook that has become almost un-American. In enclaves there are often strong ties forged by similar occupations or, as in Hasidic Williamsburg, by religious practices. Enclaves can also be economic, for instance, Manhattan's Silk Stocking district, too expensive for most people to afford, or Brooklyn's Brownsville, too run-down to attract all but the poor. But generally, enclaves are places where the residents want to live with kindred souls, and so they barely change. Gerritsen Beach ranked third among middle-class Brooklyn neighborhoods in displaying the least racial change between the 1990 and 2000 censuses; it was topped only by Mill Basin and Bergen Beach, its next-door neighbors.

Gerritsen Beach's nearly 7,000 residents like the fact that their neighborhood is on the Shell Bank Creek and a perpendicular canal. They can dock their cruisers and fishing boats alongside their homes and teach their children to row dinghies just about the same time they teach them to ride bicycles. Indeed, the water bonds fathers and sons, mothers and daughters, around boats and their overblown rituals. Gerritsen Beach's residents like the alphabetized narrow side streets—Abbey, Beacon, Canton, Dare, Eaton, Frank, Gain, and so on—that are safe for children to caper in. They like a neighborhood dominated by two churches, Resurrection Roman Catholic and St. James Evangelical Lutheran, which simplifies religious relations. They like sending their children either to the half-century-old elementary school, PS 277, or to Resurrection's parochial school; deep affection grows for those schools when children often have the same instructors the parents did and legends are passed along about eccentric gym teachers or cafeteria rituals. Gerritsen Beach's residents like having a Kiddie Beach for $285 a season, a Little League, and three or four homespun parades a year. They like a neighborhood where there's nothing to attract strangers—like popular restaurants; Gerritsen Avenue has a pizzeria, a bar, and three delis. They like a neighborhood where many men, including Benecke, consider it a moral obligation to serve in the military and work for the twenty-eight-member volunteer fire company, the only remaining volunteer company in Brooklyn.

Gerritsen Beach was named for Wolfert Gerritsen, an adventurous Dutchman who in the 1630s heeded Henry Hudson's call to settle his newly discovered patch of earth and built a flour mill on Gerritsen Creek, now Marine Park. (The mill stood there until the 1930s, when it burned down.) Until 1920 the only houses were occupied by squatters, but then a developer imagined the area's prospects as a summer resort and packed it full of one-story bungalows with pitched roofs and dormers, though no basements, backyards, or sewage lines. For many years, Gerritsen Beach was considered not much better than a shantytown.

Still, the houses were snapped up by Irish and German families of modest income like Lorraine DeVoy's grandparents. The grandfather, Cormac Divine, had a government job, but he bought a summer house at 9 Ebony Court in 1924. "My grandmother heard she could put two hundred dollars down," DeVoy told me. "That's how the Irish and Germans moved into Gerritsen Beach. It was something they could afford."

Another set of grandparents, John and Catherine Bennis, had already moved to a house on Dare Court in 1922. Four of the Bennis children bought houses in Gerritsen Beach when they grew up, and so did three of the Divine children. Lorraine DeVoy was born in Gerritsen Beach in 1938. She remembered returning from school, changing into a bathing suit, and going swimming with friends at the end of Gerritsen Avenue—something she did for years, until outsiders began to use the spot as a dumping ground.

Bungalows were soon winterized, particularly during the housing shortage that followed World War II. Developers capitalized on year-round buyers and built two-story homes north of the canal. In the 1950s, after a campaign by the civic association, the city built sewers and paved them over, and paid residents $2,500 apiece to have their homes elevated with hydraulic jacks to the new street grade. The newer section boasts sidewalks, something the older section does not.

Through the Depression and the war years, and for many years afterward, medical services were provided by one man—Dr. Louis Baronberg, a distinguished-looking physician who made $3 house calls in a Thunderbird. One writer on a Gerritsen Beach blog, Annette Marchan McKean, remembered gashing her knee after disobediently riding her bike when her parents weren't home, then running to Dr. Baronberg. "Dr. Baronberg put three stitches in it and after I told him the circumstances, he covered it with a Band-Aid and told me to keep it dry and come back in a week to have the stitches taken out. Never told my parents and never asked for a penny of money." Until the end of the twentieth century, Gerritsen Beach residents borrowed books out of a storefront library branch on Gerritsen Avenue. But they fought for and won a well-stocked modern building with a clock tower, a cathedral ceiling, and a maritime view out a two-story window. It has become the unofficial community center. "They fought for everything they got,"

DeVoy said. "Nothing came easy. They found in fighting for the community they improved the community."

Those early homeowners kindled a rebellious, do-it-yourself spirit that persists today. A good illustration came when residents wanted to create a memorial on the Marine Park baseball field to Lawrence G. Veling, who was killed in the World Trade Center collapse. Another native firefighter and four other residents were also killed, but Veling's ties to local baseball were special. Veling had grown up on Eton Court and for a time he and a partner operated a deli on Gerritsen Avenue. Like many other Beachers, he worked two jobs—as a fireman with Engine 235 in Bedford-Stuyvesant and as a high school custodian. A burly, balding man with a gravelly voice and kind face, he liked doing guy things—playing softball and coaching Little League—but he was also a man mushy enough to delight his two-year-old, Kevin, with his suddenly discovered knack for drawing characters from the Nickelodeon show *Blue's Clues*. "I knew my kids would grow up to be great adults because they had a great father," Diane Veling told an interviewer for a snapshot of her husband that became part of *The New York Times*' "Portraits of Grief." When he was killed at forty-four, he left behind three children, Ryan and Cynthia as well as Kevin. Residents felt it only natural to honor him in one of the ways he honored the community—on the baseball field. But the effort to build a monument got mired in red tape. So did the plucky residents take that passively? No, they brought in a cement truck and bulldozer and built it themselves.

The barriers that have kept Gerritsen Beach isolated have attracted a certain human specimen—people who are not all that dazzled by Manhattan's glitz. George R. Broadhead, a retired advertising executive who left the Beach in disenchantment when he was younger but returned in 2001, told me of one such incurious neighbor. The man came up to him and asked somewhat sheepishly, "You go to the city a lot—do you know where the Metropolitan Museum is? I got a nephew visiting from Ireland."

"I had to explain to him how to get to the Met," Broadhead told me. "When I was a kid it was that way in Gerritsen Beach."

That provincialism is nurtured by the fact that when houses come on the market, they are usually passed around among relatives or friends.

Those clapboard wood-frame houses on lots typically forty-five feet by fifty feet had an average value of $189,320 in 2000, which makes them affordable by Gerritsen Beach residents, whose median household income was $52,582. All that tight-knitting gives the Beach a distinctive pioneer camaraderie that residents boast of to an extent that residents of, say, the Upper East Side would never do. Doreen Greenwood, a local real estate broker, told me, "You can live in an area and that's all it is, but Gerritsen Beach is a true neighborhood. If you go away, people will take care of your dog and water your plants if you give them a key." Greenwood, a woman in her early fifties who drives the volunteers' fire truck, grew up in Gerritsen Beach in a two-bedroom bungalow on Eaton Court. Three children slept in one bedroom, two in another, and her parents slept in the living room on a pullout couch. When it was time to start her own family, she didn't want to leave and bought her own house in 1975. "We didn't want to live anyplace else," she said. "It was great growing up. There was always something to do—either fishing, boating, or playing ball. And now my children are buying houses and having children in Gerritsen Beach." She counts two grown sons, a daughter, two grandchildren, and a sister as neighbors.

The flip side of all that togetherness is a wariness of outsiders. Beachers acknowledge that not everyone would feel welcome in so clannish a neighborhood. "Anyplace that small and close-knit, you're going to have a distrust of outsiders," DeVoy says. "We like our community to stay the way it is. Doesn't everybody?" Still, Gerritsen Beach residents deny that they willfully exclude people, and when I checked with the city's Commission on Human Rights, officials there told me they had no record of any overt discrimination by Gerritsen Beach homeowners or brokers.

Yet Gerritsen Beach is changing, however imperceptibly. The 2000 census counted 293 Hispanics, 151 Asians, and 27 blacks among the 6,877 residents, numbers larger than in the 1990 census. Although the number of residents who had not graduated from high school still stood at a hefty 16 percent, the number of college graduates had increased: 15.5 percent of residents twenty-five or older have a BA degree or better. "Up to the seventies, most people here were firemen, sanitation men, police, post office, or DEP," DeVoy said. "It's only been since the seventies that you had kids who grew up, went to college, and would move out of the Beach and do other work." Rising home values—winterized houses on the water can fetch $400,000 or more—are also spurring more residents to put their homes on the market, with some going to stockbrokers and lawyers. And changing tastes are also changing the composition of the Beach. Four of DeVoy's sisters didn't want to live in a place where "your mother-in-law is in your house all the time" and settled in New Jersey and Pennsylvania. "You used to go to church and you knew everybody," lamented DeVoy. "Now you don't."

Broadhead, a blue-eyed descendant of the English and Dutch colonists who is now in his early seventies, forsook Gerritsen Beach after serving as a marine in the Korean War, where he was wounded on the day of the truce and awarded a Silver Star. He wanted out because he remembered the Beach as the kind of neighborhood that "if you were to tell the kids, 'I went to a museum,' they'd say, 'What are you, a sissy?' " Growing up there, he would sneak away to readings by e.e. cummings at the 92nd Street Y (he owns a painting by cummings of his wife). After graduating from St. John's University, he spent much of his adult life as an advertising executive for the Newhouse newspaper chain and other publications, living in Greenwich, Connecticut, Nashville, and Beverly Hills, marrying three times, and fathering a son and three daughters. All the while, he collected first editions by writers such as John O'Hara, Robert Benchley, and T. S. Eliot.

But after his mother died, he moved back into her house in Gerritsen Beach. He found he liked hanging out among the gruff-talking, jocular veterans at the Veterans of Foreign Wars Hall who understood his brutal war experiences. He even became the unit's commander. He was surprised to find less narrowness of outlook and was pleased to see what he called Gerritsen Beach's "creeping diversity." There was a Chinese American neighbor next door on Knapp Street and a black former marine sergeant in the VFW hall. Although he frequents such Manhattan restaurants as Balthazar, he also likes dining again at Brennan & Carr, a nearly seventy-year-old Irish tavern just outside Gerritsen on Nostrand Avenue and famous in southern Brooklyn for its hot roast beef sandwiches dipped in broth. "When we started taking girls out to the movies, some of us thought we were more sophisticated taking them here," he told me over a lunch of hot roast beef. Most of all he was pleasantly surprised by how much he liked, now that he was older, being in a neighborhood where people knew him in their marrow, knew him, despite his age, as "Belle's son," and could gently scold him, "Georgie, you need a haircut!"

"From Beverly Hills, where I used to eat at Spago, the Grill, and Musso and Frank's," he said, "I walked into a place where people called you Georgie."

GERRITSEN BEACH

...

WHERE TO GO

Gerritsen Beach Public Library (CHECK OUT THE VIEW FROM THE PICTURE WINDOW) 280 GERRITSEN AVENUE; *(718) 368-1435*

Gerritsen Beach Volunteer Fire Department 52 SEBA AVENUE; *(718) 332-9292*

WHERE TO EAT

Brennan & Carr Restaurant (IRISH TAVERN KNOWN FOR BROTH-DIPPED ROAST BEEF SANDWICHES) 3432 NOSTRAND AVENUE; *(718) 646-9559*

Victoria Pizzeria 2716 GERRITSEN AVENUE; *(718) 891-9496*

BROAD CHANNEL, AN ISLAND of tumbledown bungalows in the middle of Jamaica Bay, has much in common with Gerritsen Beach. It too is a neighborhood peopled by blue-collar civil servants who like to live around boats, and it too is fairly inbred. But only it has Charles W. Howard, the man who styles himself as the duke of this Queens duchy by dint of the fortune he has made in a rather unconventional enterprise.

Howard rents out portable toilets, a business he operates right on Broad Channel. Call-A-Head Portable Toilets is one of the state's biggest suppliers for construction sites, rock concerts, and, yes, outdoor weddings and bar mitzvahs. Running such a business in a waterside bedroom community on the edge of the protected marshland of Jamaica Bay has earned him more than a few detractors, but by the time I met him, he was drawing even more criticism with his outsize ambitions to remake Broad Channel itself. He wanted to reshape the occasionally woebegone mile-long island into something closer in splendor to Newport, Rhode Island, or at least to Cape May, New Jersey. He wanted to build shops, restaurants, and other amenities that, as he put it, might re-create the elegance of the Gilded Age yet have the fun of Disney World. "My goal is to make Broad Channel like America's great seashore communities," he told me. "And the reason I'm doing it here is because I can't think of a better place to live."

A stout man in his early forties who carries his girth with Orson Welles–like confidence, he clearly sees himself as the island's benefactor and speaks of his role in Broad Channel as one of noblesse oblige. "I want to help the town I grew up in," he said. "I want to protect the town." What frustrates him, he said, is that neighbors unhappy with his toilets are casting aspersions on his development plans. They accuse him of building flamboyant castles out of character with an island that has all the trappings of a forgotten fishing village—ramshackle bungalows standing on stilts over marshland, backyard canals clogged with boats. Howard thinks their real gripe is with his toilets and that they should get over it. "This company's what's rebuilding Broad Channel, and a lot of people who don't like portable toilets don't appreciate that," he said. "People will appreciate it in the end, but people should appreciate it now."

In Broad Channel, it's hard not to appreciate Call-A-Head. A visitor entering the island over the only northern approach—a bridge spanning Jamaica Bay and its wildlife refuge—will immediately see some of the company's 4,000 fiberglass booths and a fleet of stainless-steel pumping trucks bearing the slogan "We're #1 at Picking Up #2." Howard estimates that he is New York State's biggest supplier of portable toilets, though rivals dispute that assessment. Still, Call-A-Head's more than $10 million-a-year business has allowed Howard to become Broad Channel's Donald J. Trump. He owns twenty properties that will eventually include an ornate pharmacy, medical offices for eight doctors, and a Venetian café. (When I visited, the island did not have a single drug-store, doctor, or sit-down restaurant.) He also envisions opening a year-round Christmas store and a hotel to be called Howard's End Inn, not after the E. M. Forster novel but because, he said without a shred of irony, "it's at the end of town and my name is Howard."

The toilet business has been good to him, giving him the island's most opulent home, a $1.5 million house with an indoor pool and Jacuzzi that he says was inspired by those Newport mansions and Dis-ney pavilions, a forty-six-foot yacht moored right alongside that sleeps six, and a Jaguar and two Porsches that help him tool around the island with the swagger of its leading citizen. While his critics have not been especially vocal—in a neighborhood of just 3,000 residents, people know one another and choose words carefully—many do complain that Howard's structural confections dwarf the landscape.

Frank Harnisher, a retired New York Stock Exchange broker who was born in Broad Channel, told me, "Everything he builds is like a castle. I don't want to be criticizing him, but he's worked hard and he wants to leave his mark." Then there are the next-door neighbors of Call-A-Head. "At times the smell is obnoxious," said John F. McCambridge, eighty-seven, a veteran wounded in the Battle of the Bulge who still runs an ac-counting and insurance office on the main street. "My wife was here for sixteen months sick with cancer and I'd be there screaming."

It's not just neighbors who have objected. Investigators for the State Department of Environmental Conservation have accused the company of washing potties next to Jamaica Bay's wetlands, and city inspectors have issued the business seventeen summonses since 2000. In Novem-ber 2004, Call-A-Head reached an agreement with the Queens district attorney's office in which the company, without admitting wrongdoing, paid fines of $100,000 to clear charges of polluting protected wetlands.

Howard is unrepentant. "We've been under the microscope for twenty years," he said. Indeed, he thinks there's a certain degree of envy by the city inspectors. "You can't have a city worker who gets sixty or seventy thou-sand dollars a year relate to me," he said. "It's a power issue." He took me on a tour of his toilet business and vigorously argued that waste collected in the portable toilets was pumped out at sewage treatment plants; then the potties were steam-cleaned in Broad Channel, with the dirty water draining down catch basins that lead to the sewer system. In his earthy way, Howard volunteered that his business might be out of place in Beverly Hills, but Broad Channel is no Beverly Hills. "Nobody likes portable toilets until they have to run into one," he said, adding that when his company supplies portable toilets for an event such as a Bruce Springsteen concert at Shea Stadium, "It helps the environment."

There is something utterly disarming about his guilelessness. He has adopted the language of the architects he deals with, throwing around such design terms as "vernacular" as if he were building a skyscraper instead of a drugstore on a low-rise street. "We wanted this to become an anchor," he said of the drugstore. His concepts are borrowed from trips he's made to places like Disney World, where as someone growing up in modest Broad Channel he was clearly awed. "The thinking is that by putting in old-style architecture it would start a renaissance that would elevate Broad Channel's style," he told me. He also has wistful notions of what Broad Channel could be, a neighborly, Frank Capra kind of small town that Broad Channel never was. His reason for building the mansionlike medical center—it will have six cupolas and fifteen gables—is telling. "I want to make the island a place where you can hear, 'Good morning, Doctor.' You don't hear that now."

It is a fair bet that most New Yorkers have never been to Broad Channel, which lies between Howard Beach and the Rockaways and is connected to them by two bridges and the A train. As Jamaica Bay's only inhabited island, it was until late into the last century a backwater whose inhabitants were derided as "swamp rats." They lived in fishermen's shacks and other run-down dwellings that they seldom bothered to fix up since they were tenants on land owned by the city, which had visions of the island as a preserve. What the residents had, though, was what some called "a poor man's paradise"—long, misty views of the Manhattan skyline, emerald marshes, and skies graced by the flight of egrets, oyster catchers, and laughing gulls.

All that began to change after 1982, when the city allowed residents to buy their properties for bargain-basement prices. Homeowners winterized bungalows and added second stories. Among those who bought shortly after the city surrendered the island were Fred and Barbara Toborg. She edits the newsletter of the northeast chapter of the American Littoral Society, which works to protect the seashore. He retired as a gym teacher and soccer coach at Trinity High School in Manhattan, where his players included John McEnroe. They live on the edge of a marsh where herons and egrets feast and where the rhythms of daily life are often governed by the tides. The marsh they look out on is unusual because it is bisected by the tracks for the A-line subway and every few minutes the train roars through. "This is a field in Kansas and that's the Transcontinental Railroad going by," Toborg likes to say about his view. The Toborgs cautioned me about not misunderstanding Broad Channel. "To live out here you have to be of a certain mentality," Mrs. Toborg said. "We're not a neat community. One yard is grass, another cement. No two houses are alike. It's very individualistic."

But word about Broad Channel has gotten out, and outsiders have been buying. Properties that cost $10,000 in the early eighties now fetch $400,000, and developers are putting up brick houses. The island now styles itself as "the Venice of New York" because of canals that allow residents to live on the waterfront, swimming from childhood in the brackish waters and docking their boats there. They play in Broad Channel Park, with its well-tended tennis, handball, and basketball courts, and use the public library branch, which has a maritime rotunda with ceiling windows. The favorite gathering spot on Cross Bay Boulevard is a bar called Grassy Point, known as Grassy's, but for dining on something fancier than pizza or a bagel, residents go over a bridge to the Rockaways peninsula.

Lawyers and stockbrokers have been moving in, subtly changing the character of a community known for the kind of rough-edged city workers responsible for a notorious incident in 1998. Broad Channel's Labor Day parade indulges in humor that satirizes multiethnic New York; Hasidim and Asians were skewered in previous parades. But the 1998 parade went too far. A police officer and two firefighters wore blackface and Afro wigs while riding on a float called "Black to the Future: Broad Channel 2098." One firefighter spoofed the killing a few months before of James Byrd, Jr., a black Texan who had been dragged to his death behind a pickup truck. Mrs. Toborg told me, "I saw it go by and I knew it had crossed the line. You don't make fun of people dying." Mayor Rudolph Giuliani fired the city workers.

No one is moving faster to remake Broad Channel than Howard, who grew up fishing and swimming on the island that his great-great-grandfather had settled on. His father, Charles P. Howard, had worked as a truck driver for a portable-toilet company and started Call-A-Head in 1976 out of what had been a gas station. In 1981, when the business had just 150 plywood toilet booths, the father turned it over to his teenage son, who had grander ideas and artful ways of promoting them. "We didn't see eye to eye," he said of his father, who still lives on the island. "He was very conservative. He didn't like to take chances." With just a degree from Beach Channel High School, Howard built up the business from one that had just two employees to one that has fifty-six. It generally charges $165 a month for renting a portable toilet. That means that when all 4,000 toilets are being used, the business is grossing more than $660,000 a month.

Howard, a father of three who proudly describes himself as a workaholic, thinks his business has boomed because of his "forte for marketing." For construction sites, he paints toilet booths orange and gray to match the colors of bulldozers and concrete and charges 30 percent more. He has improvised a five-by-five-foot shed that he says amounts to a conventional bathroom, with a flush toilet, a sink, and a towel dispenser, that customers are also willing to pay more for. He feels he is bringing the same inventive design to his buildings, adorning the pharmacy, for example, with mahogany shelving and a cathedral ceiling painted light blue and soft pink. His decorating schemes might not pass muster on Park Avenue, but he is proud of them nonetheless.

Take the drugstore. "When you walk in you'll think about being in an English library, but when you look up it will be like the Bahamas," he said. "It's kind of like a Nordstrom. It's different than walking into a Target. It's a high-end store."

Howard projects a beguiling artlessness, as when he talks about the great pleasure he takes in finding catchy names for his properties. The pharmacy is being called Wharton's Apothecary because he noticed that the names of many great American companies—Wal-Mart, Woolworth's, Waldbaum's—start with the large letter *W*. He is calling a deli he is converting into an old-fashioned grocery Hamberry's, because it will sell meat and fruit. "Ham, which is the butcher, and berry, which is the market," was the way he put it. "It's going to be a grocery store like a hundred years ago." A café he plans to renovate will be called Victoria's Café. "Very Victorian," he explained. "It also has the word 'victory' in it. It's very hard to lose with the word 'victory.' " His yacht is named *Both Ends,* another playful allusion to his main business.

His motive for developing parts of Broad Channel is not just to make money, he assured me. "I'm here to make art," he said. "If it makes money, fine. That's the key to creating—someone sees it and does it. That's what makes the world." Then he added, with shameless nobility, "It's the greatest thing a person can do—to leave something behind."

In a neighborhood where he has donated lighting and bleachers for sandlot baseball, Howard has some supporters, including Seth Silverman, a lawyer who thinks some of the gripers are in essence Luddites. "It's the old-timers versus the new-timers, and what the new-timers are going to do to change everything," he said. But Howard doesn't seem rattled even by his detractors. When they wonder whether his pharmacy will prosper in a world of chain drugstores that accept numerous prescription plans, Howard counters that people will shop there "because it's going to be an event to go into that store." They will pay more for his shampoo, he predicts. Indeed, he suggested, figuring out how to sell pricier items will be a piece of cake for someone with his track record. "If you can sell a toilet," he said, "you can sell anything."

BROAD CHANNEL

...

WHERE TO GO

Call-A-Head (PORTABLE TOILET RENTALS) 304 CROSS BAY BOULEVARD; *(718) 634-2085*; WWW.CALLAHEAD.COM

WHERE TO EAT

THERE'S NOTHING BUT BAGELS AND PIZZA ON THE ISLAND, BUT PLENTY ACROSS THE BRIDGE IN THE ROCKAWAYS, INCLUDING SOME WATERFRONT SPOTS.

Chapter 17

Factories of Revival Around the Town

. . .

IN THE SUMMER OF 2004, A HIPSTER NAMED TODD FATJO STEPPED out on the roof of a onetime piano factory in the notorious South Bronx and fell in love with the jagged panorama—the grid of bridges along the Harlem River, the blur and purr of three highways, the rooftop water tanks, the gaudy billboards, the hulking housing projects. Most people would not find that view to their liking, but Fatjo, a rangy late-twentyish man raised in the foothills of the Catskills, was smitten, like Beauty with the Beast. "It's great at sunset," Fatjo told me a year later. "I like the industrial scene, the metal, the brick. I've seen enough sunsets over mountains."

Fatjo, who supports himself by deejaying and other odd jobs, is part of a crop of improbable newcomers who are making the South Bronx a vanguard address. Hundreds of artists, Web designers, photographers, journalists, even doctors, many of them refugees from the rising rents of Brooklyn's Williamsburg and Manhattan's East Village, have been seduced by the mix of industrial lofts and nineteenth-century row houses in the Port Morris and Mott Haven neighborhoods. Some now even call the area SoBro. Yes, it's the very South Bronx notorious for squalor and arson, the very South Bronx where Tom Wolfe set the opening of *The Bonfire of the Vanities,* in which a Master of the Universe driving with his mistress in his Mercedes-Benz gets lost on creepy Bruckner Boulevard and triggers a race-relations nightmare.

Well, Bruckner Boulevard and the blocks radiating off it now boast two tidy bars that a Master of the Universe would feel comfortable having a drink in, including one, the Bruckner Bar and Grill, that serves pear and arugula salad. There are a dozen antique shops; a new lively art gallery, Haven Arts, to join three older ones; and a wannabe European café that sells bourgeois bohemian delights such as croissants and veggie wraps.

What is happening in the industrial lofts of the South Bronx is happening as well in fabled factory neighborhoods such as Brooklyn's Red Hook and Gowanus and the Garment Center in Manhattan. The hunger to live in a newly vibrant—and safe—New York, particularly in neighborhoods a short subway ride from midtown, has turned roving eyes to the noisy, smelly, greasy, ratty places no one would have chosen to live in a few decades ago. And they are choosing those neighborhoods not just out of need, but out of desire. These young homesteaders don't cotton to streamlined Trump apartment houses or picket-fenced suburban homes, but prefer the authenticity of a 1950s cityscape. They are moving alongside a canal, the Gowanus, which despite improvements still has a nasty smell when the wind blows with a certain malice, into the Garment Center, where sewing machines still shriek, and into a forgotten bleak Brooklyn corner, Red Hook, where the rumble of waterfront-bound trucks over cobblestone streets is background music.

In the South Bronx and Red Hook, they are moving next door to public housing projects, once known as sources of neighborhood crime, but now, with crime so low, the buildings are seen as treasure troves of ethnic diversity, experience, and adventure, just as polyglot immigrant neighborhoods are. Perhaps it's the result of growing up in less segregated neighborhoods and attending more polychrome schools and colleges, but young people today simply are far more willing than their parents or grandparents to live with people different from them. That explains the increasing presence of whites and Asians in the brownstones of Harlem and Bedford-Stuyvesant and the increasing presence of blacks from Harlem and Bedford-Stuyvesant in the Victorian houses of Ditmas Park. The activity in New York both spurs and mirrors what is happening in older sections of such cities as Boston, San Francisco, Chicago, and Philadelphia, as younger people spurn the well-groomed acres of the suburbs they grew up in for the electricity of city living.

The trend testifies to the fact that immigration isn't the only force that is reshaping the city in dramatic ways. In fact, it is not too far-fetched to say the two trends are related. As the city becomes more of a patchwork of peoples, it is also becoming more of a patchwork of places to live. As immigrants infuse the oddest corners of the city, young men and women are injecting themselves into places young people would not have chosen to live decades ago. Just as almost any person, no matter what color or language, is increasingly welcome almost anywhere in the city, so anyplace with four walls becomes suitable for a dwelling—with a bit of imagination.

It all began with SoHo, which proved in the 1970s that artists would live among the pounding, grinding, and dust of machinery if they could have charming buildings—in SoHo's case, the fabled cast-iron warehouses—with acres of space and tall windows that soaked in light. When lawyers and stockbrokers followed in the 1980s and 1990s, and boutiques, galleries, and restaurants started cropping up, developers and city officials took notice. They learned to stop making a neat division between places where people live and places where they work. Much of the movement was driven by the decay in manufacturing. In 2004, the New York State Department of Labor counted 120,492 industrial employees in the city, while a decade before there were twice that many. The decline has left lofts going begging for tenants, while a booming residential market spurred landlords to improvise ways of converting them into living spaces.

In the South Bronx, the area beguiling artists and Internet jockeys is still dominated by factories such as the Zaro's Bread Basket bakery and warehouses such as Shleppers Moving and Storage as well as by car washes and gas stations, all framed by the elevated Major Deegan Expressway and ramps for the Willis and Third Avenue bridges. In the 1970s the neighborhood went into a tailspin of torched buildings, foreclosures, and runaway crime that led to its christening by police as Fort Apache. The embarrassing nadir came during the second game of the 1977 World Series at Yankee Stadium when Howard Cossell noticed ABC's camera-toting helicopter focusing on a fire consuming an abandoned elementary school west of the ballpark and told the national audience, "There it is, ladies and gentlemen; the Bronx is burning." But during the next three decades, programs by the city and church and nonprofit groups reclaimed scorched and abandoned buildings and built thousands of new ranch houses and imitation town houses on vacant lots. When the Giuliani administration's tough policing caused crime to plunge, people who never would have thought of the Bronx as a place to live reconsidered.

On Bruckner Boulevard specifically, a mixed-use rezoning of five industrial blocks in 1997 created at least 200 new apartments and other homes. Most of the new tenants were single people or childless couples, so the quality of the local schools—among the city's worst—was not an issue. By 2000, Linda Cunningham, an Ohio-born sculptor whose outdoor installations have been exhibited near the United Nations, felt secure enough to buy a five-story loft on East 140th Street with two partners for $660,000. "When I got off the subway, white faces were distinctive," she said. "Someone would stop me and ask if I needed directions." Now she feels comfortable getting off the subway at 2 a.m. She notices that a local Western Beef supermarket has accommodated the tastes of the newcomers, selling alfalfa sprouts, mesclun, and "a decent yogurt."

"I get to the Metropolitan Museum much faster than I could from SoHo," she told me as she boasted of another neighborhood asset, the number 6 train, which is a quick ride to Lexington Avenue and Eighty-sixth Street.

Now anyone strolling on Bruckner can see boxes of geraniums and satellite dishes adorning the industrial windows of a five-story redbrick former piano factory known as the Clocktower. It was converted into seventy-five apartment lofts by Isaac Jacobs, a Hasidic Jew, experienced with adapting lofts in East Williamsburg. The Clocktower lofts rent for between $1,000 and $2,000 per month, according to Fatjo, who helps pay his rent by working for the landlord as a real estate broker of sorts, showing apartments to young artists and bohemians. Jacobs explains this odd symbiosis between a Hasid and a hipster by saying, "He talks their language." Partly as a result of this new influx, the neighborhood's ranks of college-educated residents grew by 86.5 percent between 1990 and 2000.

The artists and hipsters are also drawn by the long-standing Latino and African American culture—sidewalk dominoes games, well-tended vacant-lot gardens, restaurants with fried plantains—that give the neighborhood a populist authenticity that cannot be matched in Manhattan's decorous precincts. Porfirio Díaz, who owns the Maybar Cafe and Piano Bar on Third Avenue, put it simply: New customers are "very happy with Spanish food because the prices are low."

The artists are also happy to have sidewalk entrepreneur Angel Villalona. For sixteen years this Dominican immigrant has been selling papayas, coconuts, and mangoes from the side of a battered truck. He also makes *batidas*—fruit milkshakes—that he stirs in a riveting ritual that would probably not pass muster with the health department. He yanks the cord on a greasy generator propped on the sidewalk, and it feeds electricity to an Osterizer that whips fruit and milk into a tasty malted. One customer, Charles Bachelor, a truck driver who immigrated from Antigua, told me, charmingly describing white Americans as Europeans, "White Europeans used to be afraid to walk in this neighborhood. Now they walk comfortably."

The newcomers, some of whom have spent much of their lives abroad or in the hinterlands and are not put off by the Bronx's outdated reputation, say they have felt welcomed. Still, no one expects the area to become another TriBeCa anytime soon, because the South Bronx has a longtime population of poorer Latinos and blacks that are braced to resist gentrification that will price them out of the neighborhood. "It's going to attract a class of people whose incomes and lifestyles are going to be radically different from those in the South Bronx, which is one of the poorest areas in the city," Hector Soto, a lawyer active in developmental issues, told me.

Many of those fears coalesced around a rezoning measure passed by the city council in March 2005 that essentially added another eleven square blocks of Port Morris to the 1997 rezoning. Soto and other critics—backed by newly settled artists and professionals—fought in vain for provisions reserving half of any new apartments for low-income families, losing to those who felt set-asides would hinder development.

Now a few longtime locals are defending the rezoning because they want the lofts as well. José Baez, a thirty-six-year-old photographer who grew up in the Bronx, rents a 1,000-square-foot loft in the Clocktower for $1,350 a month. "For what you get here, you get a closet in Manhattan," he said. And local merchants are thankful for the infusion of new money. Ronald Trinidad, a twenty-seven-year-old Dominican immigrant, started the Open House Café a year ago with his partner, Eric Beroff, and sells croissants to artists heading to the subway at 138th Street. "Lots of people come here from downtown Brooklyn and ask me, 'Where do I rent?' " he told me.

Paradoxically, there are newcomers who worry that gentrification will lead to an unappetizing blandness that will leave the neighborhood as mainstream as SoHo, with its branches of Bloomingdale's and the Gap. Fatjo, a canny trend spotter, is already worried that the South Bronx may soon be played out. "This neighborhood is already happening," Fatjo said. "I may have to move soon."

SOUTH BRONX

...

WHERE TO GO

Antique District (A DOZEN ANTIQUE SHOPS) ALEXANDER AVENUE
AND BRUCKNER BOULEVARD

Clocktower (ONETIME PIANO FACTORY, NOW APARTMENTS)
112 LINCOLN AVENUE

Haven Arts (GALLERY) 235 EAST 141ST STREET; (718) 585-5753

WHERE TO EAT

Blue Ox Bar (MUSIC AND DRINKS) THIRD AVENUE AND 139TH STREET;
(718) 402-1045

Bruckner Bar and Grill (PLEASANT RESTAURANT) 1 BRUCKNER
BOULEVARD; *(718) 665-2001*

Open House Café (COFFEE AND CROISSANTS) 2559 THIRD AVENUE;
(718) 292-3606

M&J TRIMMINGS' BUSINESS is buttons and bows—and ribbons, rhinestones, beads, cords, tassels, braids, feathers, flowers, and fringes—

everything one might imagine to embellish an article of clothing. In two storefronts and nearby stockrooms in the Garment Center, the firm stocks more than 600,000 items in a compulsive's dreamscape of meticulously arranged cubbies and reels that run from floor to ceiling. But where its owner, Michael J. Cohen, once sold his remarkable cornucopia to the gritty factories and flamboyant designer showrooms south of Times Square, his trade has shifted to craftspeople and hobbyists. The ranks of genuine garment manufacturers keep dwindling.

"It's a very romantic notion—Seventh Avenue as a fashion capital," Cohen told me over a cup of coffee at one of the area's rising crop of outdoor cafés. "But I don't think manufacturing has a long life."

The Garment Center, the storied heart of the city's largest industry, continues to recede, buffeted by cheap overseas labor, rising rents, and an exodus of skilled workers. The talk in the district is that it is going the way of SoHo, drawing artists, actors, and white-collar professionals into the cavernous lofts where immigrants once sat hunched over pummeling needles to make clothing for the nation. One barometer of the Garment Center's fate: When a small building on Avenue of the Americas housing one of M&J Trimmings' firm's stores burned down in 1997, Cohen joined with a developer to erect a forty-six-story building in its place. It contains upscale apartments, not sewing lofts.

These days, the area—roughly stretching between Fifth and Ninth avenues and Thirty-fifth and Forty-first streets—is often called the Fashion Center rather than Garment Center or District. It is a nod to Seventh Avenue's enduring stable of designers, including Ralph Lauren, Bill Blass, Tommy Hilfiger, Donna Karan, and Liz Claiborne, but the name betrays the sharp dwindling of actual factories and dusty stores selling notions and bolts of fabric. Already eleven small theaters, including two called the Zipper and the Belt, and three founded by Mikhail Baryshnikov, have opened in lofts that once produced dresses or suits. Marriott has built a 240-room Courtyard hotel on Fortieth Street and a forty-three-story tower around the corner on Sixth Avenue that combines a Residence Inn with ten floors of condominiums. The latter is constructed around the hoary Millinery Center Synagogue, a remnant of days when Jews like my mother knit hats. By 2006, there were a dozen new upscale restaurants and three Starbucks, to join such pricey garmento stalwarts as Arno Ristorante on West Thirty-eighth Street and Jack's Restaurant on West Fortieth Street.

The district's decline as a manufacturing hub is visible not only in the absence of "push boys" weaving racks of dresses through clogged midtown canyons but also in the presence of young thirtysomething couples pushing strollers, among them Laurie Elvove, a graphics designer, and her husband, Andy Shen, a photographer, who have a toddler, Sofia. When they moved into their co-op, Shen spied sweatshop needles in the floorboards and Elvove was struck by how deserted the neighborhood was after work. But the streets have grown livelier.

"What we still need is a grocery store," she demurred.

Hard statistics confirm the anecdotal impressions. New York State Labor Department figures show that there were only 25,956 jobs in apparel and textile manufacturing and wholesaling in the center's 10018 zip code in 2003. That contrasts with 39,700 workers in 1996 and 159,000 employees in 1975. The once-mighty garment unions are down to 3,000 members who actually work at turning out garments. There is concern that all these trends will accelerate as the city works to revitalize the far West Side between Thirtieth and Forty-second streets. There is one plan to expand the Jacob K. Javits Convention Center and build thousands of apartments on the West Side rail yards and another to transform the James A. Farley Post Office on Eighth Avenue into both a grand entrance for the underground Penn Station as well as a new home for Madison Square Garden.

What will be lost if the Garment Center fades is not just another bygone iconic neighborhood like Tin Pan Alley, but the Manhattan patch where generations of immigrants—Chinese and South Americans being the latest—have found the low-skill jobs they need for a foothold. "People should care," says Sarah O. Crean, director of the Garment Industry Development Corporation, a nonprofit group trying to sustain manufacturing. "The industry in New York has shrunk, but it is still an industry that attracts new people and new talent. It's also part of the city's cachet. High fashion is what makes New York a cultural capital, much in the way that Milan is one and Paris is one."

Her vision of the neighborhood, though, contrasts with that of many landlords, who want to condense the district largely into haute couture and off-the-rack showrooms—there are now 1,200—and free up one-time lofts for architects, advertisers, sculptors, and SoHo-like home-steaders. With rents nearly doubling between 1999 and 2004 to $25 a square foot on Eighth Avenue and $14 a square foot on the side streets, battle lines have been drawn. The unions and apparel firms want the city to enforce a 1987 zoning resolution that requires landlords to replace closed garment factories with other garment firms. But Barbara Blair Randall, executive director of the Fashion Center Business Improvement District, which largely represents property owners, contends that enforcing that zoning rule would leave hundreds of lofts empty. She points out that there is so little demand for lofts by garment businesses that they barely take up half the district's floor space. "The days of mass production in midtown Manhattan are over," she said.

Most people expect the designers to remain because they need to be close to advertisers, buyers, and the fashion press. But Crean warns that they too will leave if they cannot find places that make samples or supply fabrics and buttons.

Not everyone blames cheap overseas labor and high rents for the district's decline. Bud Konheim, chief executive of Nicole Miller, which makes dresses priced from $300 to $2,000, said that he still manages to manufacture half his line here because he is willing to take the trouble to supervise the scores of intricate details that go into making a dress, while a new breed of clothing maker would rather write a single check to an overseas firm. He specializes in producing dresses in two or three weeks after they've been ordered, giving him an advantage over manufacturers beholden to Chinese or other Asian subcontractors, who may require a nine-month lead time. That's why at his Seventh Avenue showroom and factory, he houses a full range of artisans: sample makers, sewers, cutters, and pressers, not to mention the designer Nicole Miller herself. "There's tremendous efficiency in that," he said. "If someone finds something wrong at nine a.m., we can fix it here in a minute and a half. If the problem is in China, it never gets fixed."

Nicole Miller had its origins in a firm started by Konheim's great-grandfather, a pushcart peddler. Konheim himself grew up in the bed-

GARMENT CENTER

...

WHERE TO GO

Elizabeth Foundation for the Arts (WORKSPACE FOR 110 ARTISTS
AND A GALLERY) 323 WEST 39TH STREET; *(212) 563-5855,
ext. #203;* WWW.EFA1.ORG

Zipper Theater 336 WEST 37TH STREET; *(212) 239-6200*

WHERE TO EAT

Arno Ristorante (FINE ITALIAN DINING) 141 WEST 38TH STREET;
(212) 944-7420

Ben's Kosher Delicatessen (CAVERNOUS JEWISH DELI) 209 WEST
38TH STREET; *(212) 398-2367*

Jack's Restaurant (FINE DINING) 147 WEST 40TH STREET;
(212) 869-8300

room mecca of garmentos—the Five Towns of Long Island—and worked his way through Dartmouth by folding corrugated cartons for shipping clothes. He is a suave, urbane man who does not play down his rag-trade roots and likes to underscore how they give him an edge over today's more generic breed of manufacturers. "My family, we understand cutting, we understand pattern making, we understand seam allowances," he told me. "Those talents are not irrelevant. Manufacturers today just give the factory in China a picture out of a magazine. There are very few guys that understand the process. They didn't grow up in it."

Like other Garment Center veterans, he worries that the mix of adverse forces is setting off a vicious cycle where so many zipper makers and button makers leave for other fields that even seasoned dressmakers like his firm must farm work out overseas, which compels more specialists to leave. "If you want a fourteen-inch cobalt blue zipper, you can't go out in the street and get it anymore," he said.

. . .

RED HOOK COULD'VE been a contender, just like Marlon Brando's character in *On the Waterfront,* a film that immortalized the bleak, harsh atmosphere of the Brooklyn docks (even if it was filmed in Hoboken). With acres of piers for hauling cargo and sweeping views of the Manhattan skyline, Red Hook should have become a leading industrial port or another charming Brooklyn village like nearby Carroll Gardens. But a series of government miscalculations—including cutting the neighborhood off from the rest of Brooklyn with the Gowanus Expressway and the Brooklyn Battery Tunnel—left the square-mile peninsula with tumbledown houses, hollow-eyed factories, and forlorn lots.

In recent years, however, Red Hook has become vigorous again, so much so that it is now a battleground for rival visions of the city's future. Apartment developers want to cash in on the spectacular waterfront views. Artists and restaurateurs are scouring the neighborhood for cheap space. Factories pushed out by gentrification elsewhere are fighting to sustain one of their last havens. Old-time residents want to keep the old-time flavor.

Big changes are already here. In April 2006, the *Queen Mary 2,* at 1,132 feet and 150,000 tons the largest passenger ship ever built, docked at a newly built gangway and cruise-ship terminal at Pier 12, inaugurating a site that the neighborhood hopes will funnel many of the 200,000 passengers a year through Red Hook's streets, shops, and restaurants. A month later and not too far away, the terminal was joined by a giant Fairway, a branch of the gourmet cornucopia on the Upper West Side set inside what was a brick civil war–era warehouse where coffee and cotton were stored. Meanwhile, Ikea was poised to demolish a row of factories to build an elephantine warehouse store with 1,500 parking spaces for its assemble-it-yourself furniture.

Yet the neighborhood's future is still the subject of one of those battle royals that are the glory and the bane of a city with so many gadflies, factions, and enthusiasms. Daniel Doctoroff, the deputy mayor for economic development, described Red Hook as the city's "single most complex land-use issue" because it has potential in retailing, housing, and manufacturing, uses that are not necessarily compatible. "Every conceivable issue is wrapped up in this one community, which makes everything you do there very sensitive and very difficult," he said.

Factory owners and cargo haulers particularly fear that well-heeled residents in luxury apartments would not take kindly to their trucks barreling through narrow cobblestone streets or their middle-of-the-night foghorns and bright lights. Eventually the newcomers would pressure the city to restrict industrial uses. "You're going to be doing something they don't like, even if it's interfering with a guy barbecuing on the block," said Michael DiMarino, owner of Linda Tool and Die Corporation, a precision metal fabricator with clients such as NASA. "I don't blame them, but we were here first."

Most of the antagonists in the debate seemed to dread the prospect that Ikea could trigger a wave of big-box stores that would clog Red Hook's streets with traffic and shatter the sleepy ambience. But there was one notable exception. Residents of the housing projects, whose 8,000 tenants represent three-quarters of Red Hook's population, were thirsting for the 500 jobs Ikea was dangling. Dorothy Shields, president of the Red Hook Houses East Tenants Association, pointed out that one of four of the projects' tenants is unemployed.

Any change in the neighborhood's direction, even toward prosperity, would unsettle the artists and craftsmen trickling in from the once industrial waterfront neighborhood known as Dumbo and from Williamsburg. They suspect they again will be priced out of another blossoming Brooklyn neighborhood. Madigan Shive, a twenty-nine-year-old cellist, moved from San Francisco into a rental house with three other artists: "There's a good chance we could lose our house in the next year," she said. "If I lose this space, I don't know that I can stay in New York."

The neighborhood quarrel is embodied in two men, John McGettrick, copresident of the Red Hook Civic Association, and Gregory O'Connell, a former city detective who is one of Red Hook's largest property owners. O'Connell, a ubiquitous figure who uses the paperstrewn dashboard of his pickup as his desk and file cabinet, wants to expand blue-collar businesses. He has revamped civil war–era warehouses and filled them with wood and glass workers. But McGettrick, the manager of a private investigations agency and the son of a man who slung cargo on the docks, favors more housing. Speaking forcefully through a waxed handlebar mustache, he contends that the city hurt Red Hook in 1961 when it zoned as industrial numerous blocks in which modest houses had always been mixed in. Homeowners could not renovate or expand because banks would not offer mortgages. The result was abandonment and arson. "There is a desperate need to rebuild the population that was lost," he said.

Much of the war in the neighborhood has crystallized around a mammoth concrete former book-storage warehouse at 160 Imlay Street. A Manhattan developer bought the building in 2000 for $7.2 million and received a zoning variance allowing conversion into 144 condominiums whose price might total $100 million. Standing on the windswept sixth floor overlooking the harbor, with the building shrouded in netting, the developer, Bruce Batkin, said, "We're not here to rape and pillage. We're going to do something beautiful. How can we do something worse?" But the project, supported by McGettrick, has been mired by stop-work orders resulting from a two-year-old lawsuit brought by eighty-five local businesses. They argue that fancy apartments could spell the death knell for manufacturing. In 2006, they succeeded in getting a state supreme court justice to overturn the controversial zoning variance, halting the project possibly for good. "Imlay Street could be the tipping point that affects all the zoning in Red Hook," O'Connell said. "You pay one million dollars for an apartment, you don't want to hear trucks loading or unloading early in the morning."

Actually, the outlook for industry in Red Hook is no longer bleak. According to Phaedra Thomas, executive director of the Southwest Brooklyn Industrial Development Corporation, the number of industrial businesses has grown 60 percent since 1991, to 455, and jobs have increased 19 percent, to 5,000. Waterfront activity has also rebounded. The Erie Basin Bargeport was vacant fifteen years ago, but it now provides staging for hundreds of barges used for repairing bridges or shooting off Macy's Fourth of July fireworks, and it employs more than 600 workers. Another pier operator, John Quadrozzi, Jr., president of the Gowanus Industrial Park, has taken a forty-six-acre complex of grain silos and docks and uses it, in part, to unload hundreds of thousands of tons of Chilean salt for deicing the city's streets.

On a brisk winter morning, I went out to his huge dock and spoke to him in his office trailer. Quadrozzi told me that while he opposes Ikea, he is finding it hard to resist offers from megastores that want to move in nearby. "If I'm a salmon, I can only swim upstream so long," he said. "I get tired."

Factory owners also fret when they see fashionable shops new to Red Hook sprouting on the commercial spine of Van Brunt Street: Baked, a SoHo-like bakery with delicious brownies; 360, a well-regarded French restaurant; and LeNell's, a specialty liquor store that sells 100 brands of bourbon.

Until now, the administration of Mayor Michael Bloomberg has encouraged apartment and office development along the waterfront. The city and the Port Authority of New York and New Jersey gave American Stevedoring Inc. only a short-term extension of its lease on three piers where it operates gantry cranes for moving large containers. There has been talk of new parks and office complexes.

But in January 2005, the administration seemed to respond to an outcry that persistent rezoning had destroyed manufacturing in Dumbo and Long Island City. Bloomberg announced a new policy that, when finalized, would designate fifteen "industrial business zones" as neighborhoods protected from rezoning, and would give companies relocating there tax credits of $1,000 for each employee. The new zones would include portions of Long Island City in Queens, Hunts Point in the Bronx, and Red Hook and Gowanus in south Brooklyn. Such a move would protect Linda Tool and companies like it from speculative landlords who might force them to relocate by raising their rents or offering them only short leases.

Many old-timers would like to see the neighborhood livened up with apartment dwellers. Sue and Annette Amendola, two of the ten children of an immigrant longshoreman who hauled bags of coffee on his back, live in the same apartment in which they were born in the 1940s and do not want the neighborhood moribund.

Sunny Balzano, seventy-one, a painter whose family has owned a bar on Conover Street since 1890, wants more housing too but worries that the big-box stores would destroy the neighborhood's singular character. He remembers when the noon whistle blew for lunch and children had to flee the sidewalks because of the stampede of beefy dockworkers try-

RED HOOK

...

WHERE TO GO

Brooklyn Cruise Terminal (DOCKING FOR LARGE PASSENGER SHIPS)
PIER 12 (TAKE VAN BRUNT STREET TO BOWNE STREET ENTRANCE);
WWW.NYCRUISETERMINAL.COM

Fairway Market (SOME OF CITY'S BEST FRUITS, VEGETABLES, CHEESES,
SMOKED MEATS, ON THE WATERFRONT) 480 VAN BRUNT STREET;
(718) 694-6868; WWW.FAIRWAYMARKET.COM

WHERE TO EAT

Baked (SUPERB BROWNIES, COOKIES, AND LATTES) 359 VAN BRUNT
STREET; *(718) 222-0345*; WWW.BAKEDNYC.COM

Hope & Anchor (FUNKY DINER, WITH KARAOKE ON SATURDAY)
347 VAN BRUNT STREET; *(718) 237-0276*

360 (FRENCH BISTRO) 360 VAN BRUNT STREET; *(718) 246-0360*

ing to grab lunch or a shot of whiskey at one of the forty bars in the neighborhood.

"In the summer, you can hear the water lapping against the docks and the foghorns and the ships going by," he said. "But if you're going to have thousands of cars, the quality of life is about to change."

THE GOWANUS CANAL often stinks and is almost always spotted with slicks of oil. The streets alongside it are practically deserted, the silence broken by the rumble of concrete mixers and oil tankers or the screech of buzz saws. Graffiti abounds, and no one would use the word "harmonious" for the landscape, where ramshackle wood-frame and brick row houses are tucked higgledy-piggledy among factories and two housing projects.

Yet many of the 14,500 people whose homes flank the canal love the neighborhood's rough, anarchic feel. They want to preserve a vanishing urban way of life where lunch-bucket workers lived among their workplaces. "To me, it's comfortable. It's not phony; it's not pristine," said Linda Mariano, who has lived in a brick row house in Gowanus with her husband since 1974. "It's a mishmash, and I like the variety. You take two steps and you're someplace else."

In recent years, residents of this slender neighborhood squeezed between prosperous brownstone Brooklyn neighborhoods such as Park Slope and Carroll Gardens have had to grapple with a number of proposals to convert Gowanus factories and warehouses into apartments. The reason is the residents' own success in getting the city to clean up the inky waters of the mile-long canal. Already, striped bass and jellyfish swim in its waters and canoeists paddle along the surface. New benches dot the canal's banks and cormorants perch on its old pilings. With the canal more attractive, landlords of factory lofts, sniffing the higher prices they can command for apartments, are holding their industrial properties off the market or offering the briefest of leases.

So the working-class residents who do not want their neighborhood of oil depots, brass factories, and workers' homes transformed by apartments with Sub-Zero refrigerators and Viking ranges have formed impromptu groups such as Friends and Residents of Greater Gowanus, or FROGG. They have been joined in opposing the conversions by sympathetic residents in Carroll Gardens such as Celia Cacace, who savors her family's blue-collar stripes. "My sister Linda worked in Bush Terminal making envelopes," said Cacace, who is sixty-nine. "My brother Ralphie worked cleaning septic tanks in ships. Tony, he's the one born before me, he got a job in Long Island City for a sheet metal factory. My sister Esther, she passed away, she worked for American Can Company." She wants the hundreds of factories in Gowanus and nearby Red Hook to be able to provide jobs for a new generation of immigrants and blue-collar workers. "They call it gentrification; I call it genocide," she said. "They're killing neighborhoods."

So far, these activists have successfully blocked requests for variances to convert a four-story warehouse at Butler Street, a graffiti-scarred plant at Union Street, and an export-import company on Third Street into apartments. When we spoke, they were gearing up to fight one of the city's more well-heeled development firms, a venture of the billionaire diamond entrepreneur Lev Leviev and the builder Shaya Boymelgreen. The developers want to tear down a factory and dig out a chemically contaminated patch of ground known as a brownfield to create Gowanus Village, a large condominium complex of loft buildings and town houses.

FROGG and its allies are defying powerful trends that view Gowanus as a reinvigorated residential bridge from Park Slope on the east to Carroll Gardens on the west and Boerum Hill on the northwest. When I visited the neighborhood in 2005, a 100-room Comfort Inn was rising on the edge of Gowanus, and Whole Foods, the giant gourmet purveyor, had cleared a nearly square-block space at Third Street for its first Brooklyn market. Gowanus is also less than a half mile away from the Atlantic Yards, railroad yards where the developer Bruce Ratner is planning to build a basketball arena for the Nets and sixteen buildings with 7,300 apartments, a project that has drawn a determined opposition from some neighborhood groups.

Neighborhood activists were heartened that Gowanus was included in the Bloomberg administration proposal for industrial business zones. But they were upset that the draft maps protected only southern Gowanus, not the blocks north of Third Street where the conversion of lofts into residences has been proposed. Carl Hum, director of the Mayor's Office for Industrial and Manufacturing Businesses, defends the plan as a way to strike a balance between places to live and places to work in a city with a growing population.

Not everybody in the Gowanus area opposes more housing. Some residents, such as Sandra Mineo, a longtime homeowner, are tired of the perennially ragged look of the neighborhood and think ugly properties should be gussied up—even if that means making them residential. "I'd rather see something done with it than nothing done with it," Mineo told me. Buddy Scotto, founder of Gowanus Canal Community Development Corporation, a nonprofit group, has been pressing for converting buildings into housing for the elderly and moderate-income families. Gowanus' days as a manufacturing hub are passing, he claims, because its loft buildings don't have the tall, cavernous, column-free spaces that forklifts can easily navigate. "These industrial buildings are obsolete," he said. "Nobody wants to load elevators anymore."

But Thomas of Southwest Brooklyn Industrial Development argues that Gowanus industry is still vibrant. Her group's survey in 2005 counted 500 industrial firms, a 25 percent rise since 1997, and found that only 3 percent of industrial spaces were vacant. What she doesn't acknowledge easily is that many newer occupants are hardly industrial at all—blueprint-drafting firms and costume assemblers. And while the debate rages on, landlords are finding artists and other illegal tenants to live in their lofts, trends that often presage full-blown conversion to residences. Twelve artists live legally in a former factory building at 280 Nevins Street. One of those is Margaret Maugenest, who moved from SoHo in 1984. "SoHo was an interesting neighborhood," she said. "You had the trucks and the rag industry. You had the artists, who are workers also because that's what we are. Now you have a neighborhood that doesn't have much character."

There are so many artists in Gowanus now that in October 2005, 115 of them took part in the Annual Gowanus Artists Studio Tour. But the inevitable drift to upscale housing for lawyers and stockbrokers is clear to people who have seen it all before. Jozef Koppelman, a cabinetmaker in a former garage on Baltic Street, has had his small firm pushed successively out of SoHo, Hell's Kitchen, Williamsburg, Chelsea, and Dumbo, and worries about being forced out of Gowanus. "I'm a textbook example," he said. "I think about how many buildings I've worked in that now have a doorman."

GOWANUS

...

WHERE TO GO

Gowanus Canal (A CHARMING URBAN CANAL; WALK IT FROM BUTLER
STREET TO THE BROOKLYN-QUEENS EXPRESSWAY BY WEAVING IN
AND OUT ALONG THE BRANCHING STREETS, AND CHECK OUT THE
HISTORIC BRIDGES—UNION STREET, CARROLL STREET, THIRD
STREET, NINTH STREET—EACH WITH ITS OWN PECULIAR SYSTEM
OF RETRACTING WHEN BARGES SAIL BY)

President Street (NINETEENTH-CENTURY BROWNSTONES)

WHERE TO EAT

Monte's Venetian Room (AT 100 YEARS OLD, CLAIMS TO BE THE
CITY'S OLDEST ITALIAN RESTAURANT) 451 CARROLL STREET;
(718) 624-8984

Sweet Melissa (DESSERTS) 296 BOND STREET; *(718) 797-2840*

Vinny's of Carroll Gardens (PIZZA AND PASTA) 295 SMITH STREET;
(718) 875-5600

Chapter 18

Crisscrossing Generations on the Lower East Side

. . .

No NEIGHBORHOOD IN NEW YORK CITY HAS BEEN AS ENTANGLED with immigrants as the Lower East Side. It was where the Irish settled when they fled the potato famine and where their gangs made stinking, treacherous pockets such as Five Points the stuff of urban legend. It was where Chinese men came to build the nation's railroads and do its laundry and Italians to build underground subways and water tunnels. And it was where Jews such as George Gershwin, Irving Berlin, Eddie Cantor, Al Jolson, and Sophie Tucker transformed the squalor and absurdities around them into the jokes and songs that etched this pushcart maelstrom on the nation's consciousness.

But over the last two or three decades, it seemed that the neighborhood had spent its immigrant vigor. By the 1990s, the last major immigrant groups—Dominicans and even some Chinese who had spilled over from Chinatown—were also forsaking its unkempt streets. After all, more than a few New Yorkers concluded, why would anyone want to live in those cold-water railroad flats with the bathtubs in the kitchen and the toilets in the hall? Well, such cynics were spectacularly wrong. Immigrants might not want to live there, but new Generations X, Y, Z of young people raised on grunge, slacking, and postmodern irony have found this neighborhood to their liking. So, of course, have landlords, who discovered that for a minimal investment—stick a toilet inside the apartment and shower stall alongside it—they could rent railroad flats for $2,000 a month that not too long before had been renting for less than $300. So valuable was an empty flat that landlords were paying long-settled families $50,000 to leave. In these spruced-up hovels were living Web designers, blog and zine writers, fashion photographers, makeup artists, even tenderfoot lawyers and stockbrokers, their rents often paid by their parents.

Ratner's, the venerable temple of dairy, and Schmulka Bernstein, which introduced generations of Jews to the pleasures of kosher Chinese, may have closed, but I kept reading about voguish restaurants opening on shabby streets such as Clinton and Rivington that were charging more than $30 for entrees: 71 Clinton Fresh Food, WD-50, Faila, and Schiller's Liquor Bar. They had pedigreed chefs and distinctly unkosher nouvelle dishes right next to dusty cluttered stores where hunched men in yarmulkes were selling bolts of fabric and discount underwear. I took a walk with my wife one evening and could not believe the exuberant night scene of twenty- and thirtysomethings enchanted by this latest outpost of freedom and inventiveness. Just as Greenwich Village had once been, this was a new frontier of bohemia.

More than a few of these nonconformists, I was to discover, were children and grandchildren of earlier inhabitants who fled the Lower East Side in disgust for cleaner, lighter apartments in the Bronx or Flatbush. Janet Nelson, who grew up in suburban Massapequa, Long Island, with Jerry Seinfeld and Joey Buttafucco and managed 71 Clinton Fresh Food before it closed, told me, "We have a lot of customers who come in and say, 'I used to live here and now my grandson lives here.' " I wondered what the long-ago residents and merchants would make of the wholesale revolution in this neighborhood that off-the-boat Jewish and Italian immigrants both treasured and cursed and finally escaped more than a half century ago. I particularly wondered about old-timers who were now seeing their children and grandchildren return.

My curiosity came with long tendrils attached. This was the neighborhood where my immigrant parents took me in the 1950s and 1960s to get decent clothes at cut-rate prices. If you didn't mind threading through narrow streets and jostling crowds, then shopping in dust and disarray with hurried and sometimes outright rude salesmen, you could come away from Orchard Street with a fine suit or a package of underwear at half the price those items sold for the year before at Macy's or Gimbels. My father took my mother down to Levine & Smith on Division Street under the Manhattan Bridge to buy her a winter coat. Not too far away, at Louis Kaplan, they ordered bespoke bar mitzvah suits for my brother and me. Kaplan, a master tailor, wielded chalk and measuring tape over the contours of your body with no respect for the privacy of any sensitive parts. He dictated what you were to wear, and any dissent was greeted with a look of disheartenment that made it difficult to differ. But at the end you came away with a Savile Row suit at Salvage Row prices.

In later years, both as a single man and as a young family man, I sometimes went down to Allen and Grand streets to buy sheets and towels at the Ezra Cohen overstock emporium and somehow never came away without a haul of nostalgic treats: a jar of Guss' Pickles, maybe a salami from Katz's Delicatessen, herring and Nova Scotia salmon from Russ & Daughters, and dried fruits from one of several burlap-bag purveyors. Sometimes I stopped in to see my father. Late in his life, with ruptured discs in his back and clogged arteries in his legs, he took a part-time job on Orchard Street as a salesman in J. S. Hosiery, a store that sold underwear and socks and was owned by an Orthodox couple from Brooklyn. On those benumbed legs, he clambered up two and three flights of stairs several times an hour to get sample boxes to show the wholesale customers. Sometimes, he brought home packages of underwear and socks for my brother and me or a cake from Gertel's Bakery. He had become a fixture of this neighborhood. So without ever living there, I was pulled into the neighborhood's orbit.

Over the years as a reporter, I often wrote about the neighborhood and looked for fresh ways to illuminate its past or unravel its present. In 2004, I learned that the Seward Park Public Library, an old redbrick and stone palazzo on East Broadway, was reopening after two years of renovations. For that event, librarians had located archives of its earliest days that chronicled year by year—sometimes in prosaic bureaucratese, sometimes in vivid, tender fashion—changes in the neighborhood's makeup and also singled out the books that riveted readers. In a 1920 report, the branch librarian took admiring note of how the neighborhood's tenement dwellers and sweatshop workers were thirsting for Dickens and Hawthorne, but she also lamented the "disorderliness, disregard of the rights of others, mental defectives and 'queer' characters on the borderland of sanity, thefts and book mutilations." Other reports describe how embryonic socialists intoxicated by volumes of Marx crowded next to bearded men bent over *The Last of the Mohicans* in Yiddish and working women drinking in Byron and Poe.

By the Depression, another branch librarian was struggling with "undesirables" dozing on radiators, but she was charmed by the resilience of unemployed men searching for books on syrup flavoring and stocking manufacture so they could start businesses. In later years, the archives contained other tasty sociological morsels, recording how prospering Jews were moving to the Bronx and Queens, leaving behind poorer Orthodox brethren. The waning of the 1940s brought Puerto Ricans to the neighborhood, and the librarian in 1951 lamented that while the enthusiasm of the children required the library to buy Spanish titles, the adults do not "find their way to the library."

"Most of them," the librarian wrote, "are young people busy with home and babies, trying to adjust where adjustment is particularly difficult; a new language; a large and bewildering city, especially since they come from rural communities; laws and regulations which seem purposely bent on plaguing them."

Whatever their country, fresh immigrants sought out the library like a life raft. In 1971, the librarian described the increasing numbers of Chinese youngsters in the reference room as "the most methodical and thorough little researchers." She was "cutting back on the purchase of Jewish materials in order to build up the Chinese." The 1998 librarian, Susan Singer, noted how immigrants from China's Fukien Province "are escorted in by relatives to apply for a library card only days after arriving in the United States." More recently, Mary Jones, the current branch librarian and herself an immigrant from County Roscommon, Ireland, pointed to a bookcase that captured an era's passing. The Yiddish and Hebrew collection was reduced to three forlorn shelves.

Jones' observation pained but did not surprise me. Whenever I visited in recent years, I noticed how much of the Jewish past had vanished or faded. Louis Kaplan and Levine & Smith were gone, and Ezra Cohen was a shrunken version of its former self. Yes, there were places with evocative names such as Goldberger Draper, Fishkin Knitwear, and Fine & Klein Handbags, but most of these stores were owned by Chinese, Korean, Indian, or Pakistani shopkeepers or, increasingly, by avant-garde entrepreneurs selling the kinds of frivolous frills that the Lower East Side never understood. Sam Goldstein, owner of Sam's Knitwear—Wholesale and Retail at 93 Orchard Street and a man whose yarmulke covers the few wisps of hair on his balding crown, put the transformation simply: "The neighborhood went up, but the old-time merchants went down."

Everywhere I went, there were cafés for laptop peckers with really good latte at really high prices, but no more merchants of dried fruits. There were modern dancers in an old school building on Rivington Street, Bikram yoga classes in a loft on Allen Street, and a restaurant on Orchard Street called Café Lika with an interior that looked like a bohemian bordello, though it had a splendid Tuscan garden out back. But Gertel's, a seventy-five-year-old neighborhood institution famous for its rugelach and chocolate babka, was looking woebegone, barely holding its head above water. And so was Yonah Schimmel Knish Bakery, founded as a pushcart in 1910 by a Romanian rabbi. This shop on Houston Street still retains a dumbwaiter for delivering trays of knishes from the basement ovens. It draws older customers such as eighty-year-old Frank Ligotti, who remembers living on Orchard Street in the 1930s and paying $12 a week for an apartment heated by a coal stove. "The toilets were in the hall—one for the two front apartments, one for the two rear," he remembered. But Joseph Yagudaev, a manager, told me that Yonah Schimmel now endures by selling many of its knishes over the Internet through knishery.com. "All the Jews who went to Florida and California still order knishes," he informed me. "They're willing to pay shipping. They love these knishes."

Still, the neighborhood was pulsating again, brimming with young hipsters in black clothing, tattoos, and pierced tongues, peddling new art that didn't arouse me but surely excited younger strivers with the cash to spare. The stores and restaurants were of a type never imagined by the homespun, unembellished peddlers of yore: 360 Toy Group, a boutique stocked with expensive action figures; Recon, which offers "graffiti-inspired clothing" such as jazzy knit shirts priced at $45; Girls Love Shoes, which sells—and rents—vintage footwear and is run by a woman whose great-grandfather had opened a yeshiva on East Broadway; and Il Laboratorio del Gelato, which has luscious gelato in more than twenty flavors including cheddar cheese and wasabi. Then there was the incomparable Fusionarts Museum. In 1983, Shalom Neuman paid $100,000 for a run-down corner building on Stanton Street that was surrounded by crack dealers and doorways sheltering prostitutes. He turned it into an art gallery that features large animated robots with arms made of plastic ducts and hair salvaged from brooms. "Fusion golems," Neuman called them, christening one zany figure with erotic overtones as "Womanizer." His tale of the museum's history seemed to capture the new Lower East Side ethos.

"People would go into a building and shoot up and end up on my doorstep," he told me. "I could barely get a mortgage. No one wanted to come here. Now it's totally different—the antithesis of what had been here. We essentially promote art which is hybrid. We will not show pure painting. We will not show pure sculpture. We are looking for artists who break the barriers between disciplines and cultures."

My quest for a pair of relatives who could embody the dramatic changes I had witnessed took weeks of calling around; there were many eligible young people, but their grandparents or parents either were dead or lived in Florida and could not easily revisit the Lower East Side they had forsaken decades ago. I finally came up with a good enough match in Brenda Zimmer and her daughter, Amy. Brenda Zimmer's father was born on Delancey and Eldridge and she had spent much of her life working at H. Eckstein and Sons, a cramped and hectic clothing store on Orchard Street that her family owned until it succumbed in 1998. "I went to help and I never left," she told me, relating how in 1983 she was asked to lend a hand just for the Christmas season and ended up spending fifteen years haggling with customers. Yet when she tells friends that Amy, a Yale graduate and freelance writer, had moved into one of the neighborhood's storied tenements, "they look a little shocked." "Everybody spent their lives trying to get out of there, and my daughter is trying to come back," Mrs. Zimmer told me.

I met Mrs. Zimmer and Amy at Gertel's Bakery. The mother was a plump, dark-haired Bette Midler carbon copy, high-spirited and outrageously playful in her bona fide NooYawk accent. She worked as a guidance counselor in Brooklyn. Amy was slim and serious, a writer for alternative publications such as *City Limits* and *Metro*. She had long sandy hair and a chiseled face that made her seem younger than her age at the time, twenty-eight, and was dressed in an old-fashioned man's shirt, a droll statement on her part, since the shirt was inherited from H. Eckstein's.

In the bakery's dowdy dining corner, we had a cup of coffee and some rugelach, and then we began our stroll through the old neighborhood. Mrs. Zimmer seemed tickled that her daughter had actually settled a few blocks from where Amy's grandfather was born and where the family store stood. Sure, only a handful of the hosiery, lingerie, and handbag stores—wholesale or retail—were still around, and even many of the bodegas of a more recent era of migration were gone. But the neighborhood had once again quickened to life, to something closer to the bustle of the days when the walk-up tenements were teeming and the stores drew shoppers from all over for their Sunday bargains. "Now it's exciting; it's prestigious to live there!" Mrs. Zimmer observed with a wry edge.

A few doors down from Gertel's was Brown, a hole-in-the-wall café with outdoor tables and seats made artfully—if not quite comfortably—of wooden blocks, and its gourmet market spin-off, Orange. "Who would think it, a café on Hester Street?" Mrs. Zimmer said as Amy chuckled. "It's all new to me."

We could see that dry-goods shops had been replaced by French, Japanese, and other exotic restaurants with such eye-popping adornments as leopard-skin upholstery, and boutiques where the tastefully spaced wares were fashionably retro but the prices decidedly nouveau. One shop, Toys in Babeland, both amused and embarrassed Mrs. Zimmer as she browsed through. It sells dildos and vibrators in a variety of raunchy styles. "A very unusual store," Mrs. Zimmer observed, gathering up her dignity. "Colorful!"

Some new shops are beguiling in their deceptions or laced with contradictions. A store on Stanton Street that still carries the original overhead sign "Louis Zuflacht-Smart Clothes" actually sells offbeat glassware and pottery. The dramatic yellow and black sign for Sol Moscot, the optician on the corner of Delancey and Orchard whose horn-rimmed-glasses logo reminded me of the eyes of Dr. T. Eckleburg looking over the valley of ashes in *The Great Gatsby,* actually contains an espresso shop, the Bean. (The fourth-generation family-owned glasses maker, which has been on the Lower East Side since 1915, has moved to the second floor, above the sign.) The vintage sign "Pianos, New & Used, Bought & Sold, Incredible Prices" lingers over the entrance to a bar that features live bands and mango martinis. Lolita Bar on Broome Street is around the corner from Lolita Bras. Others are just sadly altered. The Garden Cafeteria is now the Wing Shoon Seafood Restaurant. Garden was a proudly working-class eatery with long steaming tables of standard cafeteria fare highlighted by Jewish delicacies. When you walked in, you were given a ticket with columns of numbers and, as you ordered, servers would punch in the running total. Emma Goldman, Trotsky, even Fidel Castro went through this ritual. Isaac Bashevis Singer chronicled the customers ensconced at tables for hours at a time "shouting their opinions of Zionism, Jewish Socialism, the life and culture of America." Not only is the cafeteria gone, but the building it is in, the Forward building, which once housed the left-wing Yiddish newspaper, then went through several Chinese incarnations, is now a luxury condo apartment house, with the penthouse selling for $4.5 million and onetime movie stars such as Tatum O'Neal coming to look.

As the Zimmers, *mère* and *fille,* ambled with me, the sounds of renovating hammers and saws could be heard everywhere. We learned that a condominium on Essex Street had sold for $2 million, and saw a glass-and-aluminum-walled twenty-story hotel rising on Rivington Street with the self-conscious name the Hotel on Rivington. This is on a block where pushcarts once plied and where seventy-year-old Economy Candy still sells its cornucopia of 1950s candy—Mary Jane nougat bars, Good & Plenty, Jordan almonds, and chocolate cigarettes. Jerry Cohen, who was born on Suffolk Street and now owns the store where his father worked as a salesman, remembered that just ten years before "we used to lock the door and run and never look behind us—it was so drug infested." Now he stays open after dark. Unlike the out-of-fashion clothing merchants, he has something the young people still want—an encyclopedic variety of sweets at decent prices. But he is himself surprised by the glittery influx. "When grandchildren tell the grandparents, they say, 'We were always trying to get out of here; why would you want to come back?'" he told me. Cohen also has to explain such old-fashioned treats as halvah. Some of the young newcomers think it's a kind of cheese.

Tenement apartments still sit above the clusters of vanguard stores. Young people like Amy Zimmer appreciate this stock of brick walk-ups laced with fire escapes—the unmall, unhomogenized feel of the place. And they say they like the human mix of Chinese, Latinos, bohemians, along with the barely clinging Old World shopkeepers. Amy lives in a fourth-floor studio in a tenement below Delancey Street where the boiler frequently breaks down—letting her claim the fashionably ironic distinction of living in a cold-water flat. Her older brother Larry lives on the second floor, and so, their mother says, he can keep an eye out for her when she comes home late. After growing up in a ranch house in the homogeneous suburb of Pomona in Rockland County, Amy likes having neighbors who are Cantonese, and she likes shopping at the stalls in the Essex Street Market, an indoor city run market created by Mayor La Guardia to lure the pushcarts off the narrow streets. "I knew I was crossing the threshold and walking into a different era," she told me.

In that she is representative of the changes in the neighborhood, as young, degree-laden professionals from the Midwest or eastern trust-fund babies move in among the Chinese and Latino immigrants. The census shows that 7 percent of the neighborhood's 51,500 residents had graduate degrees in 2000 compared to 4.8 percent ten years before. The average household income had shot up to $40,884 from $25,327 in 1990, in inflation-adjusted dollars. The median value for an owner-occupied dwelling doubled to $170,588 from $85,725. Among the more recent residents are Greenwich-raised techno-musician Moby, who has a loft here and opened a vegan bistro called Teany on Rivington. Another resident is the Russian émigré novelist Gary Shteyngart, who worked for a time as a grant writer for the neighborhood's bedrock cultural center, the Educational Alliance (one grandmother I knew of long ago called the place "the Education of Lions"). While living in a Clinton Street tenement, he wrote much of his breakout comic novel, *The Russian Debutante's Handbook*, which pays homage to the changing streets of the Lower East Side. With his writer's earnings, Shteyngart now lives in one of the middle-class co-ops on Grand Street.

Amy and her mother finally arrived at the corner of Orchard and Grand, where Eckstein's once thrived. Its place was now taken by Sheila's Decorating, an upscale fabric and furnishings store. Eckstein's was started by Amy's great-great-grandfather and his three sons in 1916 as a pushcart and grew into a rambling, two-level store that sold jeans, sportswear, and sweaters. As a teenager, Amy helped out on weekends and recorded her affectionate memories on the website "Mr. Beller's Neighborhood." "Mounds of jeans were piled in the basement and since the store had no dressing rooms, people would try things on behind stacks of Wranglers and Levis," she wrote. "Shelves of brown cardboard boxes stuffed with underwear lined the walls; to get a pair, a salesperson would climb wooden ladders precariously affixed to a bar just below the tin ceiling."

When Mrs. Zimmer stepped inside Sheila's Decorating, the ghosts overwhelmed her. "There was the hosiery department," she said, pointing to where bolts of damask and silk had replaced the socks. "There was ladies' sweaters. When you walked back there you had the underwear department. Hanes! Jockey!" She recalled how hundreds of people would crowd the store every Sunday. "When you went into the store you were mesmerized," Mrs. Zimmer said. "There was no such thing as hours. You left when the last customer left." One Sunday the wife of Yitzhak Shamir, then the prime minister of Israel, dropped in to bring some bargains back to Jerusalem.

Even in 1998 the store never accepted credit cards and the sales taxes were pasted on a chart on the ancient cash register, though Amy's brother Larry, who worked there full-time, could figure out the tax in his head. Amy and her mother remembered how Amy's dogged great-uncle Herbert would not let anyone leave the store without buying something. "He had an interesting rapport," Mrs. Zimmer said. "He found out your whole life history in five minutes." If someone haggled, Herbert might be called in and use code to offer his bottom line. "Give it to them for S.E.X." might mean $8.50. His salesman's zeal made him such a prominent local personality that the now-defunct Grand Dairy Restaurant named a sandwich, "the Professor," after another one of his attributes. It was an open-face tuna on whole wheat with coleslaw on the side.

As she gazed around, Mrs. Zimmer patted a spot over her heart. "It's sad when I come here," she said. "I grew up here and now it feels foreign."

To Amy, the Lower East Side was "my family's second home," and as a child and teenager Amy was bewitched by the clamorous streets and the dinners at Ratner's or Schmulka Bernstein. Still, she recalled how she "wasn't allowed to walk anywhere by myself" because of the neighborhood's other large commerce—crack cocaine. Seward Park, across from the high school her mother had attended, "was a flea market for drugs."

As we continued our tour, there were places that brought out laughter as well as tears. At Gorelick's clothing on Orchard Street, Mrs. Zimmer offered a cheery greeting to the owner, Bernard Gorelick, whom she hadn't seen since Eckstein's closed.

"How are you, Bernie?" she said.

"I'm an old man," he answered plaintively.

Irving Gellis, his wizened salesman, waxed lyrical about the old days. "There was room for everybody; everybody lived in peace," Gellis said of the rival merchants. "They were all invited to each other's affairs. It was one big family, Orchard Street. But the whole neighborhood has changed with all these yuppies moving in. They must have money like dirt. They're paying a dollar seventy-five for a cup of coffee. We thought these people are crazy. You pay fifty cents for a cup of coffee on Delancey Street. It's a different world."

Gorelick informed Mrs. Zimmer that the battered seventy-year-old store—a warren of steel shelves filled with untidy cardboard boxes thick with underwear—was closing. He didn't need to bother. A hand-lettered sign in the window said, "Going Out Sale."

The old wholesale and retail stores have been hit hard by converging trends—the rise of national discounters such as Wal-Mart, the end of blue laws that once gave the Lower East Side a monopoly on Sunday business, and the long shutdowns on the Williamsburg Bridge for repairs that halted traffic into the Orchard Street district. Always an optimist, Joseph E. Cunin, until 2006 the executive director of the Lower East Side Business Improvement District, told me that "there is no point in selling a cheap handbag on the Lower East Side. You can go to Kmart. But if you want a beautiful handbag at a good price, you come here." Perhaps the biggest catalyst for the neighborhood's turnover was the paradox of retailing success—the storeowners sent their children to college, and with their degrees the children were not about to take over the family businesses. Jerry Cohen sent his son to the Wharton School at the University of Pennsylvania. While the son works at the store during the summer, the father says flatly, "Do I need him here at six dollars an hour?"

When Amy announced in 2000 that she was moving to the Lower East Side, Mrs. Zimmer was candidly concerned. The streets were noirishly desolate at night and still not carefree in the daytime. Now, on the walk, Amy wanted her mother to share her delight in the neighborhood's quirky liveliness. She showed her 88 Orchard Street, a popular watering hole that sells panini and herb omelets, not to mention prosciutto.

"This is something—prosciutto on Orchard Street," Mrs. Zimmer said. "And I bet they're open Saturday."

"I bet they are," Amy shot back with a laugh.

Amy likes the human scale of the Lower East Side, the narrow streets, and the relatively low-slung buildings. She likes such places as the Pink Pony Café and the Sunshine Bakery on Rivington Street. She and her mother passed the Michele Olivieri shop, which was selling alligator shoes for $399—on sale—and advertised a website—moshoes.com.

"Website?" Mrs. Zimmer remarked. "We didn't have a computer. Everything was on paper. We added up bills in our head. We had a calculator, but it was for emergencies." The new neighborhood was no longer the old neighborhood.

"I'm not used to it," she said, passing a final judgment. "It's too modern for me. It's not authentic Orchard Street. You could be on Madison Avenue."

Madison Avenue? On the Lower East Side? That *was* an exaggeration. But Mrs. Zimmer's remark reflected the astonishing arc not just of the neighborhood but of all of New York City, as the pressures of immigration, real estate development, and the eternal attraction of this throbbing, enchanting metropolis for young people from the hinterland make over its face and soul. New York is always transfiguring, and when this book is read twenty years from now, much of it will be badly outdated, so rapidly will the city's neighborhoods continue to change. New immigrants will become old immigrants and they will forsake lower-rung neighborhoods for ones further up the ladder, transforming both the places they leave and the places they move into. And who can predict who will take their place—perhaps some newer immigrants from some country New Yorkers have scarcely encountered as yet or another generation of Amy Zimmers looking for something novel their parents never imagined. With all that swirling change, it is important to take snapshots in time, as the Zimmers and I were doing, to hold on to what's there for a fleeting moment in conversation and memory because one day soon, what's there will be very different indeed.

As we were about to turn the corner onto Houston Street to conclude our tour by savoring pastrami and corned beef sandwiches at Katz's, the last of the great Lower East Side delis, we passed a store called Las Venus. The sign in the window claimed that the store sells "vintage" furniture. The furniture, though, is from the 1950s, '60s, and '70s.

"This," Mrs. Zimmer asked, "is vintage?"

With matchless indiscretion, she once again captured the shifting, mutating, regenerating character of this remarkable city and its people.

LOWER EAST SIDE

...

WHERE TO GO

Economy Candy (RETRO AND CONTEMPORARY CANDY) 108 RIVINGTON STREET; *(800) 352-4544*; WWW.ECONOMYCANDY.COM

Eldridge Street Synagogue (FIRST EASTERN EUROPEAN ORTHODOX SYNAGOGUE, DATING TO 1887) 12 ELDRIDGE STREET; *(212) 219-0903, (212) 219-0888*

Essex Street Market (CREATED BY FIORELLO LA GUARDIA TO LURE THE PUSHCARTS OFF THE STREETS) 120 ESSEX STREET, BETWEEN BROOME AND STANTON STREETS; WWW.ESSEXSTREETMARKET.COM

Forward Building (WHERE THE YIDDISH PAPER WAS PRODUCED) 175 EAST BROADWAY

Orchard Street (A ROW OF OLD, CLUTTERED CLOTHING SHOPS—A HANDFUL STILL JEWISH-OWNED)

Russ & Daughters (LOX, HERRING, AND DRIED FRUITS) 179 EAST HOUSTON STREET; *(212) 475-4880*; WWW.RUSSANDDAUGHTERS.COM

Seward Park Public Library 192 EAST BROADWAY; *(212) 477-6770*

Tenement Museum (A TOUR THROUGH AN ACTUAL TENEMENT, HISTORICALLY FURNISHED, AND STORIES OF THE ACTUAL RESIDENTS) 108 ORCHARD STREET; *(212) 431-0233*; WWW.TENEMENT.ORG

WHERE TO EAT

Falai (NEO-ITALIAN, NEO–LOWER EAST SIDE) 68 CLINTON STREET; *(212) 253-1960*

Gertel's Bakery (JEWISH PASTRIES) 53 HESTER STREET; *(212) 982-3250*

Katz's Delicatessen (PASTRAMI PARADISE SINCE 1888) 205 EAST HOUSTON STREET; *(212) 254-2246*; WWW.KATZDELI.COM

Schiller's (STYLISH, POPULAR BAR WITH GOOD FOOD) 131 RIVINGTON STREET; *(212) 260-4555*; WWW.SCHILLERSNY.COM

Yonah Schimmel Knish Bakery (ICONIC KNISHES IN MANY FLAVORS) 137 EAST HOUSTON STREET; *(212) 477-2858*; KNISHERY.COM

Epilogue

As Goes New York . . .

. . .

IN DECEMBER 2006, NEWSPAPERS AND TELEVISION STATIONS HUMMED with stories about a sweeping raid by immigration agents at six meat-packing plants across the West and Midwest. Hundreds of illegal immigrants had been seized, and many were to face either jail or deportation. What particularly struck me about the raid was *where* it was taking place. These plants were not in such traditional immigrant hubs as Chicago or Miami, but in the towns of Hyrum, Utah; Grand Island, Nebraska; Marshalltown, Iowa; Greeley, Colorado; Cactus, Texas; and Worthington, Minnesota. More than a few Americans reading those stories must have wondered, What were thousands of Latino immigrants doing living in the heartland?

The truth is that immigrants, legal and illegal, are firmly anchored in the heartland and indeed are now woven throughout this country. Not only are there 3,000 Somalians in once-lily-white Lewisboro, Maine, but there are lots of Laotian Hmong in St. Paul, Minnesota; Dominicans in Hazelton, Pennsylvania; Mexicans in Billings, Montana; and Afghans in Fremont, California. The number of Latinos in the Deep South—once defined solely by the uneasy encounter of blacks and whites—has quadrupled from 1990 to 2005 to 2.4 million, as Mexicans and other Hispanics pour in to take low-wage agricultural and factory jobs. A sleepy place such as Atkinson County, Georgia, within twenty miles of the Florida border, is now one-third Hispanic. We learned emphatically in December 2006 that Dearborn, Michigan, has the largest community of Iraqis outside Iraq when the makeshift souk along Warren Avenue exploded in celebration at the hanging of Saddam Hussein.

Many of those honking horns and waving flags had lost fathers and brothers to the Saddam regime.

Statistics confirm this historic transformation in the United States. In just the five years between 2000 ands 2005, Indiana's immigrant population grew 34 percent, South Dakota's 44 percent, and New Hampshire's 26 percent. Los Angeles County has 1.2 million Asians, the largest concentration in any American county. According to a study by the Pew Hispanic Center, immigrants in this country under questionable circumstances now constitute a major share of low-wage occupations: 24 percent of all farm workers, 17 percent of cleaning workers, 14 percent of construction workers, and 27 percent of butchers and other food processors.

So the story of polyglot, multicultural New York, with all its attendant tensions and cultural curiosities, is fast becoming the story of all of America. Sometime toward the end of 2006, the 300 millionth American was either born or entered the United States to live, and of those 300 million, 37 million were born in another country. As a result, the culture and cadences of cities and towns across the country are being irrevocably reshaped. The nation has so many Latinos that the Irish-dominated Roman Catholic Church of Leo McCarey's classic film *Going My Way* is now 39 percent Hispanic. Many northeastern urban police forces are no longer predominantly Irish and Italian and in not too many decades will no longer even be predominantly white. At the end of December 2006, New York City's police department graduated its latest class at Madison Square Garden, and among the 1,359 cadets were 284 immigrants who hailed from 58 nations including Albania, Barbados, Malaysia, Myanmar, and Romania.

In late 2006, I visited the University of Texas at Austin to write a column for *The New York Times* on the university's plan to modify its nine-year-old effort to diversify the flagship campus, which assures freshman spots to students ranked in the top 10 percent of their high school graduating classes. I was not surprised that the formula had increased the proportions of blacks and Mexicans. This was Texas, after all, whose history was formed in the cauldron of Anglo-Mexican conflict. But I was astonished to learn that Asians now made up 14.4 percent of a campus where 81 percent of the students hail from within the state. While

Asians do constitute a disproportionate share of top-flight American campuses, who knew there were so many Asians living in Texas? But there are. Houston alone has 32,261 Vietnamese, 22,462 Chinese, and 20,149 Indians. Texas' Asians come to the nation's attention when there are ethnic dustups, such as the effort to exclude Vietnamese-owned shrimp boats from the Gulf Coast industry in the 1970s and 1980s. But Texans will also remind you that an Indian-born woman from Houston, Kalpana Chawla, was one of seven crew members aboard the Space Shuttle *Columbia* when it exploded on reentry in 2003.

Around the same period, I visited Hamilton College, a few miles outside Utica, New York, for a talk about how immigration is altering America, and I soon discovered that I'd landed in a hotbed of immigrants. For most of the second half of the twentieth century, Utica was a down-at-the-heels milltown, pocked with empty factories and vacant wood-frame houses and losing its population. But in the mid-1970s a group of clergy conspired to fill the hollow spaces with refugees. It seemed that every time there was news of war or disaster, the exiles were invited to Utica. Those refugees have helped stabilize Utica's population at 60,000. One in six Uticans is now a refugee—from Bosnia, Vietnam, Cambodia, the former Soviet Union, Somalia, and twenty-five other countries. There are Vietnamese restaurants, Russian Pentecostal churches, and Bosnian mosques, hair salons, nightclubs, and ethnic stores that sell Bosnian meats and chocolate. According to *Refugees*, the magazine of the United Nations High Commissioner for Refugees, thirty-one languages are spoken in city schools, the local newspaper runs a Bosnian column, and large billboards carry advertisements in Bosnian. The refugees have breathed new life into Utica's industrial base. ConMed, a maker of surgical instruments that is one of the city's largest businesses, employs 1,300 people, and half of them are refugees.

"The town had been hemorrhaging for years," Mayor Tim Julian told the magazine. "The arrival of so many refugees has put a tourniquet around the hemorrhaging. They have saved entire neighborhoods which were ready for the wrecking ball."

Dr. Judith Owens-Manley, Hamilton's associate director of community research and a sparkplug in the Mohawk Valley Resource Center for Refugees, told me that many Bosnian doctors, scientists, and nurses, fleeing the tumult of war, arrived without the paperwork they needed to resume their occupations and so swept floors and emptied bedpans until they could requalify. Yet with cash in their pockets, they purchased abandoned two-family houses and fixed them up, though, she added mischievously, they have sometimes avoided sprucing up façades so as not to alert the tax assessor. There have been fistfights with non-Bosnian students in the schools, and some conservative Uticans have lamented how their city has been altered. But those seem to be aberrations. "For the most part people have welcomed refugees," she said. "They like the mix of cultures and think of Utica as an immigrant community."

There have been strains almost everywhere large numbers of immigrants settle because old-timers are unhinged by the changes in the rhythms and contours of their cities and towns. The public learned about the Hmong in Minnesota and Wisconsin in 2004 because of a notorious incident in which a Hmong hunter, crossing over private property, was confronted by a group of angry white hunters and shot six of them to death, a crime for which he was later convicted and sentenced to life in prison. There are 100,000 Hmong in both states and they have brought their traditional love of game hunting to the north woods. White hunters say Hmong do not respect private property, while the Hmong say they are often the target of racial slurs.

Most clashes between immigrants and longer-settled Americans stem from the fact that illegal immigrants are taking jobs Americans won't do at low wages or are using schools and hospitals that taxpayers finance. Even such small cities as Altoona, Pennsylvania, with just a tiny fraction of immigrants, have passed ordinances threatening the licenses of employers who hire illegal immigrants and the licenses of landlords who rent to them. My colleague Rachel Swarns reported on the reactions of whites and blacks in Atkinson, Georgia, to the growing presence of Mexicans in the schools and on the one-stoplight main street, where a Mexican video store has cropped up and the supermarket's aisles are now stacked with tortillas and cilantro.

"The way Mexicans have children, they're going to have a majority here soon," Elton Corbitt, a white businessman whose family has lived in Atkinson since the 1800s, told Swarns. "I have children and grandchildren. They're going to become second-class citizens. And we're going to be a third world country if we don't do something about it."

In Longmont, Colorado, a town thirty-five miles north of Denver where 20 percent of the 80,000 residents are Latino, the city council decided to hire an "immigrant integration coordinator," and that set off a raucous debate. Some whites wondered whether the town should stanch rather than encourage the flow of immigrants. Conversely, many Latinos resisted the effort at assimilation implicit in the job's title, worried that it would mean a loss of ethnic identity and culture.

"It's the ones coming here who don't want to fit in, who don't want to live the American dream, that bother me," Fred Schotte, a retired banker, told my colleague Kirk Johnson. "I feel like someone has come into my house and now I have to accommodate to them."

A hopeful lesson in how immigrants can integrate rather smoothly into all parts of this country is provided by the saga of Indian motel keepers. The 1991 movie *Mississippi Masala* alerted Americans to the odd phenomenon of an Indian man owning a motel in a godforsaken corner of the planet. But that phenomenon is no longer odd. Many Americans have by now experienced the sensation of pulling off the highway in the true-blue hinterlands of Wyoming or Iowa for a night's rest at a motel and encountering an Indian man or woman at the check-in desk. During the last three decades, Indian immigrants have quietly acquired more than one-third of America's 53,000 hotels, most of them budget and midpriced franchises. Indians own half the nation's Days Inns, half of its Ramadas, 40 percent of its Holiday Inns. Most of these hotel-owning Indians come from a single state—Gujarat, on the western coast of India, just above Bombay—and are named Patel, which is more common in the region than Smith is in middle America.

Indians came here in large numbers after the loosening of immigration laws in the 1960s, most with advanced degrees in chemistry, engineering, medicine, and other specialties. It happened also to be a time when the hotel business was at a watershed. Interstate highways were spreading like tendrils across the country and travelers were bypassing tumbledown roadside motels run by retired couples and checking in at sleek new franchise operations popping up at the exits. Many of these franchise motels were put up for sale because of the gas and savings-

and-loan crises of the 1970s and 1980s, and some could be picked up cheaply enough for immigrants to afford. The Indians' knowledge of English, professional credentials, and a traditional commercial savvy gave them a leg up on other newcomers. They also had a network of relatives and friends to help out and a national ethic of hospitality. "There's actually a phrase in Hindi: 'A guest is like God,'" Dr. Chekitan Dev, a professor at the Cornell University School of Hotel Administration, told me.

The guest may be divine, but ministering to that guest is not. Running a hotel is a twenty-four-hours-a-day, 365-days-a-year business, often operated in circumstances that foster loneliness and dislocation. Many Indians were tough enough to make those sacrifices. "If you want to improve your lot in life, educate your children, then maybe you have to go to Minnesota where no one else will go," Hitesh Bhakta, chairman of the Asian American Hotel Owners Association, said.

Like the Filipino trailblazers in nursing, Indians are seeing their children branch away from the family occupation, but the Indian offspring are taking hotel-keeping to a more sophisticated level. The children don't want to spend their days changing sheets and checking in tired guests, so they are enrolling in hotel schools such as those at Cornell, New York University, and San Diego State to study how to manage chains of hotels, work in corporate headquarters, and acquire more upscale properties, Marriotts and Hiltons, for instance. Call them the Cornell hotel Patels. Their path is no different from that taken by the children of Jewish cutters and sewing-machine operators who became dress designers and manufacturers or the children of Italian stonemasons who became construction contractors.

Vinu Patel realized his immigrant dreams by working 100 hours a week to turn a profit on a struggling motel. Morning and night, Patel, a Gujarati, manned the front desk and did repairs on a sixty-room EconoLodge in Bordentown, New Jersey, while his wife, Indu, son, Montu, and daughter, Payal, hauled suitcases, made up beds, and vacuumed rooms. The work paid off. At age fifty-seven, Patel owns not only the EconoLodge but, with other relatives, four more hotels. Yet, he wanted something better for his children. He wanted them to work with bankers rather than as bellhops and helped put Montu and Payal through the Preston Robert Tisch Center for Hospitality, Tourism, and Sports Management at New York University.

"What we did, we did the practical way," Vinu Patel said of his own generation. "But with their educational background, the children can work for corporate America. They understand what corporations are looking for in the hotel industry—how to market and acquire the product better than we do." Montu received his master's degree in 2003 and began advising his father on acquiring hotels while working as director of sales for American Express' travel agency network. Payal, who attended NYU's undergraduate hospitality program, took a job evaluating hotels and other real estate for Standard & Poor's.

Despite all the changes this book has recorded in a single city, the bigger American story today may be how many foreigners are living not in the city but in the suburbs. Since 2000, nearly as many immigrants have settled in New York's suburbs as in the city itself. They now constitute 22 percent of the suburban population in the New York area, double that of 1970. The share of Asians has grown tenfold, according to my colleague Sam Roberts, an expert in census data. In Palisades Park, New Jersey, Koreans now constitute a majority of the 17,000 residents and own 90 percent of the shops along the main street, and they are clamoring for more Korean police officers and political leaders. Outside San Francisco, Fremont, California, which in the 1950s was carved out of five towns that wanted to incorporate into a suburban-like city, has a population of 210,387, but of those, 95,894, or 46 percent, were born abroad—including Afghans, Indian Sikhs, and Taiwanese. One of Fremont's constituent towns, Centerville, is known as Little Kabul, with a boulevard packed with Afghan stores and such restaurants as Salang Pass. The best-selling novel *The Kite Runner* was partly set in Centerville. Another district in Fremont, Mission San Jose, is peopled by affluent Taiwanese, Japanese, and other Asians, including, when she was younger, Olympic skater Kristi Yamaguchi, whose grandparents were interned with other Japanese Americans during World War II and who graduated from Mission San Jose High School.

If Taiwanese, Korean, Indian, and Afghan immigrants who came here during the past forty years are staking out firm plots of earth in the nation's suburbs, then they have indeed become full-fledged Americans.

They are living the same American dream of a house and a backyard that generations of Italians, Eastern European Jews, Irish, Germans, and Scandinavians pursued. Count in the immigrants in the nation's prairies and mountainsides, and it seems increasingly obvious that the world is not only in a single city; the world is in the entire country. New specimens from far-flung specks on the globe are settling in once-immutable corners of the nation, transforming them, yes, but, for the most part, realizing the classic immigrant dreams of solid anchors in quiet communities where they can freely choose to cleave to their heritage or strip it off. They are merging—conspicuously or inconspicuously—into the mighty American river. It is a very different river from the one that flowed a half century ago, fed by streams and rivulets we knew little about only yesterday, but still it rolls mightily and charmingly along.

Acknowledgments

. . .

THIS BOOK WOULD NOT HAVE BEEN POSSIBLE WITHOUT THE generous indulgence of *The New York Times,* which let me spend three years running around New York's most exotic and beguiling neighborhoods, exploring, delving, schmoozing, and noshing to my heart's content. They let me be a roving foreign correspondent, but I got to sleep at home. To the editors who made that possible: Jon Landman for lapping up the notion of a neighborhoods beat when I broached it, and Susan Edgerley and Joe Sexton for wholeheartedly letting me persist when they took over as Metro editors. Jill Abramson was a welcome cheerleader. Most of all, though, I am grateful to Anne Cronin, whose passion for vivid stories encouraged me to come up with one colorful idea after another, who wielded her editor's rudder with intelligence and discretion, and who dressed articles up with glorious special effects—makeup, photographs, and maps. Her deputies—Bill Goss, Monica Drake, and Diego Ribadeneira—always edited sensitively.

At *The Times,* a special thanks goes to Alex Ward, who was gracious in letting me craft a book out of stories that first appeared in sparser, more reportorial form in *The Times.* I'd like to thank Charlie Bagli and Fernanda Santos, who worked on two of those original articles with me. Other colleagues, including Sam Roberts, Nina Bernstein, Kirk Johnson, David Gonzalez, Rachel Swarns, Sewell Chan, Sabrina Tavernise, Andrea Elliott, Jennifer 8. Lee, Yilu Zhao, Lee Romero, and Angel Franco, have written about or photographed immigrants, neighborhoods, and shifts in population, and their reporting enlightened mine. Jim Perry kindly helped with the map. It would be neglectful to fail to pay tribute to two of *The Times'* departed—Dick Shepard and Murray Schumach—who taught me about the zest you can feel writing about the city's charming ethnic groups and its hidden corners. Finally, a special credit goes to the unparalleled Arthur Gelb, a mentor to many, who offered me a tall shot of enthusiasm as well as some shrewd suggestions about the book's direction and the title.

There were many experts who illuminated the book's larger thoughts, and they include Joseph Salvo, William Helmreich, Jerome Krase, Jon Rieder, John Mollenkopf, Barry Lewis, Mitchell Moss, Gay Talese, Madhulika Khandelwal, Jenna Weissman Joselit, Sam Heilman, Yaakov Kornreich, Philip Kasinitz, Sharon Zukin, Richard Alba, Neal Gabler, Cynthia Lee, Maxine Margolis, Fred Siegel, Felix Matos Rodriguez, Pyong Gap Min, Harry Daskalothanassis, Lloyd Ultan, Phaedra Thomas, Judith Owens-Manley, and Jack Ukeles. Still, the lion's share of gratitude must go to the dozens of neighborhood personalities who were willing to open their hearts and intimate stories to me—including Claudio Caponigro, Zhong Wen Jiang, Manizha Naderi, Masuda Sultan, Intesar Museitef, George Alexiou, Mavis Theodore, Hynda Schneiweiss, Kwasi Amoafo, Nicholasa Mohr, Mario Romero, Aurora Flores, Maggie Leung, Bernard Haber, Anatoly Alter, Jay Graber, Raphael Wallerstein, Shlomo Nisanov, Lana Levitin, Jesus Peña, Latchman Budhai, Shariar Uddin, Robert Gangi, Lorraine DeVoy, George Broadhead, Linda Cunningham, Bud Konheim, Charles Howard, and Brenda and Amy Zimmer. Without them, the book would have been undoable.

Without my editor, Nancy Miller, there also would not have been a book. Reading *The Times* pieces, she thought there was a larger work to be hatched, and she guided me in shaping it into a thematically consistent and engaging whole. With help from Lea Beresford, she shepherded me through the hundreds of painstaking steps that lead to an actual book, all with grace, ardor, and intelligence. My agent, Jane Dystel, once again saw to it that the book was handled respectfully, and her enthusiasm and attention to detail pushed me onward.

My parents—my late father, Marcus Berger, and my mother, Rachel Berger—as well as my siblings, Josh and Evelyn, bred in my bones an immigrant perspective that surely enriched the book—as did their love. Friends Alon Gratch, Michele Sacks, Jerry and Eva Posman, Jack Schwartz, Gina Schwarz, David Aftergood, Victor and Lois Neufeld, Phyllis and Elliott Rosen, Andrea Gabor, Nancy Rabinowitz, Jack

Kadden, Clyde Haberman, Joyce Purnick, Connie Rosenblum, Jacques Steinberg, Jules Bemporad and Nancy Albertson, Steve Greenhouse, Miriam Reinharth, Carolyn Hessel at the Jewish Book Council, and others space won't allow me to mention were bountiful in their exuberance, and that nourished me. Most of all my wife, Brenda, and daughter, Annie, were there mornings and evenings to share my pleasures, tolerate my worries, and step in with always-brilliant suggestions. Their love made the work of the past five years a high point in my life.

ABOUT THE AUTHOR

JOSEPH BERGER is a reporter and columnist for *The New York Times*, where he writes about education, religion, and the New York region. During his thirty-five-year career in journalism, he has covered the 1973 Mideast war, the Watergate scandal, and Pope John Paul II's trip to the United States, among many other events. Berger is a recipient of the Education Writers Association Award and a three-time winner of the Supple Award, the highest honor given by the Religion Newswriters Association. He is the author of *The Young Scientists: America's Future and the Winning of the Westinghouse* and *Displaced Persons: Growing Up American After the Holocaust*, which was named a *New York Times* Notable Book of the Year. He lives with his wife, Brenda, a psychoanalyst, and his daughter, Annie, in Westchester County.

ABOUT THE TYPE

This book was set in Caslon, a typeface first designed in 1722 by William Caslon. Its widespread use by most English printers in the early eighteenth century soon supplanted the Dutch typefaces that had formerly prevailed. The roman is considered a "workhorse" typeface due to its pleasant, open appearance, while the italic is exceedingly decorative.

RECEIVED NOV 1 4 2007